Fundamentals of Performance Modeling

Fundamentals of Performance Modeling

Michael K. Molloy, Ph.D.

Computer Science Department
Carnegie-Mellon University
Pittsburgh, PA 15213

Macmillan Publishing Company
NEW YORK

Collier Macmillan Publishers
LONDON

Macmillan Publishing Company
866 Third Avenue, New York, New York 10022

Collier Macmillan Canada, Inc.

LIBRARY OF CONGRESS CATALOGING IN PUBLICATION DATA

Molloy, Michael K.
  Fundamentals of performance modeling / Michael K. Molloy.
     p.   cm.
  Includes index.
  ISBN 0-02-381910-3
  1. Computer simulation.   I. Title.
QA76.9.C65M64 1988
001.4'34—dc19   88-3950
                                                                      CIP
Printing: 1 2 3 4 5 6 7 8   Year: 9 0 1 2 3 4 5 6 7 8

Preface

This book has been written to fill an observed need for an introduction to performance modeling (specifically of computer systems) which does not rely so heavily on an extensive mathematical background. In computer science departments, the normal mathematical preparation for undergraduates is a course in calculus and a course in discrete mathematics. In some cases even a course in formal logic is included. However, very few computer science programs include courses in probability theory, complex analysis, transform theory, or linear algebra, all of which are normally assumed in textbooks about performance modeling.

The entire topic of performance modeling could be presented in a "cookbook" fashion by avoiding mathematical foundations entirely. That would not be addressing the basic problem of an incomplete background. Instead, this text is designed to establish that background of fundamental concepts. It is not intended for an established computer scientist who wants a quick "HOW TO" reference. It is intended to provide all of the necessary material to introduce the basic concepts of performance modeling to undergraduate students in computer science. By clearly explaining the fundamental concepts and providing intuitive insight into why the mathematics works, a course using this text will provide a comprehensive introduction and a foundation for more advanced work.

For that reason the majority of the book is devoted to explanations and examples on fundamentals. The question addressed by this textbook is more "WHY" than "HOW". This is illustrated in such sections as Generating Pseudo Random Numbers. The student may never again write a random number generator, but this section teaches the reader why some random number generators are better than others and how to compare them. It is the author's belief that too many erroneous performance studies are caused by the lack of a clear understanding of why a simulation or equation works.

The book is based upon the concept that performance analysis cannot be studied by simulation or analytical models alone. Both techniques are required, and each has its place in a good analyst's repertoire. The first four chapters develop the normal background; modeling, probability theory, transform theory, and simulation. An important difference in these introductory sections is the treatment of probability theory and transform theory. In Chapter 2, both continuous and discrete are carried through together. In fact, contrary to classical probability theory, the discrete case is treated as a special case of continuous where probability densities are made up of all impulses. Although this makes discrete more complicated in a formal mathematical sense (which is not discussed in the text) it allows the student to relate continuous and discrete concepts more easily. In Chapter 3, transform theory is developed as a simple tool without relying upon complex analysis. Chapter 4 concentrates on pseudo random number generators and the basic structure of simulation programs.

The advanced sections (5-8), Markov Models, Single Queue Models, Queuing Network Models, and Computer Applications, follow the natural and normal ordering. In Chapter 5, both discrete time and continuous time Markov chains are covered. In Chapter 6, single queues are introduced as birth-death systems which are a special case of the continuous time Markov chain developed in Chapter 5. In Chapter 7, single class queuing networks are introduced in successively more complex stages, starting with open networks of feed forward queues and ending with closed queuing networks. Numerical algorithms, such as convolution and mean value analysis, are stressed in this section. Chapter 8 is devoted to larger case studies to provide some guidance to the student in how to use the new techniques. Each of these advanced sections includes both the analytical and simulation techniques. Finally, the appendices are included to provide all of the algebraic formulas, transforms, and statistical tables necessary to solve the problems in the text. This avoids the usual requirement for students to search mathematical textbooks for a few, simple relationships.

The reader is assumed to have already studied calculus and discrete mathematics. Since this text is oriented toward the modeling of computer systems, it is also assumed that the reader has a knowledge of the architecture of computer systems and has done some programming. Since many of the examples of systems are multiprogramming systems, it is helpful if the reader understands the basic problems and has observed the real time behavior of such systems. It is assumed that a course in Performance Modeling would be an advanced undergraduate course, following courses in data structures, computer architecture, and operating systems.

In order to improve the comprehension and utility of the text, three types of problems are included. First, the example problems will be given in the actual text of the material. These will help the student understand the operations and approaches to the solutions of such problems. Second, a series of exercises are given after each section of material. The answers to these exercises appear in the appendices. These exercises are intended to help the student study independently. Third, a series of problems are given at the end of each chapter. These problems may be used as graded homework assignments.

ACKNOWLEDGMENTS

The author wishes to thank all of the people who made this textbook possible. Special thanks is due to the reviewers and to Richard Gail in particular who always has a sharp eye for details. In addition, the author wishes to thank Leonard Kleinrock, Mario Gerla, and Richard Muntz for the inspiration and motivation the author received at UCLA as a graduate student.

Contents

3 Transform Theory 65

4 Simulation 83

5   Markov Models   117

6   Single Queues   157

Introduction to Modeling

1

1.1 What Is a Model?

To many people the term *model* represents a small toy or replica of an airplane, automobile, or ship. In a narrow sense this association is correct. The small object represents (duplicates) the outward physical appearance of the original object. The fact that a measurement of a section of the model can be used to predict the measurement of the same section of the larger object suggests the term *scale* model.

We can generalize this example into a useful definition of a model in a very straightforward manner. Recall the fact that the scale model represents the outward appearance, but not the functionality (it does not run) or the weight (the same scale does not apply to the weight relationship). So a model may represent some, but not all, of the aspects of the original. Some models will represent more aspects of a system than others. It is common to construct flying models (functional models) of airplanes that sacrifice a little (sometimes a lot) of the scale aspect. The particular features of the model that are implemented depend only on the user's requirements and desires.

To summarize, a *model* is a representation (physical, logical, or functional) that mimics another object under study. The fact that it mimics the object under study allows the user to manipulate the model, observe its behavior, and infer the behavior of the actual object under the same circumstances. This ability to predict some behavior of the original object is the critical feature of a model. Since the model will represent only certain features of the original object, it will usually be much less complex and it will therefore be easier and cheaper to study.

Once a model is constructed, it is often desirable to extend its capabilities by adding features of the original. In model airplanes, functional flying models are refined so that they appear more and more like actual airplanes. In model

FIGURE 1.1 A Model and Its Real Counterpart

railroading, scale models are modified to move more like the actual locomotives on a railroad. There are inherent limits to each model's capabilities. The engines of model airplanes cannot be built to look like the actual airplane's engines and still propel the model. The actual distances of a HO model railroad layout of a town cannot be to scale because of the fact that 1 mile equals approximately 63 feet in the scaled layout. The limits of a model must be as clearly understood as its representative aspects are understood.

1.2 Kinds of Models

The variations in models (even of the same original object) are virtually unlimited. We can, however, classify models in three ways. The model may be classified in terms of what aspects of the original object the model represents, how completely they are represented, and in what way the aspects are represented. As an example, a model airplane could be classified as a scale model since it implements the relative physical appearance of the object. The model could be made up of plastic parts and so be referred to as a plastic scale model airplane.

For our purposes we will break down the aspects of an original object represented by a model into two basic categories.

1. *Scale.* Linear measurements represent a fixed percentage of the same measurement on the actual object.
2. *Functional.* Some facet of the operation (flying, climbing hills, or sailing) is represented.

The representation need not be complete. It is possible that only some features of the original object are represented in the model. So, we can also separate the level of representation a model employs.

1. *Concrete.* The aspects are represented as precisely as your observations can be made.

2. *Abstract.* The aspect (usually function) is represented imprecisely so that general (or average) behavior and not complete behavior is modeled.

The techniques for constructing functional models are even more varied, but again, we will try to describe three main categories.

1. *Physical.* The model is constructed out of plastic, wood, metal or other physical material and its operation follows the same mechanisms as the real object.

2. *Simulation.* The functional model is a procedure whose execution mimics the behavior of the object through the manipulation of values that represent physical observations. Each manipulation corresponds to some actual operation on the real object but uses different mechanisms.

3. *Analytical.* The model does not have operations that mimic the behavior of the object. Instead this model is constructed using mathematical operations (such as multiplication, integration, etc.) to capture the relationships between observable quantities. The computations have nothing to do with operations in the real object.

Example 1.1: As an example, let us consider some different models of a single object, an airplane.

1. A simple toy airplane for young children which has the correct ratio of wing span to length, but is missing small breakable pieces like antennas, would be an abstract, scale, physical model.

2. A flying model airplane with a single piston gas engine and string controls instead of a pilot would be an abstract, functional, physical model.

3. The complete aeronautical engineering drawings of the actual airplane would be a concrete, scale, simulation model. The mechanisms used to represent the dimensions in 2-D are not the same as the original object in 3-D.

4. A computer graphic image of the plane created by fitting cubic-spline functions to a given set of points for the aircraft is an abstract, scale, analytical model.

1.3 Who Uses Models

Models are used by everyone at various times. Often, the actual use of a model is not conscious. Researchers in the human thought process talk of the cognitive models for objects and relationships that exist in our memories. Think for a moment about how you identify an object (associate it with a concept). As an example, how do you classify a particular structure made out of wood or metal as a chair? Is it identical to the other chairs you have seen? No, you have observed certain aspects of the object that match all the aspects in the concept "chair" in your memory. You identify objects by retaining a model of the physical object.

The use of functional models is a little less familiar but nonetheless broad. Physicists have in mind many complicated models of the universe. Many are constructed from mathematical entities. However, automobile mechanics also have in mind models of the functionality of the automobile engine. Although these are probably not mathematical, they are still functional.

1.4 How We Use A Model

Modeling is very important to human thought processes and to our ability to solve problems. Because of the inherent complexity of the real world and our limited capacity for thought, we tend to manipulate simple models of the real world. However, even simple models can be used in very complex ways.

Before delving too far into a philosophical discussion, let us define an abstract concept. A *process* is something that will produce some measurable outputs for some given inputs. There are three types of questions about processes where models provide significant help.

1. How does it work?
2. What will happen if I do this?
3. What happened to cause this?

Each question is different in its viewpoint and in the kind of information required. The first considers a known set of inputs and outputs and asks for a process description consistent with those known observations. The second considers a known set of inputs to a known process and asks for a prediction of the outputs. The third considers a known process with a set of known outputs and asks for the appropriate inputs.

We say that we know (i.e., have a model) how a process functions if our model can be used to answer the questions about the process. The scientific method for establishing knowledge about the world around us is simply an application of these questions to both a model of the process and the actual process.

Step 1: Experiment with the actual process. Here the inputs are measured, the unknown process proceeds, and then the outputs are measured.

FIGURE 1.2 An Abstract Process

Step 2: Conjecture a model of the process. This is the creative part. The scientist must "dream up" a model that behaves in the same way as the process has been observed to behave. That means that the model, when given the previously observed inputs, produces the previously observed outputs. (Question 1)

Step 3: Validation. This step is the "proof of the pudding." If the model of the process is accurate, when both the model and the process have the same input conditions, they should both give the same output conditions. If not, then we must start over again. This step uses the predictive nature of the model and checks that prediction. (Question 2 or 3)

This interactive process is precisely the method humankind has used to amass the volume of "knowledge" that has allowed us to reach the moon. You can rightly say that this knowledge could be in error. We may not have run enough validation experiments. But my response is that "it is good enough" and does not need to be proved to be free of error.

Clearly, this method is useful in establishing an "acceptable" model. On the other hand, how can we use an acceptable model to solve other problems, such as questions 2 and 3? In our normal construction of the model, we "built" it to do just what question 2 needs, so we simply subject the model to the given inputs and retrieve the outputs. Question 3 provides a more difficult problem. How can we determine the inputs given only the model and the outputs?

1. *Invert the model.* Switch the inputs and the outputs while retaining their relationships.
2. *Trial and error.* Guess at the inputs, apply the model to that guess, and check the outputs against the given outputs. If they match, you have "discovered" the appropriate inputs.

As an example of the first technique, consider a common mathematical model of the motion of physical objects, $F = ma$. Here the model has been accepted after countless applications of scientific technique. If the output F (force) is known and one input m (mass) is known, we can construct an inverse model, $a = F/m$, where the inputs are F and m and the output is a (acceleration). The relationships among the components of the model are preserved; only the inputs and outputs are changed.

As an example of the second technique, consider an automobile mechanic. The mechanic has been presented with a problem, some malfunction in an automobile engine. Logically, we understand that the symptoms of the malfunction indicate exactly what the cause is. In other words, certain conditions hold for the operation of engine. One or more of these are incorrect. The actual operation of the engine transforms these input conditions into observable symptoms (output conditions). Were it possible to "invert" the operation of the engine, we could apply the output conditions and observe the cause as before. This, unfortunately, is not usually possible. So we resort to a more tedious technique familiar to all detective story buffs. It is the proverbial "what if" question. We suppose a set of input conditions to a model of the object under study and observe the output conditions. If we have a match with the output conditions of the actual object, we have now established its input conditions and know which are in error.

1.5 Why Model Computers?

A computer system is simply a collection of components that cooperate to accomplish a task (i.e. process data). However, computer systems are probably one of the most complex objects human beings have created. They operate faster and have more input conditions than a person can cope with. The sheer complexity of the system forces users to keep in mind a simplified model of the system. An overly simplified model is adequate for a casual user but entirely insufficient for a system developer or system programmer, who need more complex models of the computer system.

Many of the models needed by such people are not quantifiable. This is one reason why people who have constructed correct models in their minds are in such demand. Attempts to establish formal models are continuing. An aspect of computer systems that has been successfully modeled formally is the overall or average performance of a system. Since the computer performs so many operations in a period of time, its actions begin to appear similar to some physical processes. These physical processes are termed *stochastic* since they appear randomly as a function of time.

A stochastic model is very different from the models we normally consider because it models systems that will have many possible outputs for a single set of inputs. In the next chapter we describe the basic concepts of this new model.

1.6 Performance Measures for Computer System Models

Before becoming too involved in the details of constructing models of computer systems, it is necessary to clearly understand the objectives of the modeling analysis. The performance of a computer system can be described in many different ways, depending on your point of view. You can characterize the speed of the computer in millions of instructions executed per second (MIPS). You can consider the usefulness of the computer in terms of ease of use, quickness of response to your commands, and other factors. Although many of the aspects of the computer which may loosely be labeled as performance are important to the user, many are not quantifiable, such as the usability of the interface. We will restrict our models to quantifiable measures.

Typical performance measures we will be interested in determining from our models (or real experiments on the computers) are listed in Table 1.1. The collection of these measures can then be used to answer specific questions about the performance of a computer system.

Performance Measures

Measure	Units	Potential Use
Throughput	Processes/unit time	Productivity evaluation
Capacity	Processes/unit time	Planning
Response time	Units of time	Usability evaluation
Utilization	Percent of time	Configuration
Reliability	Mean time to fail	Maintenance scheduling
Availability	Percent of time	Usability evaluation
Speedup	Number of effective PUs	Configuration
Backlog	Number of processes	Usability evaluation

Table 1.1

With a little thought it becomes clear that these measures will depend on the current workload on the system. It must be remembered that no performance measure is useful, or even valid, without a description of the workload under which the system labored while it was being evaluated. The workload for a system can be characterized by another series of measures which are made on the input to the system. However, errors in characterizing the workload may have serious consequences. Even slight variations of the input workload to a system, such as rearranging job submissions, can significantly affect the performance measures of the system.

Workload Parameters

Parameter	Units	Potential Variations
Interarrival time	Units of time	Change the offered load
Task size	Units of time	Amount of processing
I/O request rate	Number per unit time	Type of processing
I/O service rate	Number per unit time	I/O device type
Memory size	Kilobytes per task	Multiprogramming level
Task mix	Number of tasks	Interactive/batch
Parallelism	Percent of program	Vector/sequential

Table 1.2

1.7 Problems

1.1 Construct a model of a four-dimensional cube. (*Hint:* Begin by constructing a one-dimensional model of a two-dimensional square, then a two-dimensional model of a three-dimensional cube.)

1.2 List some aspects of the motion of ''real'' objects that are not modeled by the equation $F = ma$.

1.3 List some additional performance measures.

1.4 List some additional workload parameters.

Probability Theory $\boxed{2}$

2.1 Observations versus Long-Term Behavior

An important distinction that is often misunderstood is the difference between a single experimental measurement (or outcome) and the long-term behavior (or limiting behavior) of a repetitive system. The models we are normally familiar with are structured in such a way that the model predicts every occurrence of a phenomenon. It is therefore easy to see the relationship between an experiment and use of the model. In probability theory, the model represents the behavior of the system over a large number of experiments and does not predict a particular outcome.

In the case of probability, we are dealing with a multiplicity of possible outcomes for an experiment. We cannot predict a particular outcome, only the number of observations of a particular outcome with respect to a large number of repetitions of the same experiment.

$$\text{relative frequency} \triangleq \frac{\text{number of observations of an outcome}}{\text{number of repetitions of the experiment}} \quad (2.1)$$

Consider a simple performance model of a program running on a computer. The program is made up of some instructions, each of which will take a fixed period of time to execute. We can "count up" those periods of time and tell precisely how long that program will execute. We have assumed, of course, that the computer will not, for some reason, do anything other than execute that program and will execute the program in exactly the same way that we counted the instructions.

If we now consider that program running on a time-sharing computer system that uses virtual memory, we are faced with a problem. Each time we run the program it takes a slightly different amount of real time (response time) to execute, even when it is run using the same data. We know that if an instruction causes a page fault, it will take substantially longer to execute. We realize further that if more users are on the system it will take longer for the program to finish. The complexity of the environment has made a deterministic model intractable. We can, however, run the program a large number of times while the load on the system is stable. These observations will form some pattern and we can calculate an average value from them. But to predict results, we need to have a model of the program executing on the system.

This series of observations could be used to characterize the relative frequency of the possible outcomes. It was, of course, not an infinite sequence, and if we tried it again, we might not get exactly the same relative frequencies. There is a point (we will discuss how to determine the point when we study simulation techniques) where the number of trials is large enough so that the differences in relative frequencies become negligible. Therefore, we have approached (within the error we termed ''negligible'') that elusive description of the relative frequency of the possible outcomes from an infinite number of trials.

We can now construct a mathematical model that *represents* the relative frequency of an outcome for an *infinite* number of repetitions of the experiment. This abstract model (clearly, an infinite number cannot actually be performed) is referred to as *probability theory* and will be used as our model of complex computer systems.

2.1.1 Experimental Environments

The actual type of measurement for both the inputs and outputs of a process depend upon the environment. Two basic types of environment can be modeled. Outcomes may be selected from a discrete or a continuous set.

The observation (measurement) in a *discrete* environment is quite straightforward. Even though there are many possible outcomes, we can count them. Sometimes, there are even a finite number of possible outcomes which makes the problem even simpler.

Consider a simple (and very common) example of such an experiment. The input conditions are a two sided coin with no weight bias or flat edges (so that it will always fall on one side or the other) and an action of flipping the coin into the air. Therefore, a particular experiment amounts to flipping the coin and observing the side that faces up after the coin hits the ground. For any such experiment, only one of the two outcomes can occur.

The observation (measurement) in a *continuous* environment is a little more subtle. Here we have an uncountably infinite number of possible outcomes, and even when we limit the range of possible outcomes, we still have an uncountable number of them.

Consider an example of a continuous environment experiment. A measurement of the temperature in a room is such an example. We would normally measure the temperature of the room with some device that has, say, a single decimal point of accuracy. Then a possible measurement would be 74.2 degrees Fahrenheit. But what does that measurement really mean? Does it mean that the room temperature is 74.2000000 . . . . degrees? Of course not. What it really means is that the temperature is "around" 74.2 degrees. In other words, the measurement is not a value but a range of values. Clearly, the room was at a particular temperature when the measurement was made. The outcome was some exact temperature, but its value cannot be determined. In fact, there are an uncountable number of such temperature values that could have resulted in a reading of 74.2 degrees. We could decide to "assign" the value of 74.2 to any temperature that we would measure as 74.2 on our device. This is a way of discretizing the continuous environment. But this will not be necessary. We will return to this concept when we discuss events and probabilities of events.

2.2 The Basic Model

To work effectively with a model, we need to describe the objects and rules of the model more precisely. This more disciplined approach will enable us to manipulate relatively complex models. There is always the danger of losing track of the basic ideas behind the model as we begin to manipulate symbols. To avoid problems in the future, it is important to understand the material at each step of development.

Probability theory is based firmly on the theory of sets (or collections of objects). This is a natural result of the idea that outcomes may not be unique and may have a number of possible values. To manipulate the potentially large group of possible outcomes, we use the notation of set theory.

2.2.1 Review of Naive Set Theory

First we define the objects in our theory. Basically, we can start with the simplest and most basic component, the element.

Definition 2.1: An *element* is an instance of an object of interest.

Example 2.1: If the objects of interest are fruit, an apple would be an element.

Definition 2.2: A *set* is a collection of distinct elements. (Usually written as a list of elements, in arbitrary order, enclosed in braces.)

Since the elements of a set are distinct, then two or more elements in a set cannot be the same. Elements that actually occur in a set are called members of that set and membership is denoted as $1 \in \{1,2,3\}$. That translates as "one is a member of the set one, two, three". We often do not actually list all the elements (especially if it is an infinite set). In those cases, we give a rule "such that" any element can be generated. For example, $\{m \mid m = 2\,n, n = 0, 1, 2, \cdot\cdot\cdot\}$ in English means the set of positive integers m such that m is an even number.

Example 2.2: For sets made up of integer elements, $\{1,3,4\}$ is a legal set, whereas $\{1,1,3\}$ and $\{1,\frac{1}{2},2\}$ are not.

We have not ruled out the possibility of a set being made up of elements which are themselves sets. This brings forth an image of a picture of a man holding a picture of himself holding a picture of himself, ...

There is another twist to the concept as well. We have not restricted the number of elements in a set. It is quite possible (and very useful to us) to have an uncountable number of elements in a set, or no elements at all in a set.

Example 2.3: The set of all positive integers $\{0,1,2,3, \ldots\}$ has a countably infinite number of elements and the set of all real numbers between and including 0 and 1 (i.e., the line segment $[0,1]$) has an uncountably infinite number of elements.

Definition 2.3: The *null* set (denoted as $\varnothing$) is the set containing no elements at all.

We also can abstract the idea of a set and replace any actual set with a symbol that represents a generic set. We will use capital letters (e.g., A, B, C, etc.) for sets and lowercase letters (e.g., a, b, c, etc.) for elements of sets.

Now that we have described the objects that make up this model, we consider the operations that can be applied to these objects.

Definition 2.4: The *union* of two sets A and B is a set (denoted as $A \cup B$) that contains all the elements found in *either* of the two sets.

Example 2.4: The union of the set $\{1,2,4\}$ and the set $\{1,3,5\}$ is a new set $\{1,2,3,4,5\}$.

Example 2.5: The union of the set of real numbers $[0,1]$ and the set of real numbers $[1,2]$ is a new set of real numbers $[0,2]$.

Note: Only one occurrence of an element is allowed in a set by definition, so the element 1 occurs only once in the union even though it occurred in both of the initial sets.

Definition 2.5: The *intersection* of two sets A and B is a set (denoted as $A \cap B$) that contains only the elements that appear in *both* sets. It is the set of elements that both sets have in common.

Example 2.6: The intersection of the set {1,2,3} and the set {2,3,5} is a new set {2,3}.

Example 2.7: The intersection of the set of real numbers [0,2] and the set of real numbers [1,3] is a new set of real numbers [1,2].

Note: Since the intersection of two sets must contain elements that occur in both sets, the number of elements in the intersection must be less than (or at most equal to) the number of elements in the smaller of the two sets.

Definition 2.6: A set A is a *subset* of a set B (denoted as $A \subset B$) if all the elements in the set A are also in the set B.

Example 2.8: A set {2,3} is a subset of the set {1,2,3,4}.

Example 2.9: A set of real numbers [1,2] is a subset of the set of real numbers [0,2].

Note: By definition, the intersection of two sets is always a subset of *both* sets.

As is true in most discussions, unless the realm of discussion (potential pool of concepts) is accepted and is common to the participants, numerous disagreements due to misunderstandings will occur. For discussions about sets of objects, the same is true. If we are discussing sets of students, and you think we are talking about students at all levels and I think we are discussing students at the college level, we are going to have difficulty. We must establish the overall set of objects we are dealing with. This set is called the universal set or just the universe in set theory.

Definition 2.7: The *universe,* denoted as Ω, is the set of all elements that can possibly be included into any set. Therefore, all other sets will be subsets of the universe.

Example 2.10: In considering sets of students for each letter grade, the universe is the students enrolled in the class. (This is not the only possible universe. Some professors include past courses for comparison.)

Example 2.11: In considering sets of temperatures in Fahrenheit, the universe is all real numbers between -459.72 and $+\infty$.

Many times, it is easier to describe a set by describing what is *not* in the set. This leads to the concept of the complement operation.

Definition 2.8: The *complement* of a set is the set of all elements in the universe that are *not* in the set.

Example 2.12: For the universal set {1,2,3,4,5}, the complement of the set {1,2,3} is the set {4,5}.

Example 2.13: For the universe of all positive real numbers [0,∞], the complement of the set [3,∞] is the set of real numbers [0,3). (We denote the exclusion of the number 3 by a parenthesis instead of a bracket.)

Using the concepts above, we can describe very complex collections of objects. Certain relationships between sets are important enough to have special names.

Definition 2.9: Two sets A and B are termed *mutually exclusive* (or *disjoint*) if they have no elements in common (i.e., $A \cap B = \varnothing$).

Definition 2.10: Two sets A and B are termed *mutually exhaustive* if they contain between them all the elements of the universal set (i.e., $A \cup B = \Omega$).

Definition 2.11: Two sets A and B *partition* the universal set Ω if they are both mutually exclusive (A ∩ B = empty) and mutually exhaustive (A ∪ B = Ω).

A useful example of sets are areas of the plane. A set may consist of all the points on and inside a closed contour such as a circle. The universe is usually denoted as a large box. These drawings, called *Venn diagrams,* are often useful to help you think about a set-theoretic concept. Let us review the previous definitions using Venn Diagrams.

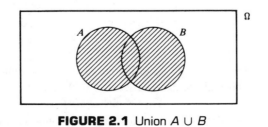

FIGURE 2.1 Union $A \cup B$

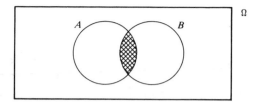

FIGURE 2.2 Intersection $A \cap B$

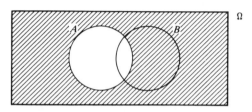

FIGURE 2.3 Complement of A

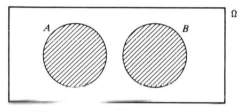

FIGURE 2.4 Mutually Exclusive

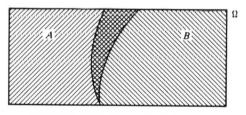

FIGURE 2.5 Mutually Exhaustive

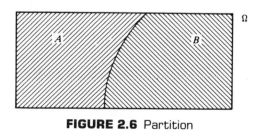

FIGURE 2.6 Partition

The theory of sets has its laws, or axioms, which the objects and operations must obey. They are simply listed here, but you may want to try convincing yourself of their truth by using Venn Diagrams (see the exercises).

Laws of Set Theory

1. Commutative	$A \cap B = B \cap A$	
	$A \cup B = B \cup A$	
2. Associative	$A \cap (B \cap C) = (A \cap B) \cap C$	
	$A \cup (B \cup C) = (A \cup B) \cup C$	
3. Distributive	$A \cap (B \cup C) = (A \cap B) \cup (A \cap C)$	
	$A \cup (B \cap C) = (A \cup B) \cap (A \cup C)$	
4. Identity	$A \cap \Omega = A$	
	$A \cup \varnothing = A$	
5. Inverse	$(A')' = A$	
6. DeMorgan's	$(A \cap B)' = A' \cup B'$	
	$(A \cup B)' = A' \cap B'$	
7. Exclusion	$A \cap A' = \varnothing$	

Table 2.1

Exercises

2.1 List, in set notation, the set of elements formed by each of the following operations:
   a. $\{1,2,3,4\} \cup \{3,4,5,6\}$
   b. $\{1,2,3,4\} \cap \{3,4,5,6\}$

2.2 Sometimes, the notation $A - B$ is used to denote the set of all elements in A that are *not* in B. Write out an expression, using our notation of $\cap$, $\cup$, $'$, and Ω, which is equivalent to $A - B$.

2.2.2 Sample Space and Event: Some Special Sets

Now that we have established a method for discussing collections of things, let us return to the original problem. We wish to construct a model of processes where multiple possible outcomes of an experiment can occur. Since we have a collection of possible outcomes, we can describe that collection as a set.

Definition 2.12: The *sample space* for an experiment is the set of all possible outcomes. The outcomes are elements and the *sample space* is the universal set for our model.

Example 2.14: For our example of flipping a coin, the possible outcomes were *H* (heads) and *T* (tails) Therefore, the sample space was the set {*H*, *T*}.

Example 2.15: For an experiment with multiple coins (or multiple flips of the same coin) we have outcomes such as *HTH* and *HTT*. Since the sample space is the set of all possible outcomes, it is the set of all possible combinations of *H* and *T* for the number of coins flipped. Therefore, the sample space for three coins is the set {*HHH*, *HHT*, *HTH*, *THH*, *HTT*, *THT*, *TTH*, *TTT*}.

Example 2.16: For an example in a continuous environment, consider an experiment that measures the time until the next person speaks to you. Since the split second a person speaks can be measured arbitrarily accurately, we are using a continuous environment model. The possible outcomes can be any point in time from now (a value of zero) until infinity (since some arbitrary descendent could still address you even if you had passed away) Negative values are not included since negative time refers to the preceding, not the next, person. Therefore, the sample space for this experiment is the infinite set of real numbers $[0, \infty]$.

Another concept that is *very* important to our model is the notion of an event. The idea is actually very simple. Many times, we are not as interested in the actual outcome of the experiment as in the consequence of an outcome. Consider the common example of the game of roulette. We are not interested in whether or not a particular drop of the ball occurs, but we are interested in if we win or lose. We refer to the fact that we win as an event. This event will occur if any one of a series of outcomes occurs. If we have bet on black, then any of the numbers 2, 4, 6, 8, 10, 11, 13, 15, 17, 19, 20, 22, 24, 26, 29, 31, 33, 35 is a winner. If we have bet on odd, then any of the numbers 1, 3, 5, 7, 9, 11, 13, 15, 17, 19, 21, 23, 25, 27, 29, 31, 33, 35 is a winner.

Definition 2.13: An *event* is a set of outcomes. It is a subset of the sample space.

From this definition, there are two extreme events. It may be a set with no elements or the entire sample space. If the event contains no elements, no possible outcome can lead to that event. The event can never occur. On the other hand, if the event is the entire sample space, that event must always occur, since *any* outcome will always be a member of the event.

Example 2.17: Consider the experiment of flipping two coins. The sample space is {*HH, HT, TH, TT*}. The sets {*HH, HT, TH, TT*}, {*HH, TT*}, {*HT, TH*}, {*HH*}, and {*HT, TH, HH*} are all examples of events.

It is very important in the actual use of events in this model to define the problem as simply as possible. In the example above, we could describe one event as the flipping of two coins such that we observed each coin showing heads or each coin showing tails. An alternative idea is simply to describe the event as both coins showing the same side.

Example 2.18: Consider the continuous environment example of the temperature in a room. If we describe the result of the experiment as a reading of 72.2 degrees Fahrenheit whenever the actual temperature is between 72.150000 . . . and 72.249999 . . ., the reading of 72.2 degrees is an event. We have defined a reading of 72.2 as a set of possible outcomes in the actual temperature range.

An important thing to notice (we will use it often) is the constructive nature of events using set theory. Since an event is a set, we can construct complex events from other simple events by union, complement, and intersection.

In fact, we may consider the idea alluded to earlier about sets of sets. If we think of a set of events, we are considering the set of sets concept. Let us now consider the set of *all* possible events. That set will contain the empty set ($\emptyset$), the universal set (Ω), and all other possible subsets of Ω. Some events will have all but one of the elements of Ω, some will have all but two, and so on. This set of sets has a special name.

Definition 2.14: The *power set* of a set A is the set of all possible subsets of the set A.

Exercises

2.3 Describe the set that represents the sample space for a roll of a single die.

2.4 Describe the set that represents the sample space for a student's grade-point average, where A = 4, B = 3, C = 2, D = 1, and F = 0.

2.2.3 Probability Measure: Laws of Probability

So far we have discussed only the possible outcomes of an experiment and the ways to manipulate them. We have considered events that are of a more general nature, as a sort of "result" of an experiment. Until now we have avoided the concept of relative frequency which we mentioned in the first section. For our model to be useful we need to know more than what may happen. We also need some measure of how often we can expect "something" to happen.

We will add to our model an abstract quantity, the probability measure, which will represent the relative frequency. We will use it to predict what we would measure for the relative frequency in a large number of repeated experiments. For the time being, we will concentrate on the concept itself, its behavior, and its manipulation. The discussion of exactly how we determine the probability measure for a physical process will be postponed until later.

First, let us consider the properties of this measure. The measure should give a value representing the relative frequency for any set of outcomes (an event). That value should clearly be positive for any event. (How could we have a negative relative frequency?) It should be 1 for the sample space (since every experiment will have an outcome in the sample space, every experiment will count toward the event Ω). Finally, if we consider a new event which includes all the outcomes of another event plus some extra, the relative frequency should be at least as large. Therefore, we define this part of our model in the following way.

Definition 2.15: For a sample space Ω a *probability measure P* is a function defined on all the subsets of Ω (the events) such that:

    1. $P[\Omega] = 1$.
    2. For any event $A \subset \Omega$, then $P[A] \geq 0$.
    3. For any events A, $B \subset \Omega$ where $A \cap B = \varnothing$, then $P[A \cup B] = P[A] + P[B]$.

These rules are referred to as the *laws of probability*. We will make extensive use of them. From these rules we can quickly derive a series of other relationships that will also prove very useful (see the exercises).

Example 2.19: We can show that the relationship $P[A'] = 1 - P[A]$ holds by making use of some of our set theory identities. We know that $\Omega = A' \cup A$ and $A' \cap A = \varnothing$, so we can use law 3.

$$P[\Omega] = P[A' \cup A] = P[A'] + P[A]$$
$$1 = P[A'] + P[A]$$
$$1 - P[A] = P[A']$$

As an obvious application of this new result, we can get the value of the probability measure for the empty set.

$$\Omega' = \varnothing$$
$$P[\varnothing] = P[\Omega'] = 1 - P[\Omega] = 1 - 1 = 0$$

Example 2.20: We can show that for any two sets A and B, then $P[A \cup B] = P[A] + P[B] - P[A \cap B]$. We begin by breaking the sets A and B into two disjoint sets and then use law 3.

$$P[A] = P[(A \cap B') \cup (A \cap B)] = P[A \cap B'] + P[A \cap B]$$
$$P[B] = P[(A' \cap B) \cup (A \cap B)] = P[A' \cap B] + P[A \cap B]$$

We can now break the union of A and B into three disjoint sets using law 3 each time.

$$P[A \cup B] = P[((A \cap B') \cup (A' \cap B)) \cup (A \cap B)]$$
$$P[A \cup B] = P[(A \cap B') \cup (A' \cap B)] + P[A \cap B]$$
$$P[A \cup B] = P[A \cap B'] + P[A' \cap B] + P[A \cap B]$$

We can now use the previous result for the probability of set A and set B to substitute and cancel terms.

$$P[A \cup B] = P[A] - P[A \cap B] + P[B] - P[A \cap B] + P[A \cap B]$$
$$P[A \cup B] = P[A] + P[B] - P[A \cap B]$$

Although the three laws of probability are sufficient for all sample spaces with a finite number of subsets, if there are an infinite number of subsets, we have a problem. Consider a situation where we have an infinite number of subsets that partition the sample space. We can add up any number of them to get arbitrarily close to the whole sample space, but we cannot actually reach it. In other words, not only do the rules have to hold for all points up to the limit, they must hold at the limit as well. To handle this specific case for sample spaces with an infinite number of subsets, we must add one additional law.

4. For mutually disjoint events A_m, $P\left[\bigcup_{m=1}^{\infty} A_m\right] = \sum_{m=1}^{\infty} P[A_m]$

With the addition of the probability measure, we now have two different kinds of things to deal with, each with its own set of rules. Events are sets and are manipulated by set operations. They must obey the rules of set theory. Probability measures are functions that give real values between 0 and 1. They must obey the rules of probability. We must be aware of these differences because we will use different rules for each manipulation, depending upon the type of objects.

Exercises

2.5 Which of the following can not be part of a valid probability measure for the sample space $\{a,b,c,d\}$? Why?
   a. $P[\{a\}] = 0.2$, $P[\{b\}] = 1.1$, $P[\{c\}] = 0.3$, $P[\{d\}] = 0.4$
   b. $P[\{a\}] = 0.1$, $P[\{b\}] = 0.2$, $P[\{c\}] = -0.3$, $P[\{d\}] = 0.4$
   c. $P[\{a\}] = 0.2$, $P[\{b\}] = 0.1$, $P[\{c\}] = 0.3$, $P[\{d\}] = 0.4$
   d. $P[\{a\}] = 0.2$, $P[\{b\}] = 0.1$, $P[\{a,b\}] = 0.4$

2.6 Which of the following can not be part of a valid probability measure for the sample space of points x on the real line between 0 and 1? Why?
   a. $P[a \le x < b] = a - b$ for $0 \le a < b \le 1$
   b. $P[a \le x < b] = 2(b - a)$ for $0 \le a < b \le 1$
   c. $P[x < b] = b$ for $0 \le b \le 1$
   d. $P[a \le x < b] = \dfrac{b + a}{2}$ for $0 \le a < b \le 1$

2.7 What is the probability of rolling a 5 with two dice?

2.8 Given $P[A] = 0.6$, $P[B] = 0.7$, and $P[A \cup B] = 0.8$, what is $P[A \cap B]$?

2.2.4 Conditional Probability—Adjusting the Model

We now have all the basic parts of our model. It is only necessary to learn how to use it effectively. As a first step, let us consider how the model can easily be modified after it has been defined.

Consider a simple situation. A model of a process has been established with its sample space (and resulting events) and its probability measure. We discover (or are informed) that our sample space was too general. Some of the outcomes have been ruled out. In other words, a condition has been added to our original model, namely, a restriction of the possible outcomes. The question now arises: How can we easily modify our probability measure so that it is correct and still consistent with our original?

This new probability measure is termed the conditional probability since the original has changed due to an additional condition. The actual change is a simple calculation.

Definition 2.16: The *conditional probability* $P[A \mid B]$ is the probability measure for an event A given that only outcomes which are in event

B are considered. This is sometimes shortened to read "the probability of event A given event B."

To evaluate $P[A \mid B]$, let us consider its meaning in more detail. Since we are restricted to outcomes in the event B, only outcomes in the event $A \cap B$ could result in the event A. We must also maintain the laws of probability for this new probability measure, so $P[B \mid B] = 1$. This is simply acknowledging the fact that the condition that event B did occur now limits our universe to that event. If the event B really was a restriction (i.e., $B \neq \Omega$), then $P[B] < 1$. So changing the measure such that $P[B \mid B] = 1$ implies that $P[B \mid B]$ is somehow "scaled up" from the original measure $P[B]$. The precise relationship is simply the ratio

$$P[A \mid B] = \frac{P[A \cap B]}{P[B]} \text{ where } P[B] \neq 0 \qquad (2.2)$$

Remember that we are calculating a "new" probability measure $P[A \mid B]$ using the "old" values $P[A \cap B]$ and $P[B]$. We cannot simply drop the "given" notation $\mid B$. Let us review this reasoning using the Venn diagram on p. 23.

We began by defining a probability measure on the sample space Ω. However, in conditioning on the event B, we now restrict our consideration to the shaded portion of the original sample space. Notice that the only outcomes under consideration that could result in event A are the outcomes in the event $A \cap B$ (the crosshatched region). So now, when we consider the likelihood that event A occurred given the fact that the event B did occur (i.e., only outcomes in event B are considered), we see that we need to relate the portion of the shaded region $A \cap B$ to the entire shaded region B. We already have the measure of the likelihood of each of these events with respect to Ω, namely $P[A \cap B]$ and $P[B]$. Therefore, our new model of the likelihood of $A \mid B$ is simply $P[A \cap B]/P[B]$.

Example 2.21: Consider the case of flipping two identical and fair coins. We know that the probability of getting two heads is ¼. However, what is the probability of getting two heads if I peek and tell you that at least one of the coins is definitely a head? We know that the probability of at least one of the coins being a head is ¾ since three of the four possible outcomes has at least one head. Therefore, the probability of getting two heads given that one is a head is ¼ divided by ¾, or ⅓.

We have noted that the ratio $P[A \cap B]/P[B]$ is defined only for $P[B] \neq 0$. This is more than a question of division by zero since if $P[B] = 0$ then $P[A \cap B] = 0$. What this says is that for conditioning on an event with zero

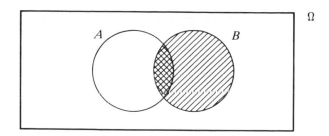

probability, the new probability measure is completely unknown. It could be anything. This is not a bothersome problem since conditioning on such an event is not useful. In fact, if we write out this concept in English, its absurdity becomes obvious. What is the probability of an event given the information that an impossible event occurred?

It is often useful to "invert" the formula for conditional probability and use it differently. If we can easily obtain $P[A \mid B]$ and $P[B]$, we can calculate the event $P[A \cap B]$. Since $P[A \mid B]$ is a restricted case, it is often easier to determine that value than $P[A \cap B]$. This idea is often drawn out in the form of a tree diagram and so has been called a *probability tree*. The tree is made up of nodes that represent the events (each level being more restrictive and complex) and the arcs that represent the conditional probability to get from one node to the next.

The calculation of the probability of a complex event such as $A \cap D$ can be visualized as multiplying the values $P[D]$ and $P[A \mid D]$ on all of the arcs followed to get to that event node in the tree.

Example 2.22: Consider the case of a game where you flip a coin to determine whether you flip one or two additional coins. When you flip a head you flip two more coins, and when you flip a tail you flip only one more coin. The problem is to determine the proba-

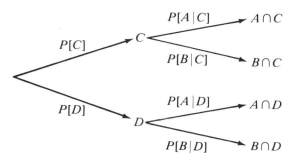

FIGURE 2.7 Probability Tree

bility of getting all different combinations of numbers of heads or tails. It is easier if we notice that we know the probabilities of getting a number of tails, say 2, if we know (conditioned upon) the flip of the first coin. If the coin was a head, we can flip two T only by flipping a T and a T. If the coin was a tail, we can flip another T only by flipping a single T. Therefore, the probability that we will flip two T is simply $\frac{1}{2} \cdot \frac{1}{4} + \frac{1}{2} \cdot \frac{1}{2} = \frac{3}{8}$. The probability tree shown below illustrates all of the possibilities.

Exercise

2.9 If a bucket contains two red and three white balls, calculate the probability that you would draw, one at a time without replacing a draw, two white balls.

2.2.5 Independence

Suppose that the probability of an event does not change when a condition is given. In other words, the information that an outcome of an experiment falls in an event B, which is a proper subset of the sample space Ω, in no way affects the predicted relative frequency of another event A.

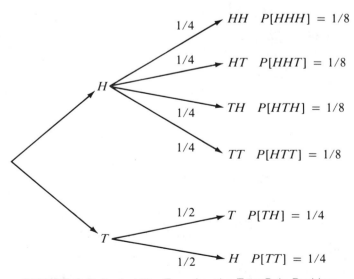

FIGURE 2.8 Probability Tree for the Two Coin Problem

We call this relationship *independence*. We consider two events independent if knowledge about the occurrence of one event does not change our knowledge about the relative frequency of the other event. Then we have the following relationship if event A is independent of event B:

$$P[A \mid B] = P[A]$$

But we know that

$$P[A \mid B] = \frac{P[A \cap B]}{P[B]}$$

So

$$P[A \cap B] = P[A] \cdot P[B] \tag{2.3}$$

Since intersection is reflexive ($A \cap B = B \cap A$), A being independent of B leads to the same relationship as B being independent of A. This is consistent with our intuitive understanding of independence.

Definition 2.17: Two events A, $B \subset \Omega$ are *independent* if and only if $P[A \cap B] = P[A] \cdot P[B]$.

We define independence in this way, rather than with conditional probabilities, to include the possibility of either event having zero probability. Since if $P[B] = 0$, then $P[A \cap B] = 0$ and event A is independent of event B. This implies that any event is independent of any other event whose probability measure is zero, such as the empty set. This makes sense if you consider the English description of the relationship. Knowledge about the occurrence of any event can give no additional information about an impossible event. If we defined independence with a conditional probability, we would have to include the cases of A and B having probability zero as special cases, since the conditional probability would be undefined for zero divided by zero.

Example 2.23: Consider the example of flipping two identical and fair coins. Now we ask the question: Is the flipping of the second coin independent of the first coin? We know that the probability of getting heads on the second coin is ¼ plus ¼ or ½ since two possible outcomes $\{T, H\}$ and $\{H, H\}$ give that case. And we know that the probability of getting heads on the second coin given that we have tails on the first coin is ¼ for $\{T, H\}$ divided by ½ for $\{T, H$ or $T\}$, which is ½, the same as the probability of the event itself. Therefore, the two events are independent.

Independence between more than two events is more complicated. We cannot simply extend our definition with more terms. Consider three events A, B, and C, and assume that B was the empty set. Then the intersection of A, B, and C would be empty regardless of the relationship between A and C. Similarly, the product of the probabilities of the individual events $P[A]$, $P[B]$, and $P[C]$ would be zero no matter what $P[A]$ and $P[C]$ were. Therefore, we would satisfy the condition $P[A \cap B \cap C] = P[A] \cdot P[B] \cdot P[C]$ if $B = \varnothing$ no matter what A and C were. So it is necessary to add additional conditions for all the possible interrelationships to be truly sure that the events are independent.

Definition 2.18: A set of events are *independent* if and only if the probability of the intersection of a set of those events equals the product of the event probabilities for *all* possible combinations of those events.

Exercise

2.10 For two independent events A and B, $P[A] = 0.2$ and $P[B] = 0.3$. What is the probability $P[A \cup B]$?

2.2.6 Bayes' Theorem

A very useful application of conditional probability is known as *Bayes' theorem*. It allows you, under certain circumstances, to invert a problem. It is based on the third property of a probability measure and the definition of conditional probability. Consider the Venn diagram in Figure 2.9.

If we start with a set of events A_i that partition the sample space Ω, we can see that $P[B] = \Sigma P[A_i \cap B]$. But for events with nonzero probability, $P[A_i \cap B] = P[A_i]P[B \mid A_i]$. Putting these together we get Bayes' theorem.

$$P[A_i \mid B] = \frac{P[A_i \cap B]}{P[B]} = \frac{P[A_i]P[B \mid A_i]}{\sum_j P[A_j]P[B \mid A_j]} \tag{2.4}$$

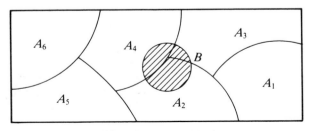

FIGURE 2.9 Bayes' Theorem

The only requirements for using Bayes' theorem are the set of mutually exhaustive and exclusive events which form the partition of the sample space and the fact that the event of interest has nonzero probability. This actually occurs more often than one might think.

Example 2.24: Consider a group of programmers who submit jobs to a system. For any job, it may run or fail to run. If we know the probability that a job submitted by a particular programmer will fail, and the relative frequency with which each programmer submits jobs, we can calculate, using Bayes' theorem, the probability that a programmer submitted a particular job, given that the job failed. Consider the case of three programmers 1, 2, and 3. Then define the following events:

Event A_1: program was submitted by programmer 1
Event A_2: program was submitted by programmer 2
Event A_3: program was submitted by programmer 3
Event B - program failed

Given the following probabilities:

$$P[A_1] = 0.2$$
$$P[A_2] = 0.3$$
$$P[A_3] = 0.5$$
$$P[B \mid A_1] = 0.1$$
$$P[B \mid A_2] = 0.7$$
$$P[B \mid A_3] = 0.1$$

we can calculate the desired probability using Bayes' theorem.

$$P[A_1 \mid B] = \frac{P[A_1]P[B \mid A_1]}{\sum_i P[A_i]P[B \mid A_i]}$$

$$P[A_1 \mid B] = \frac{0.2 \times 0.1}{0.2 \times 0.1 + 0.3 \times 0.7 + 0.5 \times 0.1}$$
$$= 0.07144$$

2.3 Combinatorics: Deriving Discrete Probabilities

We have not yet discussed how, outside of measurement, we can obtain a probability measure. One method to obtain values for a model is simply to count the number of possible outcomes N, assume that they are all equiprobable, and assign N^{-1} as the probability for each. (Such methods, of course, require a finite set of outcomes.) The general area of "counting" is historically called *combinatorics* from the counting of possible combinations of, say, playing cards, which make up all possible outcomes of a game. Although this topic is very important, we are limited in our scope in this book. In this section we only briefly introduce the basic concepts of combinatorics.

2.3.1 Basic Combinatoric Rules

There are two very basic rules in combinatorics. These rules are really common sense and are used by almost everyone.

Definition 2.19: The *rule of sum* states that if there are N outcomes in one event and K outcomes in another disjoint event, then there are a total of $N + K$ outcomes.

This can be considered as the generalization of the concept of counting each outcome, since an event can be a single outcome. Do not forget the reference to distinct events. This is the usual mistake made, where the rule of sum is invoked for two events with some common outcomes.

Example 2.25: There are three sides of a die with an even number of dots and three other sides of the same die with an odd number of dots. Therefore, since the sides are distinct and each is an outcome, the rule of sum implies that there are a total of six outcomes.

Definition 2.20: The *rule of product* states that if there are N possible outcomes in an experiment and there are K possible outcomes in another experiment, then taking both experiments as one, the number of possible outcomes is $N \cdot K$.

This is the most important rule in combinatorics. It should be clearly understood that this is a rule for combining less complex experiments into more complex experiments (e.g., flipping two coins instead just one).

Example 2.26: There are six sides on a die, so we have six outcomes in an experiment that rolls the die. If we roll two dice in an experiment, we have $6 \cdot 6 = 36$ different possible outcomes.

Exercises

2.11 After shuffling two decks of cards together, what is the probability of turning up an ace?

2.12 If you take two decks of cards and draw one card from each deck, what is the number of possible outcomes (draws)?

2.3.2 Sampling with Replacement

Assume that there is a set of N distinct elements. We wish to count the number of possible sequences of length R that we can obtain by drawing (sampling) an element from the set, noting its value, and returning it. If the sequence was of length 1, that is, a single draw, the answer is clearly N different sequences. Now consider the subsequent draws. Since we have replaced the original draw, we still have N possible values for the new draw. If one considers the two draws as separate experiments, we see that this is simply a case of the rule of product. Therefore, the number of sequences of length R, using N distinct elements with replacement, is N^R.

Alternatively, one can think of the case where the elements are the N digits $(0 \ldots N - 1)$. Then any sequence of length R is an R-digit number of base N. Clearly, there are N^R such numbers.

$$\text{Number of different samples of length } R \text{ with replacement} = N^R \quad (2.5)$$

2.3.3 Permutations

Again we begin with a set of N distinct elements. We wish to count the number of possible sequences of length R that we can obtain by drawing (sampling) an element from the set and placing it in a sequence (no replacement). Again, if the sequence was of length 1, that is, a single draw, the answer is clearly N different sequences. Now consider the subsequent draws. Since we did not replace the original draw, we have one less element to choose from in the new draw. Using the rule of product again, we see that the number of sequences of length R that can be obtained by drawing without replacement, is $N \cdot (N - 1) \cdot \cdots \cdot (N - R + 1)$.

If the sequence we are interested in contains all of the original N elements (a sequence of length N), we can substitute N for the value of R and get the number of different sequences that can be formed from N distinct objects. The result is simply $N \cdot (N - 1) \cdot \cdots \cdot 1$, which is so frequently used that the notation $N!$ (N factorial) has been adopted. Note that the value of $0!$ is defined as 1 since it is the product of no values, as with n^0.

$$\text{Number of sequences of size } R \text{ from } N \text{ elements} = \frac{N!}{(N - R)!} \quad (2.6)$$

Since each of the sequences of the entire N objects can be obtained from any other (no objects are missing or dropped) by a series of interchanges, such arrangements are called *permutations*.

$$\text{Number of permutations of } N \text{ elements} = N! \quad (2.7)$$

Example 2.27: Consider the set of elements $\{a,b,c\}$. We can rearrange them into $3! = 1 \cdot 2 \cdot 3 = 6$ different sequences: abc, bac, acb, bca, cab, and cba.

Exercise

2.13 If you deal out a sequence of five cards, how many different sequences could you deal out?

2.3.4 Combinations

Assume that there is a set of N distinct elements. We wish to count the number of possible groups of size R which we can obtain by drawing (sampling) an element from the set and placing it in the group, but we are not concerned with the actual order of the draw.

Combinations are similar to permutations, except that the actual order of the sequence is not important to us, only the identity of the elements. Therefore, if you start with a particular sequence and rearrange it, it would be considered the same combination of elements. This is very important to us, since that is exactly how a set is defined. A set is equivalent to another set if it contains exactly the same elements, regardless of the order.

If we take a sequence of length 0 we should have only one possible sequence. We would then have only one combination of N elements taken 0 at a time. Similarly, if we take a sequence of length N, it will always contain the same combination of elements. We would therefore have only one combination of N elements taken N at a time.

Example 2.28: Consider the set of $\{a,b,c\}$ again. We have several combinations of letters when we take two at a time. We can get ab, ac, and bc. Note that we do not consider ba different from ab.

How can we count such things as combinations? If you consider the combination as a permutation with many of the permutations being the same thing, you can derive the number of such combinations. Consider the number of permutations of N elements taken R at a time, $N!/(N - R)!$. Unfortunately, many of the permutations are really the same combinations. So we need to divide out the number of multiply counted combinations in those permutations. When we have a particular draw of R elements, we have fixed the first R elements of a possible sequence. However, since only the identities of the elements are important, we could have drawn those first R elements in $R!$ different ways and had the same combination of elements.

$$\text{Number of combinations of } N \text{ things taken } R \text{ at a time} = \frac{N!}{R! \cdot (N - R)!}$$

$$\frac{N!}{R! \cdot (N - R)!} \stackrel{\Delta}{=} \binom{N}{R} \tag{2.8}$$

The notation on the right is called the *binomial coefficient* since it is the coefficient of the Rth term in the expansion of $(x + y)^N$. We will use this notation often since we are normally counting sets when we are deriving probabilities.

Exercise

2.14 If you deal out five cards for a hand of poker, how many different hands could you have dealt out?

2.3.5 Size of the Power Set

The last problem we will consider in combinatorics is the counting of the number of possible subsets of a set of N elements. We find this of particular interest since this number is also the number of possible events that can be defined on a universe of N outcomes.

There are several different ways of viewing this problem. The first is the simplest to see and the most difficult to calculate. If we arrange all the subsets of a set in order by size, we see that we need to calculate the number of subsets of size R we can obtain from the set of size N. This is the same as the number of combinations of N elements taken R at a time. We then must add up all those numbers for subset sizes 0 to N.

$$\sum_{R=0}^{N} \binom{N}{R} = 2^N \tag{2.9}$$

To see how this is true, recall the interpretation that the number of combinations is the coefficient of the binomial expansion of $(x + y)^N$. To sum up only the coefficients, set $x = 1$ and $y = 1$. Then all terms in the expansion are merely the coefficients. However, the original factor is simply 2^N.

The other way of viewing this problem is to consider each element to be associated with a bit position in a binary number. If the bit is 1 the element is in the subset and zero if it is not. So each binary number with N bits represents a particular subset of the original set. So the problem is to count the number of different numbers that can be represented by N bits. That is simply 2^N.

2.4 Random Variables

Although our model is complete, its structure is a bit cumbersome. We all know that it is easier to tell someone how many apples you have in a bushel by counting the apples than to carry the bushel to show them. The same thing is true of the sets we have used as our basis for probability theory. It is much easier to use and manipulate numbers than other representations. (Try discussing the outcome of a roll of a pair of dice without counting the spots.) Therefore, we will adopt a technique to "carry" information about events using numbers in order to simplify the manipulation of events.

Definition 2.21: A *random variable* is a function that assigns a real number to each possible outcome in the sample space. (Note that these values need not be distinct for different outcomes.)

This function will allow us to discuss events as real numbers. It will also allow us to restrict our discussion to the important features of complex experiments since we can map different outcomes to the same value if we are not interested in distinguishing the outcomes.

Example 2.29: For a game of roulette, if we always bet on red with two dollars, we can describe our wins (two dollars more) or losses (two dollars less) as a random variable that assigns the value of 2 to each outcome with a red number and a value of -2 to each outcome with a black number or 00.

Note that the statement that the random variable had a value of 2 actually describes an event (we won!). Since many possible outcomes will map into the same value for a particular random variable, we now consider only a certain set of events as our objects of interest. This is sometimes referred to as the *event space*. In fact, we can discuss ranges of random variables. If we refer to the fact that the random variable defined above had a value less than 3, that includes all possible values of the random variable. We have therefore just constructed the event which is the universe for this experiment. Similarly, we can obtain the empty event by restricting the range on the values of the random variable to be less than -3.

We do not have to restrict our function, the random variable, to a finite, or even countable subset of the real numbers. It is perfectly reasonable to define a random variable as an arbitrary function.

Example 2.30: Consider an experiment of throwing darts at a rectangular piece of paper where we consider only throws that hit the paper as outcomes. Then define a random variable that measures the distance the dart hit from the left side of the paper divided by the width of the paper. This random variable can take on all values between 0 and 1. (Note that we could have defined a random variable to be the distance from the top of the paper for the same experiment.)

Example 2.31: Consider the incremental measurement of the temperature in a room. At each moment we will read a decrease or increase in the temperature. Here the random variable is the real number that indicates the amount of decrease or increase. Obviously, a different unit of measure (Fahrenheit or Celsius) has a different function (random variable) for the same actual increase or decrease in temperature.

It is important to remember that the random variable is a *function* X which assigns a *value* x to an outcome. Many times, when the statement "A random variable X is equal to 10" is made, confusion may arise because the actual meaning is forgotten. More precisely, the statement would have been: "An outcome occurred such that the function (random variable) X, when applied to that outcome, resulted in the value 10." As long as the meaning is clearly understood, the shorter statement will suffice.

Exercise

2.15 What are the possible values of a random variable that represents the counts of the number of dots showing on a pair of dice?

2.4.1 Cumulative Distribution Functions

Now that we have added the random variable concept to map all the sets we may deal with into real numbers (which are still sets of course), we need to add a feature to modify our concept of probability measure. We wish to condense all the information that was cumbersome (such as a table of values for all possible outcomes and sets of outcomes) to some easily describable function of the random variable.

How do we construct such a function? Consider the idea of counting in combinatorics. There we tried starting at some point and literally listed all the possibilities. Here we would like to have such a recursive approach, but we have outcomes mapped onto the real line $[-\infty, +\infty]$. So the function must be defined on the real line and may be defined on an uncountable number of outcomes. To provide structure, we pick an order for the real line, from left to right. To provide simplicity, instead of dealing with all events, we pick events of the form $[-\infty, x]$ and define our function at the point x as the value of the probability measure for the event $[-\infty, x]$. This makes our inclusion of additional outcomes recursive since as we increase x we include all of the previous events as well. In addition, given this form, we can construct any event from appropriate unions and intersections of events of the type $[-\infty, x]$, so it is also complete.

Definition 2.22: The *cumulative distribution function* (CDF) F for a random variable X is equal to the probability measure for the event that consists of all possible outcomes with a value of the random variable X less than or equal to x, that is $F(x) \triangleq P[X \leq x]$.

We have defined the cumulative distribution function for all $x \in [-\infty, +\infty]$ even if the random variable X is discrete and can only take on values at specific points within $[-\infty, +\infty]$. In fact, many cumulative distribution functions will be only piecewise continuous functions. In the case of discrete random variables, we will often use functions that have values defined in terms of integers. This is a shorthand notation for cumulative distribution functions that do not change their value in the range between successive integers.

Example 2.32: Recall the example of the experiment where we flip a fair coin. The possible outcomes were $\{H,T\}$ and the probability measure was $P[H] = \frac{1}{2}$ and $P[T] = \frac{1}{2}$. If we have defined the random variable x to be 1 when the outcome was H and 2 when the outcome was T, the cumulative distribution would look like a stairway starting at 0 left of 1, with a $\frac{1}{2}$ high step at 1 and a final $\frac{1}{2}$ step at 2 to a height of 1. This particular cumulative distribution function is shown in Figure 2.10.

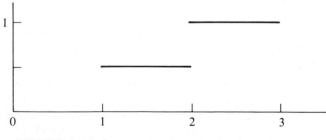

FIGURE 2.10 Cumulative Distribution for a Fair Coin

Example 2.33: Recall the example of the rectangular dart board. If we assume that the darts hit randomly on the paper (there is no bull's eye), we know that as we include more area of the paper in an event, the increase in the relative frequency (probability) will be constant for a constant area. In addition, we know that the paper is rectangular, so an equal increase in the distance from the left is an equal increase in the area. Therefore, the cumulative distribution function would appear as a line from 0,0 to 1,1. This function is shown in Figure 2.11.

We have now seen a couple of cumulative distribution functions. There are several properties that hold for these functions, simply because they are based on the probability measures we discussed earlier. Since as the value x approaches $+\infty$ on the real line, the event will approach the universal set, the cumulative distribution function must approach 1 as the value x approaches $+\infty$. Also, since as x approaches $-\infty$ on the real line, the event will approach the empty event, the cumulative distribution function will approach 0. Furthermore, since at each successively larger point on the real line the cumulative distribution function will include more of the probability measure (which is always greater than or equal to zero), the cumulative distribution function cannot decrease as x increases. We can summarize these properties for a cumulative distribution function F of a random variable X as follows.

1. $F(-\infty) = 0$
2. $F(\infty) = 1$
3. For $x_1 < x_2$, then $F(x_1) \leq F(x_2)$ [i.e., $F(x)$ is nondecreasing]

There are four particular distributions of random variables that are of great interest to us. These distributions are called the geometric, binomial, exponential, and Poisson. The geometric, exponential, and Poisson distributions are for random variables that have an infinite set of possible values. The binomial has only a finite number of possible values. The geometric, binomial, and Poisson distributions are discrete, whereas the exponential is continuous.

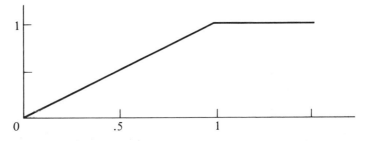

FIGURE 2.11 Cumulative Distribution for the Dart Position

Exercise

2.16 Describe the cumulative distribution function for the dart board using algebraic function notation.

The Geometric Distribution

The geometric distribution can be constructed by considering a specific experiment. Consider the case of flipping a biased coin which has a probability p of coming up tails. The experiment proceeds by flipping the coin as many times as necessary until a heads appears (a success). Even though you realize that you will probably get heads eventually, you cannot guarantee that it will not take just one more try. Therefore, the random variable K that represents the number of additional flips required to obtain a heads outcome could be infinite.

To construct the distribution, let us return to the definition of the cumulative distribution. The geometric cumulative probability distribution $F(k)$ is the probability measure for the event that $K \leq k$, that is, the event that it took less than or equal to k flips to obtain a heads. We know what the probability measure is for flipping a heads at precisely the $k + 1$st flip since that would require k tails and one head. Since the flips are independent, the probability of each flip can be multiplied to construct the probability of the complex event.

$$P[\text{flip the first heads on } (k+1)\text{st flip}] = (1 - p)p^k \text{ for } k = 0, 1, 2, \ldots$$
$$(2.10)$$

$$F(k) = \sum_{n=0}^{k} P[\text{flip the first heads on } (n + 1)\text{th flip}]$$

$$= \sum_{n=0}^{k} (1 - p)p^n = 1 - p^{k+1} \tag{2.11}$$

Alternatively, we could have asked ourselves the inverse question (remember that $P[A'] = 1 - P[A]$). The probability that no heads occur in the first $k + 1$ flips is simply the probability that we flip $k + 1$ tails in a row. That is simply p^{k+1}. So we get the same equation as before. This function is shown graphically in Figure 2.12.

The Binomial Cumulative Distribution

The binomial cumulative distribution is constructed using an experiment similar to the geometric case. The experiment is a series of precisely N coin flips (trials) and the random variable K is the number of heads (failures) appearing in those N coin flips.

Here we know the probability, p, of a particular coin flip turning up tails. So we can easily compute the probability of a particular sequence of coin flips which results in $K = k$ heads by using the independence result.

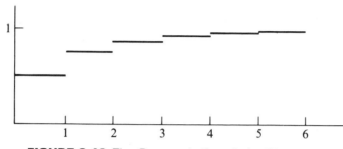

FIGURE 2.12 The Geometric Cumulative Distribution

$$P[\text{a sequence of } N \text{ flips with } k \text{ heads}] = (1 - p)^k \, p^{N-k} \qquad (2.12)$$

But there are many different sequences with k heads. In fact, there are as many sequences as there are combinations of N things taken k at a time.

$$P[k \text{ heads}] = \binom{N}{k} (1 - p)^k p^{N-k} \qquad (2.13)$$

Therefore, the cumulative distribution function for the binomial distribution is simply the equation

$$F(k) = \sum_{m=0}^{k} \binom{N}{m} (1 - p)^m p^{N-m} \qquad (2.14)$$

Note that this function does not have a closed form (i.e., something without a summation). This is unfortunately true for many cumulative distribution functions, making the use of the cumulative distribution function more cumbersome.

The Exponential Cumulative Distribution

This distribution is simply the continuous case analog of the geometric distribution. Since it is continuous, the idea of flipping a coin at specific points in times is no longer applicable. Instead, we think of successes happening at some rate λ. However, the basic idea is the same, in that the random variable T represents the amount of time until a success occurs. The difference is that a success can occur at any time between 0 and ∞.

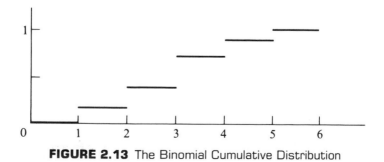

FIGURE 2.13 The Binomial Cumulative Distribution

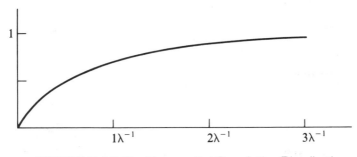

FIGURE 2.14 The Exponential Cumulative Distribution

$$F(t) = P[T \leq t] = 1 - e^{-\lambda t} \tag{2.15}$$

This distribution deals with time as a continuous quantity. We can interpret this idea of successes as an arrival of a job, a completion of a task, or a response by a user. The distribution is shown graphically in Figure 2.14.

The Poisson Cumulative Distribution

The Poisson cumulative distribution function is the analog of the binomial cumulative distribution function where trials are allowed at any moment in time (as in the exponential case). So for a fixed period of time T and a success rate of λ, we have the probability of k successes given by the equation

$$P[k \text{ successes in time } T] = \frac{(\lambda T)^k}{k!} e^{-\lambda T} \tag{2.16}$$

So we can construct the cumulative distribution function given below.

$$F(k) = \sum_{n=0}^{k} \frac{(\lambda T)^n}{n!} e^{-\lambda T} \tag{2.17}$$

Note that this distribution function does not have a closed form. A graph of the distribution function is given in Figure 2.15.

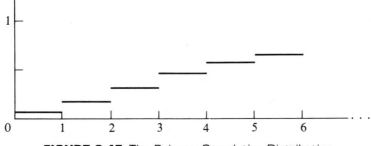

FIGURE 2.15 The Poisson Cumulative Distribution

2.4.2 Probability Density Functions

As is true in most systems, one particular representation is good for some things and poor for others. Because there are some other calculations we will want to perform on our models that are more suited to a different representation, we will discuss how we can transform the cumulative probability distribution into something called the probability density function. The relationship between the cumulative distribution and the density is simple. While the cumulative distribution continued to include more and more of the probability measure in a well-defined way, the density function is a measure of the amount of that increase in the cumulative distribution function. We can define the probability density function as the derivative of the cumulative distribution function if we include the concept that the derivative of a discontinuous jump is an impulse. In that way, we retain all of the information but represent it in a form that shows some quantification of how much of the probability measure is associated with an arbitrarily small range of the random variable. (Be careful; it does not necessarily represent the actual probability measure of a particular value of the random variable.)

Definition 2.23: The *probability density function f(x)* is the derivative of the cumulative distribution function $F(x)$; that is,

$$f(x) \triangleq \frac{d}{dx} F(x) \qquad \text{or inversely} \qquad \int_{-\infty}^{x} f(y)\, dy = F(x)$$

This form of the information is not uncommon. In fact you have often made use of a discrete example of the experimental analog of this function. If you recall our introduction to the probability measure, the probability measure was a model of the relative frequency of a particular outcome with respect to the number of experiments. A *histogram* is a particular example of such a frequency plot. In fact, for the discrete case, the probability density function is simply a functional representation of the probability measure. (But this is true only for the discrete case.)

We can list the basic properties of the probability density function simply by translating the properties of the cumulative distribution function. Since the density function is the derivative of the cumulative distribution function, we have the following properties:

1. Since $F(\infty) = 1$, $\int_{-\infty}^{\infty} f(x)\, dx = 1$.

2. Since $F(x)$ is nondecreasing, $f(x) \geq 0$.

Notice that we did not place any bounds on the value of the probability density function at a point. This is not an oversight, because the density can have an arbitrarily large value. In the case where we have a step function (like the coin flip) for a cumulative distribution function, we get an infinite value for the derivative at that point. In calculus, we really defined the derivative only for certain kinds of continuous functions (which did not include step functions). This problem is not unique to probability theory and is solved by defining a special function called the *impulse function*. This function [denoted symbolically as $\delta(x)$] has exactly the right properties to handle the discrete case.

One way of visualizing this function is to start with a bell-shaped curve that has an area equal to a specific value (the value of our step in the cumulative distribution function). We then take the limit of this function by making it narrower and narrower while raising its height to keep the area constant, until it has a zero width. So when the region of integration includes an impulse function, it contributes its area to the integral. Therefore, integrating a series of impulses results in a step function.

The normal graphical representation of the impulse function is a vertical arrow with a label, or specific height, to indicate its area. Using this notation we can graph a discrete density function in Figure 2.16. This density function corresponds to the cumulative distribution of the coin flip example.

In the case of continuous random variables the density function is very easy to derive. You simply take the derivative. (There are some cases where there is a mixture of both.) However, there is something that must always be remembered in the continuous random variable case. It is very tempting to label the discrete probability density as the probability measure. The problem is that in the continuous case, the analogy does *not* hold. In other words, the values of the continuous probability density function are not probabilities and cannot be interpreted as such. This is clear in some continuous density functions where the slope of the cumulative distribution exceeds 45 degrees. Since the derivative at that point is greater than 1 and we know that probabilities must always be less than 1, the density function cannot represent probabilities.

In the density for the dart board experiment, we see that the derivative is uniformly equal to 1 for all values of x between 0 and 1. If we had used a

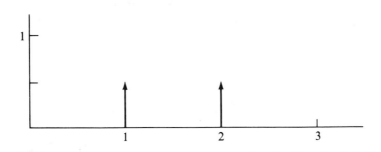

FIGURE 2.16 Probability Density Function for the Flip of a Fair Coin

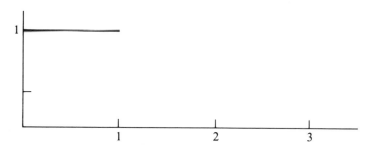

FIGURE 2.17 Continuous Probability Density Function for the Dart Board

different random variable such that the range would have been less than 1, we would have had a density that was uniform, but at a value greater than 1. Similarly, if we had defined the random variable to have a range greater than 1, we would have had a density that was again uniform, but at a value less than 1. These types of densities are common in modeling. The random variables that have this kind of density are referred to as uniformly distributed. The density functions for our four important distributions follow the same rules. See Figures 2.18–2.21.

For the geometric probability density function, differentiating the step function results in a series of impulses located at the points 0, 1, . . . , which are monotonically decreasing.

For the binomial probability density function, differentiating the step function results in a series of impulses located at the points 0, 1, . . . , N.

For the exponential probability density function, differentiating the exponential curve results in a different exponential curve which is monotonically decreasing.

For the Poisson probability density function, differentiating the step function results in a series of impulses located at the points 0, 1, . . .

$$f_k = (1 - p)p^k \qquad k = 0. 1, . . . \qquad (2.18)$$

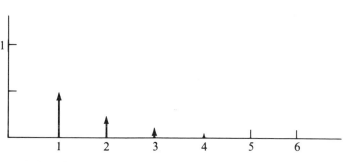

FIGURE 2.18 Geometric Probability Density Function

$$f_k = \binom{N}{k} (1 - p)^k p^{N-k} \qquad (2.19)$$

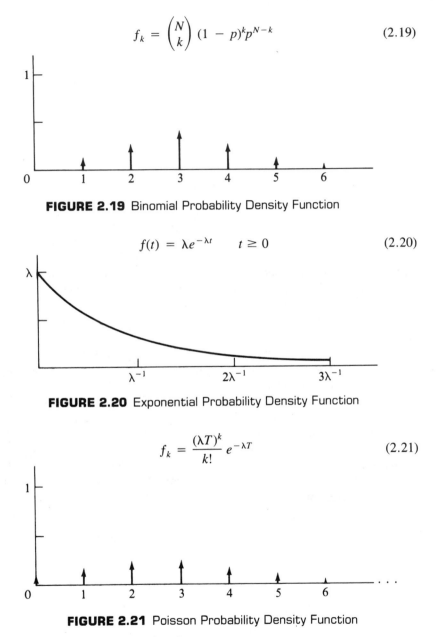

FIGURE 2.19 Binomial Probability Density Function

$$f(t) = \lambda e^{-\lambda t} \qquad t \geq 0 \qquad (2.20)$$

FIGURE 2.20 Exponential Probability Density Function

$$f_k = \frac{(\lambda T)^k}{k!} e^{-\lambda T} \qquad (2.21)$$

FIGURE 2.21 Poisson Probability Density Function

2.4.3 PDF Conditioned on an Event

It is possible to condition a density on some other event. However, when we consider arbitrary events, we must be cautious, since the event may include some restriction on the random variable in whose density we are interested.

Therefore, even though the method seems straightforward, one must be careful of the restriction imposed by the event. (Not only is the probability density function divided by the probability of the event, the range of the random variable is restricted so the probability density function is zero outside that range.)

Definition 2.24: The *conditional probability density function* $f(x \mid A)$ of a random variable X given an event A is the probability density function $f(x)$ restricted to the range of the random variable within the event A, divided by the probability of the event A, $P[A]$, that is,

$$f(x \mid A) = \frac{f(x)}{P[A]} \quad x \in A$$

2.4.4 Using CDF and PDF

The cumulative distribution and density functions are used to calculate probabilities of events (ranges on random variables) and expectations (average values of the random variables). The basic rules are simple. Cumulative distributions are normally used to calculate probabilities, and densities are normally used to calculate expected values. Since the two forms are easily derived from each other, one can always construct the cumulative distribution from the density if you need to calculate probabilities, and you can also construct the density from the cumulative distribution if you need to calculate expected values.

Calculating Probabilities

To calculate probabilities for a range of a random variable, it is a simple arithmetic operation using the cumulative distribution. To see this, recall the definition of the cumulative distribution $F(x) = P[X \le x]$. If we are interested in calculating the probability of an event where the random variable X is in the set $\{a < X \le b\}$ then we can return to our basic rules on the probability measure. We know from set theory that $\{X \le b\}$ is equal to $\{X \le a\} \cup \{a < X \le b\}$. Furthermore, we note that $\{X \le a\} \cap \{a < X \le b\} = \varnothing$ so we can apply the third law of probability.

$$P[X \le b] = P[X \le a] + P[a < X \le b]$$
$$P[X \le b] - P[X \le a] = P[a < X \le b]$$
$$P[a < X \le b] = F(b) - F(a) \tag{2.22}$$

So the calculation of the probability of any event (which can always be expressed as a combination of ranges on the random variable) is simply a series of additions or subtractions of the cumulative distribution evaluated at the points defining the ranges.

In the case of probability density functions, one must literally construct the cumulative distribution function for the values of interest. In this case we replace the cumulative distribution function in equation (2.22) with the equivalent density function evaluation.

$$P[X \le b] = F(b) = \int_{-\infty}^{b} f(x)\, dx$$

$$P[X \le a] = F(a) = \int_{-\infty}^{a} f(x)\, dx$$

$$P[a < X \le b] = F(b) - F(a) = \int_{a}^{b} f(x)\, dx \qquad (2.23)$$

Although we have consistently used the integral (or antiderivative) notation to calculate the cumulative distribution from the probability density function, in the discrete case we may note that this is just a series of increments in the distribution. In those cases, we use the summation notation Σ to indicate our action of adding up all the increments. Therefore, in the discrete case, we use summation in any place where we previously had integration.

Exercises

2.17 What is the probability that a dart lands in the middle third of the dart board?

2.18 What is the probability that a dart lands precisely in the middle of the dart board?

2.19 What is the probability that for a geometrically distributed random variable, the value is 4, 5, or 6?

Calculating Expectations

One of the most common calculations we will be performing is the evaluation of expected values. This is because the performance measures introduced in Chapter 1 are values averaged over an experiment. Such measures are modeled by the expected values of the random variable. Although there are other techniques for calculating expected values (see Chapter 3), we will define the fundamental procedure here.

Definition 2.25: The *expected value E[X]* of a random variable X is the weighted sum (integral) of all possible values of the random variable, that is,

$$E[K] \triangleq \sum_{-\infty}^{+\infty} k f_k \qquad E[X] \triangleq \int_{-\infty}^{\infty} x f(x)\, dx$$

The expected value can be calculated on a function of a random variable as well. The expected values of such functions as X, X^2, and X^3 are referred to as the *first, second,* and *third* moments of the random variable. The expected value of the random variable X (the first moment) is the same as the average value of the random variable. It is a measure of the center of mass of the probability density. Note that the expected value is not the value one "expects" to see as the outcome of an experiment. That would be the value with the highest probability. It is, instead, the value that one would expect to see as the average of the outcomes of several experiments.

Example 2.34: For the case of the random variable for the fair coin experiment, we had assigned the only two possibilities, 1 and 2, each with an impulse value of ½. Therefore, the expected value of that random variable is $1 \cdot \frac{1}{2} + 2 \cdot \frac{1}{2} = 1.5$.

Example 2.35: The expected value of a geometrically distributed random variable is a little more complicated. Here we must recognize the fact that the derivative of the summation is the same as the sum of the derivative.

$$E[K] = \sum_{k=0}^{\infty} k \cdot (1 - p) \cdot p^k$$

$$= (1 - p)p \sum_{k=1}^{\infty} k \cdot p^{k-1} \quad \text{but } k \cdot p^{k-1} = \frac{d}{dp} p^k$$

$$= (1 - p)p \sum_{k=1}^{\infty} \frac{d}{dp} p^k$$

$$= (1 - p)p \frac{d}{dp} \sum_{k=1}^{\infty} p^k$$

$$= (1 - p)p \frac{d}{dp} \left[\frac{1}{1 - p} - 1 \right]$$

$$= (1 - p)p \cdot \frac{1}{(1 - p)^2} = \frac{p}{1 - p} \qquad (2.24)$$

Example 2.36: The calculation of the expected value for an exponentially distributed random variable is, not surprisingly, similar to that for the geometric case.

$$E[T] = \int_0^\infty t \cdot \lambda e^{-\lambda t} \, dt$$

$$= -\lambda \int_0^\infty \left(\frac{d}{d\lambda} e^{-\lambda t} \right) dt$$

$$= -\lambda \frac{d}{d\lambda} \int_0^\infty e^{-\lambda t} \, dt$$

$$= -\lambda \frac{d}{d\lambda} \frac{1}{\lambda}$$

$$= \frac{1}{\lambda} \tag{2.25}$$

In a similar fashion we can calculate the second moments (expected values for K^2 and T^2) for these random variables. The second moment is a measure of the "spread" of the distribution. It is related to the common concept of variance (denoted by σ^2) by a simple relationship $\sigma^2 = E[X^2] - (E[X])^2$.

Example 2.37: In order to calculate the variance of the geometric distribution, we need to calculate the second moment, $E[X^2]$, of the random variable. With that result and the previous calculation of the first moment we can use $\sigma^2 = E[X^2] - (E[X])^2$ to obtain the variance.

$$E[K^2] = (1 - p) \sum_{k=1}^\infty k^2 p^k = (1 - p) \sum_{k=2}^\infty k^2 p^k + (1 - p)p$$

$$= (1 - p)p^2 \sum_{k=2}^\infty k^2 p^{k-2} + (1 - p)p$$

$$= (1 - p)p^2 \sum_{k=2}^\infty (k^2 - k)p^{k-2} + (1 - p)p^2 \sum_{k=2}^\infty k p^{k-2}$$

$$+ (1 - p)p$$

$$= (1 - p)p^2 \sum_{k=2}^\infty \frac{d^2}{dp^2} p^k + (1 - p)p^2 \sum_{k=2}^\infty k p^{k-2}$$

$$+ (1 - p)p$$

$$= (1 - p)p^2 \frac{d^2}{dp^2} \sum_{k=2}^\infty p^k + (1 - p) \sum_{k=0}^\infty k p^k$$

$$- (1 - p)p + (1 - p)p$$

$$= (1 - p)p^2 \frac{d^2}{dp^2} \left(\frac{1}{1 - p} - p - 1 \right) + E[K]$$

$$= (1 - p)p^2 \frac{2}{(1 - p)^3} + \frac{p}{1 - p} = \frac{2p^2}{(1 - p)^2} + \frac{p}{1} - p$$

$$= \frac{p(1 + p)}{(1 - p)^2}$$

$$\sigma^2 = E[K^2] - (E[K])^2 = \frac{p(1 + p)}{(1 - p)^2} - \frac{p^2}{(1 - p)^2}$$

$$= \frac{p^2}{(1 - p)^2} \tag{2.26}$$

Exercise

2.20 Find the average value (first moment) of a random variable K whose discrete probability density function is the Poisson density function, $[(\lambda\tau)^k/k!]e^{-\lambda\tau}$.

Other Names for the CDF and PDF

As is true in most disciplines, there are different names for similar concepts in probability theory. The entries in Table 2.2 are some of the many different labels given to the concepts. When reading other textbooks it is important to be aware of these differences.

Notice how some of the names are the same. This is the source of a great deal of unnecessary confusion. One of the major factors is the English meaning of distribution. Many authors will talk about how a random variable is distributed without making a specific reference to a function. In fact, some authors will

	Discrete	Continuous
$P[X \leq x]$	Cumulative distribution Distribution function Probability function	Cumulative distribution Probability distribution function
$\frac{d}{dx} P[X \leq x]$	Probability density Probability mass function Distribution function	Probability density Probability density function Density

Table 2.2

state that a random variable is exponentially distributed and then show a curve of the density function. As we have stated before, the distribution of a random variable is fixed by the probability measure for the events associated with the values of the random variables. We can express that distribution information in several forms, the cumulative distribution function or the probability density function. These functions each contain all the information about how that random variable is distributed.

One should note that there are still some subtle differences between some of these concepts. In this book we have adopted a notation and representation that more clearly exposes the relationships between the discrete and continuous environments. However, what has been left unsaid is that there is a problem since such a representation would require a significant amount of added complexity to handle the mathematical theory in a rigorous fashion. The traditional approach of defining a probability mass function for discrete random variables avoids the need for dealing with limit functions like impulses.

2.4.5 Multiple Random Variables

If you will recall, when we were discussing examples of random variables we alluded to the fact that you could have different functions (random variables) defined for the same set of outcomes. That is true and can often be useful. In the example of the rectangular dart board, two random variables could be defined. One was a measure of the dart's horizontal position from the left side. The other was a measure of the dart's vertical position from the bottom edge. Notice how for any specific value of one random variable there are several values for the other. But for a particular outcome, there is only one value of either random variable. This is due to the fact that we allowed random variables to map different outcomes into the same value.

Joint CDF and Joint PDF

Because we will often have more than one random variable, we need to consider the cumulative distribution and probability density as functions of more than one random variable value. We must maintain the same properties (since they are still defined in terms of the probability measure) and we will have a multidimensional space of real numbers.

Definition 2.26: The *joint cumulative distribution function* $F(x,y)$ is a function defined on all values of the random variables X and Y. $F(x,y)$ is equal to the probability measure for the event, that includes all possible outcomes that give rise to values of the random variables less than or equal to x and y, respectively, that is, $F(x,y) \triangleq P[X \leq x \text{ and } Y \leq y]$.

We see now that the multiple random variable case is no more difficult than the single case, except that the dimensionality has increased. For the two random variable case, the function is a surface that is nondecreasing in all the directions where neither random variable is decreasing.

Example 2.38: Recall the experiment where flipping the first coin determined the number 1 or 2 of the subsequent coins to be flipped. We originally were interested in the number of tails showing. So we define a random variable T as the number of tails showing. At the same time we may define another random variable, C, which represents the number of coins that were flipped. The joint cumulative distribution function for these random variables appears as the side of a pyramid built out of different size blocks. We can write down the function $F(c,t)$ in tabular form, as shown in Table 2.3.

$F(c,t)$	$t = 0$	$t = 1$	$t = 2$
$c = 2$	0	¼	½
$c = 3$	⅛	⅝	1

Table 2.3

Example 2.39: Recall the experiment with the rectangular dart board. There we saw that the random variables located the dart on the board using a coordinate system whose origin was the bottom left-hand corner. We had assumed that the dart throw was random, so that the distribution was uniform. Therefore, the joint cumulative distribution function is a surface whose value at a point is the area defined by the rectangle formed from perpendiculars lines dropped from that point to the left and bottom edges of the dart board. The function is zero at all of the points along the bottom and left-hand edges, and increasing toward the apex at the upper right-hand corner. It is easy to represent this function.

$$F(h,v) = h \cdot v \qquad \text{for } 0 \leq h, v \leq 1$$

In the same way we extend the concept of probability densities to handle multiple random variables. We will, however, need to use partial derivatives.

(Remember that partial derivatives are just like regular derivatives, where you treat the other variables as constants.)

Definition 2.27: The *joint probability density function* $f(x,y)$ is the second partial derivative of the joint cumulative distribution function, that is,

$$f(x,y) \triangleq \frac{\partial^2}{\partial x\, \partial y}\, F(x,y)$$

Example 2.40: In the case of the previous joint distribution for the coin flipping game, the joint density will be a series of impulses. The location of the impulses will be at the corner of the steps in the cumulative distribution function and they will have a value equal to the height of the step. The location and heights of the impulses are shown in the Table 2.4.

$f(c,t)$	$t = 0$	$t = 1$	$t = 2$
$c = 2$	0	¼	¼
$c = 3$	⅛	¼	⅛

Table 2.4

Example 2.41: In the case of the rectangular dart board, we had a simple function that is easily differentiated.

$$f(h,v) = \frac{\partial^2}{\partial h\, \partial v}\, h \cdot v = 1 \cdot 1 = 1 \qquad 0 \le h, v \le 1$$

Marginal Density Functions

In many cases, we have a joint probability density but wish to ignore one of the random variables and instead, manipulate a single random variable. The calculation necessary is really very simple. We simply need to "lump" all of the density spread over multiple values of the random variable that we wish to ignore onto the density of the single random variable.

Definition 2.28: The *marginal probability density function* $f(x)$ for a random variable X is the integral (or sum) over all values of the random variable Y of the joint probability density $f(x,y)$, that is,

$$f(x) \triangleq \int_{-\infty}^{\infty} f(x,y)\, dy$$

Example 2.42: In the coin flipping game, we could add up all the values for the various numbers of tails showing for each count of the number of coins flipped to get the marginal density $f(c)$. So $f(2) = \frac{1}{4} + \frac{1}{4} = \frac{1}{2}$ and $f(3) = \frac{1}{8} + \frac{1}{4} + \frac{1}{8} = \frac{1}{2}$. This makes sense when you realize that the first coin flip determined the number of subsequent flips. So the probability of flipping two coins is precisely the probability of flipping a tail on the first flip.

Example 2.43: In the rectangular dart board example, we see how if we ignore the random variable representing the vertical position, we get exactly the same density we had originally when we considered only one random variable.

$$f(u) = \int_0^1 1 \, dv = 1$$

This is true in general. The marginal probability density function is the same as the density function that would have been defined if only one random variable had been considered in the first place.

Conditional Probability Density Functions

Many times, we will be interested in determining the probability density for a random variable given some specific information about the other. This is different from the concept of marginal probability density, where we were not concerned at all with the value of the other random variable.

Definition 2.29: The *conditional probability density function* $f(x \mid y)$ of a random variable X given Y is the joint probability density function $f(x,y)$ divided by the marginal density $f(y)$ of the random variable Y, that is,

$$f(x \mid y) = \frac{f(x,y)}{f(y)}$$

One has to be careful to remember that the conditional density is a density, possibly different, for each value of the other random variable y. So if you integrate $f(x \mid y) \, dx$ over the range of the random variable x, you will get the value 1 for any value of the random variable y.

Example 2.44: As an example, let us calculate the conditional density of the number of tails for a given value of the number of coins tossed in our coin flipping game.

$f(t \mid c)$	$c = 2$	$c = 3$
$t = 0$	0	¼
$t = 1$	½	½
$t = 2$	½	¼

Table 2.5

Independence

If we look closely at the example of the rectangular dart board, we notice that the relationship between the two random variables is really very special. Note that if we know that $h \leq 0.2$, we still have no idea what v could be. Also note that the marginal probability densities for both random variables are 1, and $1 \cdot 1$ is still 1, and that the range of each of the random variables is unaffected. These random variables are independent of each other.

Definition 2.30: Two random variables are *independent* if and only if their joint probability density is equal to the product of their individual marginal probability densities. [i.e. $f(x,y) = f(x) \cdot f(y)$]

Independence of random variables is an extension of the concept of independence of events. Since a random variable may map many outcomes onto a single real value, each value of the random variable represents an event. Therefore, for two random variables to be independent, each pair of events defined by each combination of the random variables must be independent in the underlying sample space and corresponding probability measure.

Unconditioning: A Useful Tool

Sometimes, when a solution to a problem is being constructed, the usual divide and conquer strategy is useful. We can often quickly specify a conditional probability density without knowing the actual joint density. However, from the definition of the conditional probability density function, cross multiplying by the density of the conditioning random variable gives the equation

$$f(x,y) = f(x \mid y) \cdot f(y) \tag{2.27}$$

Moreover, we can substitute this relationship in the definition for the marginal density. Now we can solve for a marginal density given a conditional density and the marginal density of the conditioning random variable Y by integrating (or summing in the discrete case) on the random variable Y.

$$f(x) = \int_0^\infty f(x,y) \, dy = \int_0^\infty f(x \mid y) \cdot f(y) \, dy \tag{2.28}$$

$$f_k = \sum_{n=0}^\infty f_{k,n} = \sum_{n=0}^\infty f_{k|n} f_n \tag{2.29}$$

This last form will prove useful in manipulating probability density functions. If we know the conditional probability density function of a random variable X conditioned upon the random variable Y, and we know the marginal probability density function of the random variable Y, we can find the marginal density of the random variable X directly. This is true even if the random variables are dependent. So, as we will see, a careful choice of the random variable Y can simplify a problem immensely. This idea, if you had not noticed, is analogous to Bayes' theorem for arbitrary events.

Example 2.45: We have already calculated the marginal density of the number of coins flipped in the coin flipping game, and we have just calculated the conditional density of the number of tails showing, given the number of coins flipped. Therefore, we can easily calculate the marginal density of the number of tails showing in the coin flipping game.

$$f(t = 1) = \tfrac{1}{2} \cdot \tfrac{1}{2} + \tfrac{1}{2} \cdot \tfrac{1}{2} = \tfrac{1}{2}$$
$$f(t = 2) = \tfrac{1}{4} \cdot \tfrac{1}{2} = \tfrac{1}{8}$$
$$f(t = 3) = \tfrac{1}{2} \cdot \tfrac{1}{2} + \tfrac{1}{4} \cdot \tfrac{1}{2} = \tfrac{3}{8}$$

2.5 Stochastic Processes

In all these cases, we have only considered the manipulation of one or more random variables defined on a single sample space. Yet we introduced the concept of probability as the limit of a series of independent repetitions of an experiment. So far, we have not been too concerned with repetitions of experiments. Nor have we concentrated on what those random variables represent. Now we wish to return to the concept of a series of observations.

In the models we need for computer systems, we are more concerned with how a system performs over some period of time than with any particular observation. We want to discuss several observations (experiments) of many different aspects (measures) of a system. Therefore, we will generalize our current concepts to consider successive experiments which are performed at specific moments in time, while retaining the idea of describing each experiment as having a different pattern of potential outcomes.

2.5.1 What Is a Stochastic Process?

In our analyses we want to consider a specific kind of model that mimics our environment. We are interested in discrete events (jobs, arrivals, completions, users, etc.) embedded in some measure of time. Each of these events is an experiment with some sample space (set of possible outcomes). Therefore, each of these events can have a random variable, potentially different, defined on its sample space. These experiments will continue to be observable as a series of events over time. A process (a series of experiments) that is embedded in time is called a stochastic process.

Definition 2.31: A *stochastic process* is a collection of random variables [$X(t)$ in the continuous case or $X_t \triangleq \{X_{t_0}, X_{t_1}, \ldots\}$ in the discrete case], parameterized on time t, which are defined on a common sample space.

Note that the distribution of the random variable $X(t)$ may not be the same at different points in time t_1 and t_2. If they are the same, we refer to the random variables as identically distributed. In addition, the particular points in time t_1 and t_2 have not been restricted. To specify a stochastic process completely, we must also distinguish when the samples of the random variable occur in time (the embedding points).

Example 2.46: The successive roll of a pair of dice in a game is a stochastic process. Each roll has the same sample space (i.e., 2-12) and each roll occurs at some point in time. Each of the random

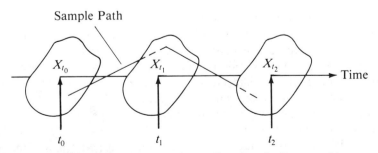

FIGURE 2.22 A Discrete Time Stochastic Process X_t

variables is identically distributed and independent (if we neglect the wear on the dice).

Example 2.47: The winnings of a player in a game based on the roll of a pair of dice is a stochastic process (sometimes called a *counting process*). Each roll has a sample space that is potentially zero to infinity. However, the distribution of the winnings depends on the amount bet and the previous winnings. So the distribution is different at each roll (a different random variable). (Note that it could be impossible to observe certain values, such as zero or a very large number, since there are limits on how much could be bet. Therefore, the probability measure would be zero in those regions.)

Recall that a random variable was defined as a function on the possible outcomes of an experiment (i.e. the sample space). Now, in a stochastic process, there are a series of outcomes (one for each repetition of the experiment) which are mapped by a series of (possibly different) random variables. This results in a real value being associated with each moment (repetition of the experiment) in time. This set of real values and their moments in time, represents a particular series of experimental outcomes (or observations) of the process through time.

Definition 2.32: A *sample path* is the set of values of the random variables for particular outcomes in a stochastic process and the times associated with those outcomes.

To describe a stochastic process completely, we need to know all of the random variables (or how they change with time) and at what points in time the variables change. That can be very complex. In many cases, the random variables do not change with time, so that a particular outcome at any time always maps into the same real number. In addition, the time between experiments (events) may have a simple form (like every minute). We will not consider stochastic processes in their most general form, but will instead concern ourselves with stochastic processes with the same distribution at each moment in time, or some easily described variation in the distribution at each moment in time.

In general, we always consider at least two random variables, which represent an event count (or an event indicator, like winnings) and a timing of the events. This concept of an underlying process is crucial to our models.

2.5.2 Some Specific Stochastic Processes

Two particular stochastic processes are of extreme interest to us, because of their properties. The Poisson process (continuous time) and the Bernoulli process (discrete time) will appear throughout this book. Two important random variables for each of these processes are an event count and a measure of time between events. These random variables have distributions which are already familiar to us.

Process Type	Event Counting	Time Between Events
Poisson Process	Poisson distribution	Exponential distribution
Bernoulli Process	Binomial distribution	Geometric distribution

Table 2.6

Notice that in the case of counting events, we have a parameter that is time but is not a random variable. We will have a different distribution for the number of events (the random variable) for a particular value of the parameter time. In the case of the time between events, time is the random variable, while the number of events becomes the parameter (a constant number of 1). In the more general cases, the time between every kth event in a Bernoulli process is distributed with a Pascal distribution, and the time between every kth event in a Poisson process is distributed with an Erlang distribution.

These processes are of interest to us because they have very nice renewal properties. These properties will make it possible for us to construct a more complex stochastic process model, a Markov chain.

2.5.3 Renewal Theory

When we consider successive experiments, we need to describe the information about the random variable for each of the successive outcomes in terms of its probability density function. (After all, each experiment may depend on the preceding one.) If we say that the information is the same (i.e., that the same probability density function is used), we say that the process is "renewed" at that time. This means that the time associated with that experiment is a renewal point. That simply means that the random variables have their original distributions.

A simple example of a renewal process (recall that a stochastic process is embedded in time) is the collection of arrival instants to some queue. If after an arrival the time before the next arrival has precisely the same distribution as the time for the previous arrival (i.e., the random variables are independent and identically distributed), this process is a renewal process.

A more complex example would be a case where a process was such that the distribution of time after an arrival until the next arrival was the same after precisely n arrivals. In this case we still have a renewal process, but it renews after every n trials. This is referred to as an nth order renewal process. This kind of process is more difficult to analyze, but we will find some use for this concept in simulation techniques.

Residual Lifetime

An important concept in renewal theory is residual lifetime. Basically, the residual lifetime is a new random variable whose distribution depends on the distribution of the original lifetime random variable at its renewal point, and some amount of expended time after the renewal point. You will often see this concept illustrated with an example of an item that can fail at any time, such as an integrated circuit.

Definition 2.33: The probability density function $r(t)$ for the random variable R representing the *residual lifetime* of a random variable A with a probability density function, $a(\tau)$, given that the original lifetime has expended t_e time is defined as

$$r(\tau - t_e \mid t_e) \triangleq a(\tau \mid \tau > t_e) = \frac{a(\tau)}{P[A > t_e]}$$

$$= \frac{a(\tau)}{1 - \int_0^{t_e} a(s) \, ds}$$

Defining $t = \tau - t_e$, we have

$$r(t \mid t_e) = \frac{a(t + t_e)}{1 - \int_0^{t_e} a(s) \, ds} \tag{2.30}$$

Of course, once we have a probability density function, we can derive the other representations of the distribution information.

$$R(t \mid t_e) = P[R \le t \mid t_e] = \frac{P[t_e < A \le t + t_e]}{P[A > t_e]} = \frac{A(t + t_e) - A(t_e)}{1 - A(t_e)} \tag{2.31}$$

Example 2.48: As an example, let us consider a consumable item such as a light bulb. The amount of time a certain kind of light bulb will stay lit can be modeled by a random variable T whose probability density function $b(\tau)$ is described by a uniform density.

$$b(\tau) = \begin{cases} \dfrac{1}{40} & 0 < \tau \le 40 \\ \\ 0 & \text{elsewhere} \end{cases}$$

If the light bulb has been on for 10 hours and has not burned out yet [which is a possibility for this $b(\tau)$], what is the residual lifetime of the light bulb?

$$b(t + t_e) = \begin{cases} \dfrac{1}{40} & t_e < t + t_e \le 40 \\ \\ 0 & \text{elsewhere} \end{cases}$$

$$1 - \int_0^{10} b(\tau)\, d\tau = 1 - \frac{1}{40} \cdot 10 = \frac{3}{4}$$

$$r(t \mid 10) = \begin{cases} \dfrac{1}{30} & 0 < t \le 30 \\ \\ 0 & \text{elsewhere} \end{cases}$$

So we see that the new probability density function is still uniform, but not identical to the original lifetime probability density function.

In order to calculate the average residual lifetime for a distribution, we need to find the first moment of the probability density function of the residual lifetime $r(t)$. That is not easy, and we simply quote the result. The average residual lifetime $\bar{r}$ is calculated from the first $\bar{f}$ and second $\overline{f^2}$ moments of the original lifetime density.

$$\bar{r} = \frac{\overline{f^2}}{2\bar{f}} \tag{2.32}$$

The Memoryless Property

Now that we understand the basic idea of a renewal process and residual lifetime, we want to look at a case that we will use extensively in the rest of the book. Whenever the residual lifetime of a process has the same distribution as the original process, we observe a property called the *memoryless property*. The property is so named because no matter how long it has been since an event has occurred, the distribution of time remaining (residual lifetime) is precisely the same as if no waiting had occurred. The process "forgot" that any time had been expended. If the process was the burnout and replacement of lightbulbs, then if we saw that the light bulb was on, regardless of how long the bulb had been on, the bulb would act as if it were brand new. This is an inherent property of Markov chains.

Only two distributions have this property. The geometric probability density is the discrete distribution that is memoryless and the exponential probability density is the continuous distribution that has this memoryless property.

Example 2.49: As an example, let us show, by finding the residual lifetime r_k, that the geometric probability density function has this property. We begin by substituting into the residual lifetime formula where k is the number of remaining trials until success and n is the number of previously observed trials (failures).

$$f_k = (1 - p)p^k$$

$$r_k = \frac{f_{k+n+1}}{1 - \sum_{m=0}^{n} f_m}$$

$$= \frac{(1 - p)p^{k+n+1}}{1 - (1 - p)\sum_{m=0}^{n} p^m}$$

$$= \frac{(1 - p)p^{k+n+1}}{1 - (1 - p)\frac{1 - p^{n+1}}{1 - p}}$$

$$= \frac{(1 - p)p^{k+n+1}}{p^{n+1}} = (1 - p)p^k$$

So $r_k = f_k$.

Exercise

2.21 Show that the exponential probability density function has the memoryless property.

Poisson Arrivals Take a Random Look

An important property of a Poisson process is that the points in time defined by the process are uniformly distributed within a fixed interval. This may seem contradictory, but it really is not, since we are no longer talking about the time between points, but their location within the interval.

To see how this is true, consider picking an arbitrary set of subintervals that partition the complete interval $[0,t]$. Denote the number of those subintervals as

k and each subinterval as h_1, h_2, . . . , h_k. If Poisson arrivals are uniformly distributed over $[0,t]$, the probability that exactly one Poisson point occurs in each of the subintervals will be the same as the probability of randomly selecting k points and finding exactly one of those in each of the subintervals.

We know the probability that exactly one of the k randomly selected points in $[0,t]$ would fall in each of the subintervals h_i. Since the probability a particular point hits an interval h_i is simply h_i/t and there are $k!$ ways to select intervals, we have the following equation.

$$P[\text{one point in each interval}] = \frac{k!}{t^k} h_1 h_2 \cdots h_k \qquad (2.33)$$

Since the Poisson process is memoryless, we know that the distribution for the time of the next arrival is the same even when conditioned on a new point in time. So each start of the subintervals can be considered as a renewal point. We can then calculate the probability of n arrivals in each subinterval independently as a Poisson distribution. Therefore, the probability that precisely one Poisson arrival occurs in each of those subintervals given that k Poisson arrivals occurred is given by the following equation.

$$
\begin{aligned}
P[\text{one point in each interval}] &= \frac{\lambda h_1 e^{-\lambda h_1} \lambda h_2 e^{-\lambda h_2} \cdots \lambda h_k e^{-\lambda h_k}}{e^{-\lambda t} \lambda^k t^k / k!} \\
&= \frac{\lambda^k e^{-\lambda[\Sigma h_i]} h_1 \cdots h_k}{\lambda^k e^{-\lambda t} t^k / k!} \\
&= \frac{k!}{t^k} h_1 \cdots h_k \qquad (2.34)
\end{aligned}
$$

So we have the same probability assuming Poisson arrivals as we do when we assume random selection. Since we did not restrict the number of those subintervals or their size, the result must be true for any number of subintervals which partition the interval in an arbitrary way. So, the location of those Poisson arrivals must be uniformly distributed in that interval $[0,t]$. We will make use of this since it implies that Poisson arrivals take a random "look" at the time line.

A Warning: The Bus Paradox

As we progress into using more complex models, we run the risk of improperly applying the methods we have studied. One such case is given here as an illustration of how easily a mistake can be made. We will solve the problem in two different ways to show how the mistake occurs.

Example 2.50: Consider a bus stop where the time between bus arrivals is exponentially distributed with a rate λ. Thus the bus arrivals form a Poisson process. If I walk up to the bus stop, how long do I have to wait until the next bus arrives?

1. *Possible solution.* Since buses arrive at a rate λ, the average time between arrivals is $1/\lambda$. But since we walk up at random, we would wait for only half an interval, on the average. So we would expect to wait $\frac{1}{2}\lambda$ for the next bus.
2. *Possible solution.* Since the time between buses is exponentially distributed, it is memoryless. So the residual lifetime for any time that I walk up should be distributed exactly the same way as the original distribution. Since the average time between buses is $1/\lambda$, the average time (residual) to wait would also be $1/\lambda$.

Which solution is correct? (You may have guessed, since this section is on renewal theory, that the second solution is correct.) Why is the first solution incorrect? The first solution is incorrect, simply because we assumed something that was not true. It is true that the "average" interval between buses is $1/\lambda$ long, but what makes us think that we would walk up during an "average" interval, to have only $\frac{1}{2}\lambda$ left?

The truth is that randomly arriving to the bus stop biases the selection toward long intervals. Consider the extreme case. Buses arrive at 8:00 a.m. and 8:10 a.m. If you randomly walk up, do you expect to wait until the 8:10 bus, or the next day to the 8:00 bus? To calculate correctly the time until we observe the next arrival, we would need to weight the interval size by the probability that we would select it. That probability will depend on the frequency of occurrences of the interval of particular size and on the size. If intervals occurred equally often, the probability would be the size of that interval divided by the length of the renewal period.

Exercise

2.22 If buses arrive at intervals of $\frac{1}{2}$ hour and 1 hour alternately, how long would you wait, on the average, for the next bus?

2.6 Problems

2.1 What are the sets resulting from the following operations?
   a. $[0,1]'$ where $\Omega = [-\infty,\infty]$
   b. $[-\infty,0] \cup [-2,3] \cup [1,5)$
   c. $\{2n + 1 \mid n = 0,1, \ldots\} \cap \{n \mid n = 0,1, \ldots\}$
   d. $\{2n + 1 \mid n = 0,1, \ldots\} \cap \{2n \mid n = 0,1, \ldots\}$

2.2 Using Venn diagrams, validate DeMorgan's laws.

2.3 Using the rules of set theory, show that for the three sets A, B, and C, $(A \cap B)' \cup C' = A' \cup (B \cap C)'$.

2.4 Reduce the following expressions.
    a. $((A \cup B') \cap (A \cup C'))'$
    b. $A \cup (B \cap A)$
    c. $B \cap (C \cup B')$
    d. $((A' \cup B') \cap (A' \cup B))'$

2.5 Describe the sample space for the following.
    a. The roll of a pair of dice.
    b. The number of jobs in a computer system.
    c. An observation of a character received by a modem.
    d. The amount of time you wait for a response from a timesharing system.

2.6 Given $P[A] = 0.6$, $P[B] = 0.7$, and $P[A' \cap B'] = 0.25$, what is $P[(A \cup B) \cap (A \cap B)']$?

2.7 A game is designed where first a coin is flipped and then some dice are thrown. If the coin turns up heads, then two dice are rolled. If the coin turns up tails, then only one die is rolled. If the coin and dice are fair, what is the probability of a total of six dots appearing?'

2.8 For which of the following, are the events A and B independent?
    a. $P]A] = 0.5$, $P[B] = 0.4$, $P[A \cup B] = 0.7$
    b. $P[A] = 0.5$, $P[B] = 0.4$, $P[A \mid B] = 0.4$
    c. $P[A] = 0.5$, $P[B] = 0.4$, $P[B \mid A] = 0.4$
    d. $P[B] = 0.4$, $P[A \cap B] = 0$

2.9 A winner in a contest is one of three winners tied for the prize. He knows that two of the three will be selected randomly and allowed to split the prize. At dinner, a judge tells him that one of the other two winners has been selected. What is the probability that he is going to get the other part of the prize? Justify your answer.

2.10 Consider a communication mechanism between a sender and a receiver (a channel). If we send binary information (1 or 0) over the channel, we may have errors where a 1 is sent but a 0 is received and viceversa. For the information we send, the probability that any bit sent is a 0 is 0.49. An error occurs with probability 0.08 given that a 0 was sent, and with probability 0.01 given that a 1 was sent. What is the probability that when a 1 is received, a 1 was actually sent?

2.11 Connections in computer or communication systems can be redundant, so there is more than one way to trace a connection from its source to its destination. Assume that each link may fail with probability 0.1 and that failures occur independently of each other. What is the probability that some connection between A and B is possible, given the configuration shown?

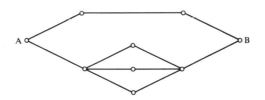

2.12 If we have a network of n computers such that each computer has a direct connection to every other computer, how many wires are there in total? (Remember that you need a separate wire in each direction in order to communicate.) How many would be needed in total if only one wire were needed for communicating in both directions?

2.13 When a byte of data is transferred, it may arrive with no bits changed, one bit changed, or up to eight bits changed. However, if the first bit is changed, that results in a different error than if the second bit is changed, so there are many possible single bit errors. How many different errors of each type (1 bit, 2 bits, etc.) could occur if a byte of data is transferred?

2.14 If the probability of a single bit being received incorrectly is p, what is probability that all 8 bits of a character are received correctly, assuming errors occur independently?

2.15 Sometimes a coding scheme called *parity* is used to detect errors. However, parity can detect only an odd (1, 3, 5, . . .) number of bit errors. What is the probability that a character (8 bits) would be either correctly received or detected as an error? Assume that the probability that a bit is in error is p and that bit errors are independent.

2.16 Which of the following are not valid cumulative distribution functions? Why?

a. $F(x) = \dfrac{1}{9} x^2, \quad 0 \le x \le 3$

b. $F_n = F_{n-1} + \dfrac{1}{10}, \quad n = 1, \ldots 10, \quad F_0 = 0$

c. $F(x) = \sin(x) \quad 0 \le x \le \pi$

d. $F(x) = \dfrac{1}{2} - \dfrac{1}{2} e^{-x}$

2.17 Which of the following are not valid probability density functions? Why?

  a. $f_n = \dfrac{n}{15}, \quad n = 0, 1, 2, 3, 4, 5$

  b. $f_n = \dfrac{n - 1}{9}, \quad n = 0, 1, 2, 3, 4, 5$

  c. $f(x) = 2x, \quad 0 \le x \le \dfrac{1}{2}$

  d. $f(x) = \dfrac{3}{2} x^2, \quad -1 \le x \le 1$

2.18 If jobs arrive to a system such that the time between jobs has an exponential distribution with a rate of two per second, what is the probability that the time between successive arrivals is between 400 and 500 ms?

2.19 After a short burn-in at the factory, integrated circuit chips fail after installation following a exponential distribution with a rate λ. What is the probability that two or more chips fail in a time t?

2.20 What is the probability that an exponentially distributed random variable is greater than its mean?

2.21 Find the expected value of a random variable K whose discrete probability density is the binomial density. See equation 2.19, p. 42.

2.22 What is the first moment of the number of dots showing in the roll of two fair dice?

2.23 Consider two random variables defined on the sample space, the roll of a pair of dice. The first random variable is a count of the number of dots on the pair of dice. The second random variable is an indicator that has a value of 0 when the dice are different (e.g., 3 and 5) and a value of 1 when the dice are the same (e.g., 2 and 2). Construct the joint density function for these two random variables and determine whether or not these random variables are independent. Justify your answer.

2.24 Calculate the residual lifetime density of the Poisson density function $[(\lambda t)^k / k!] e^{-\lambda t}$.

2.25 Two arrival processes, each Poisson with rate λ, are merged to form one process. Derive the interarrival probability density function of the merged process.

Transform Theory $\boxed{3}$

3.1 What Is a Transform?

Normally, when we are manipulating equations, we use rules that are applicable to the type of equation. For example, if the equation has sine and cosine functions, we may use equivalence rules from trigonometry. If, on the other hand, we had an equation with derivatives, we might use rules for differential equations.

Transforms give us an alternative to changing rules. We will use transforms to change the form of an equation to one where the rules we use will always be simple algebraic rules. For example, we may have some transform L which maps functions from one domain where t is the free variable, to another domain of functions where s is the free variable. Applying the transform L to a function $f(t)$ would result in a new function $F^*(s)$.

Definition 3.1: A *transform* is a function defined on a domain of functions of some variable t and produces a new function of some new variable s.

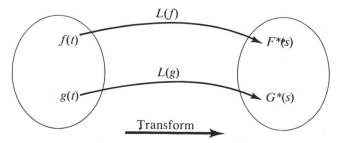

FIGURE 3.1 A Transform Mapping Functions to Functions

Transform	Types of Equations
Fourier	Sines and Cosines
Laplace	Exponentials, Differential Equations
z	Geometric Series, Difference Equations

Table 3.1

Different kinds of transforms are useful for different kinds of functions. All transforms have some basic properties. They are linear operators, which means that multiplicative constants are unaffected by the transform, and transforms of sums of functions are the same as the sum of the transforms of the individual functions. For details on these properties, see the transform tables in the appendix.

Several transforms are commonly used in electrical engineering and computer science. They are listed, along with the type of equations for which they are useful, in the Table 3.1.

Since transforms of functions are related to the original function, we will adopt the following notation. For any function, denoted as a lowercase letter, we use the capital roman letter for its transform. To avoid any confusion with the cumulative distribution functions we will add an asterisk. So a function, $f(t)$, possibly a probability density function, would have a transform denoted as $F^*(s)$. In addition, we denote the relationship between a transform pair as $f(t) \Leftrightarrow F^*(s)$.

3.2 The z-Transform

The first transform we will consider is the z-transform. It is a transform for discrete-valued functions. Since it is useful for geometric series, we will apply it to the geometric probability density function. Since it can be used to solve difference equations, we will use it for solving Markovian systems.

3.2.1 Definition

The z-transform maps a series f_k indexed by an integer value k into a function on a variable z. This mapping is accomplished by summing the series after multiplying each element by a different power of the variable z. In other words, we map the series into a polynominal in z.

Definition 3.2: The z-Transform $F^*(z)$ of a discrete function f_k is defined as follows:

$$Z(f) \triangleq F^*(z) \triangleq \sum_{k=-\infty}^{\infty} f_k z^k \quad z \neq 0 \quad (3.1)$$

Since we are using transforms in probability theory, we restrict the f_k to be a discrete probability density function. Many times, such as in the case of the geometric density, there are no values (they are zero) of the density f_k for $k < 0$. Therefore, we may omit that range from the sum, and often write the transform in the following form.

$$F^*(z) \triangleq \sum_{k=0}^{\infty} f_k z^k \quad (3.2)$$

This is not a different transform. It is simply a property of the functions f_k that we are considering. If the probability density was always zero above some point N, we could further restrict the range of the sum.

$$F^*(z) \triangleq \sum_{k=0}^{N} f_k z^k \quad (3.3)$$

3.2.2 Applying the Transform

To apply the transform, simply replace f_k with the discrete function to transform. Since any function that is a polynominal will form a simple geometric series, we can get a nice closed form for the transform of such functions. As an example, let us generate a few of the entries in the z-transform table found in the appendix.

Example 3.1: Let us find the z-transform of the discrete function $(1 - \alpha)\alpha^k$, the geometric probability density function.

$$F^*(z) = \sum_{k=0}^{\infty} (1 - \alpha)\alpha^k z^k$$

$$= (1 - \alpha) \sum_{k=0}^{\infty} \alpha^k z^k$$

$$= (1 - \alpha) \sum_{k=0}^{\infty} (\alpha z)^k$$

$$= (1 - \alpha) \frac{1}{1 - \alpha z}$$

$$= \frac{1 - \alpha}{1 - \alpha z}$$

Note that when we used the geometric series summation formula, we made an important assumption. We are restricted to values of $|z\alpha| < 1$ when we use that closed form of the transform. This normally never causes us a problem, but we should be aware of it. (Of course, if α was not already less than 1, the original function would not have been a probability density function.)

The fact that the transform is a linear operator is easy to demonstrate. Recall the fact that an operator $Z(\ )$ is linear if when applied to a linear combination $Z(\alpha f_k + \beta g_k)$, the resulting transform is the same as the linear combination $\alpha Z(f_k) + \beta Z(g_k)$. Since the z-transform is an infinite sum, it is easy to see that the multiplicative constants α, β can be factored out of the summation. In addition, since addition is commutative (reversible in order) and associative (can be done left to right or right to left), the summation of a sum $\Sigma (f_k + g_k)$ is the same as the sum of the summations $(\Sigma f_k) + (\Sigma g_k)$. So if we have a complex function, we can split it apart and take the transforms of each separately.

Example 3.2: Let us find the z-transform of the function $f_k = k + k^2$.

$$f_k = k + k^2$$

$$F^*(z) = \sum_{k=0}^{\infty} f_k z^k = \sum_{k=0}^{\infty} (k + k^2) z^k$$

$$= \sum_{k=0}^{\infty} k(k + 1) z^k = z \sum_{k=0}^{\infty} (k + 1) k z^{k-1}$$

$$= z \sum_{k=0}^{\infty} \frac{d^2}{dz^2} z^{k+1} = z \frac{d^2}{dz^2} \sum_{k=0}^{\infty} z^{k+1}$$

$$= z \frac{d^2}{dz^2} \left[\frac{1}{1-z} - 1 \right]$$

$$= \frac{2z}{(1-z)^3}$$

Exercise

3.1 Find the z-transform of the discrete Poisson probability density function,
$$f_k = [(\lambda t)^k / k!] e^{-\lambda t}.$$

3.2.3 Inverting the z-Transform

For every transform there is a corresponding inverse transform. However, using the inverse transform can be very difficult. For the z-transform, successive derivatives are required to use the intermediate value theorem.

$$\frac{1}{n!} \frac{d^n}{dz^n} F^*(z) \Bigg|_{z=0} = f_n \qquad (3.4)$$

We adopt a more pragmatic approach in this book. If we construct a table of functions and compute their transforms, we could simply "look up" the transform in the table and read across the table to find the corresponding function. We will use this table-lookup technique as our inversion technique. Clearly, this is not a general approach since our table will never be large enough for all cases. However, with the addition of the linear property of transforms, it will often be sufficient for our purposes.

Example 3.3: To find the inverse of the z-transform of the function, we need to manipulate it into a form found in the table. As an example, consider the z-transform $2/(3 - z)$.

$$F^*(z) = \frac{2}{3 - z}$$

$$= \frac{2/3}{1 - z/3}$$

$$A = 2/3 \text{ and } a = 1/3$$

$$f_k = \frac{2}{3} \left(\frac{1}{3}\right)^k$$

We can use the linear nature of the z-transform to handle more complicated functions. Anything of the form $\alpha F^*(z) + \beta G^*(z)$ can be inverted if $F^*(z)$ and $G^*(z)$ can be inverted. In some cases, we do not seem to have a linear combination of individual transforms. We often have something of the form $N(z)/D(z)$, where the numerator is an nth-order polynomial in z, and the denominator is an mth-order polynomial in z. In these cases, we must first apply the technique of partial fraction expansion (see the appendix) to create a linear combination of invertible transforms. If $n \geq m$, you must use polynomial division to reduce the function and perform the partial fraction expansion on the remainder.

Example 3.4: Let us find the inverse of the z-transform given below. We must first use partial fraction expansion, then algebraic manipulation, and finally the table lookup.

$$F^*(z) = \frac{4 - \frac{3}{2}z - \frac{1}{2}z^2}{12 - 13z + 3z^2}$$

$$= -\frac{1}{6} + \frac{6 - \frac{11}{3}z}{12 - 13z + 3z^2}$$

$$= -\frac{1}{6} + \frac{1}{3 - z} + \frac{\frac{2}{3}}{4 - 3z}$$

$$f_k = \begin{cases} \dfrac{1}{3} & k = 0 \\[2ex] \dfrac{1}{3}\left(\dfrac{1}{3}\right)^k + \dfrac{1}{6}\left(\dfrac{3}{4}\right)^k & k \geq 1 \end{cases}$$

Exercise

3.2 Find the inverse of the z-transform $(z + z^2)/(1 - z)^3$.

3.2.4 Application to Difference Equations

So far we have only defined transforms and how to manipulate them. We now look at a specific application of the z-transform. We will find this technique very useful later.

Many times, a function may be unknown, but a relationship or property of a function may be known. Such is the case in difference equations, where the relationship between relative terms is known.

Example 3.5: As an example, we may describe a relationship between a term and its successor. This is a simple difference equation.

$$3f_{k+1} = f_k \qquad \text{where} \quad k \geq 0 \quad \text{and} \quad f_0 = \frac{2}{3}$$

The function f_k that would satisfy this may be hard to determine by simple trial and error. Remember, the difference equation must hold for all $k \geq 0$. This is where the z-transform can help.

The basic idea is to note that the difference equation is really a set of equations. We can then perform some algebraic operations on those equations, as long as we do not destroy equality, to construct a z-transform. Once we have the z-transform $F^*(z)$ of the unknown function f_k, we can invert the transform to obtain the function f_k. This manipulation is easily expressed as a set of simple steps.

1. Multiply both sides of each equation (or the generic one) by z^k, where k is the index of the kth occurrence of the difference equation.
2. Add up all the equations. (That amounts to writing the summation $\Sigma_{k=a}^b$ on both sides of the generic equation. The indices a, b are the range of indices for which the generic difference equation holds.)
3. Complete the sums using boundary conditions (e.g., $f_0 = 1$) to form the z-transform ($\Sigma_{k=-\infty}^{\infty} f_k z_k$). We usually assume that any values of the function outside its range are equal to 0.
4. Solve for the z-transform.
5. Invert the z-transform.

Example 3.6: As an example, let us solve the previous example of a difference equation.

$$f_k = 3f_{k+1}$$

$$f_k z^k = 3f_{k+1} z^k$$

$$\sum_{k=0}^{\infty} f_k z^k = 3 \sum_{k=0}^{\infty} f_{k+1} z^k$$

$$= \frac{3}{z} \sum_{k=0}^{\infty} f_{k+1} z^{k+1}$$

$$F^*(z) = \frac{3}{z} [F^*(z) - f_0]$$

$$= \frac{3}{z} \left[F^*(z) - \frac{2}{3} \right]$$

$$F^*(z) \left[1 - \frac{3}{z} \right] = -\frac{2}{z}$$

$$F^*(z) = \frac{-\dfrac{2}{z}}{1 - \dfrac{3}{z}}$$

$$= \frac{\dfrac{2}{3}}{1 - \dfrac{1}{3} z}$$

$$f_k = \frac{2}{3} \left(\frac{1}{3} \right)^k$$

Exercises

3.3 Solve for the function that has an initial value of $f_0 = 2/3$ and satisfies the difference equation $3f_k = 8f_{k-1} + 8f_{k+1}$.

3.4 Solve for the function that has an initial value of $f_0 = 0$ and satisfies the difference equation $f_{k+1} - f_k = 2k + 1$.

3.3 Laplace Transforms

The second transform we will consider is the Laplace transform or, as it is sometimes called, the *s*-transform. It is a transform for continuous functions. Since it is applicable to equations with transcendental functions, we will use it for the exponential probability density function.

3.3.1 Definition

The Laplace transform (or s-transform) maps a continuous function $f(t)$ into a function of a complex variable s.

Definition 3.3: The *Laplace transform $F^*(s)$* of a continuous function $f(t)$ is defined as follows.

$$L(f) = F^*(s) \triangleq \int_{-\infty}^{\infty} f(t)e^{-st}\, dt \qquad (3.5)$$

However, if the density values are only non-zero for positive values of the random variables [i.e., $f(t) = 0$ for $t < 0$], we can write the transform omitting the negative axis.

$$F^*(s) = \int_0^{\infty} f(t)e^{-st}\, dt \qquad (3.6)$$

3.3.2 Applying the transform

To apply the Laplace transform, simply replace the function $f(t)$ with the continuous function to transform. Since we are multiplying, any function with e to some power will allow us to add the exponents. Again, as an example of applying the transform, let us generate a few of the entries in the Laplace transform table in the appendix.

Example 3.7: Let us find the Laplace transform of the continuous function $\lambda e^{-\lambda t}$, the exponential probability density function.

$$F^*(s) = \int_0^\infty \lambda e^{-\lambda t} e^{-st}\, dt$$

$$= \lambda \int_0^\infty e^{-(\lambda + s)t}\, dt$$

$$= \frac{-\lambda}{\lambda + s} \int_0^\infty -(\lambda + s)e^{-(\lambda + s)t}\, dt$$

$$= \frac{-\lambda}{\lambda + s} e^{-(\lambda + s)t} \Big|_0^\infty$$

$$= \frac{-\lambda}{\lambda + s} [0 - 1]$$

$$= \frac{\lambda}{\lambda + s}$$

Example 3.8: Let us find the Laplace transform of the function $f(t) = 8te^{-\lambda t}$, $t \geq 0$.

$$F^*(s) = \int_0^\infty 8te^{-\lambda t}e^{-st}\, dt$$

$$= 8 \int_0^\infty te^{-(\lambda + s)t}\, dt$$

$$= \frac{-8}{\lambda + s} \int_0^\infty -t(\lambda + s)e^{-(\lambda + s)t}\, dt$$

$$= \frac{-8}{\lambda + s} \left[te^{-(\lambda + s)t} \Big|_0^\infty - \int_0^\infty e^{-(\lambda + s)t}\, dt \right]$$

$$= \frac{-8}{\lambda + s} \left[0 - 0 - \frac{-1}{\lambda + s} e^{-(\lambda + s)t} \Big|_0^\infty \right]$$

$$= \frac{-8}{\lambda + s} \left[\frac{1}{\lambda + s} [0 - 1] \right]$$

$$= \frac{8}{(s + \lambda)^2}$$

3.3.3 Inverting the Transform

The inverse transform for the Laplace transform relies on techniques developed in complex analysis. It is well defined but difficult to use. However, we will not resort to complex analysis for the transforms used in this book. Instead, we will use the same table-lookup method that we employed for the z-transform.

Example 3.9: To find the inverse of a Laplace transform of a function, we manipulate it into a form found in our table.

$$F^*(s) = \frac{(\lambda + \mu)s + 2\lambda\mu}{s^2 + \lambda s + \mu s + \lambda\mu}$$

$$= \frac{(\lambda + \mu)s + 2\lambda\mu}{(s + \mu)(s + \lambda)}$$

$$= \frac{\mu}{s + \mu} + \frac{\lambda}{s + \lambda}$$

$$f(t) = \mu e^{-\mu t} + \lambda e^{-\lambda t} \qquad t \geq 0$$

Exercise

3.5 Find the inverse of the transform $\dfrac{3\mu s + 4\mu^2}{s^2 + 3\mu s + 2\mu^2}$.

3.3.4 Application to Differential Equations

The Laplace transform is very useful for the manipulation of differential equations, just as the z-transform was useful for the manipulation of difference equations. In order to solve differential equations we will need to use the following two properties of the Laplace transform.

$$\frac{d}{dt} f(t) \Leftrightarrow sF^*(s) - \lim_{t \to 0} f(t)$$

$$\int_0^t f(\tau) \, d\tau \Leftrightarrow \frac{1}{s} F^*(s) \tag{3.7}$$

By making use of these identities, we can transform each term in an equation with derivatives and integrals, immediately reducing the equation to a transform equation. Then we can algebraically solve for the transform of the unknown function $f(t)$. Finally, we manipulate that transform into a form we can find in our tables, inverting the transform by inspection.

These types of integral/differential equations occur often in the physical sciences. Most electrical engineering majors have seen these techniques many times before. In fact, many of the techniques taught in classes on ordinary differential equations (ODE) are direct results of Laplace transform theory. As an example, let us solve a simple differential equation.

Example 3.10: Solve the ODE $\dfrac{d}{dt} f(t) = af(t)$ for the initial condition $f(0) = 1$.

$$\frac{d}{dt} f(t) = af(t)$$
$$sF^*(s) - 1 = aF^*(s)$$
$$(s - a)F^*(s) = 1$$
$$F^*(s) = \frac{1}{s - a}$$
$$f(t) = e^{at}$$

3.4 Transforms in Probability Theory

So far we have simply introduced, explained, and applied transforms to a series of problems. Although we will use these techniques later in the book, we have not shown some of the most important uses of transforms in probability theory. Both the z-transform and the Laplace transform have special properties that reduce the complexity of the problems. Our main use of transforms will be as generating functions. Generating functions turn out to be very useful in calculating expectations (moments), creating new random variables from sums of other random variables, and unconditioning random variables without inverting the transforms.

3.4.1 Special Properties

Because we are using the Laplace transform and the z-transform on probability densities, we can obtain some special properties. The first property is a general property of the z-transform and gives us the initial value of a sequence directly. So, for our purposes, we can find the probability of the random variable being equal to zero simply by evaluating the z-transform at $z = 0$.

$$F^*(z) \bigg|_{z=0} = \sum_{k=0}^{\infty} f_k z^k \bigg|_{z=0} = f_0 \tag{3.8}$$

Note that we have assumed that all of the values of the probability density f_k are zero for $k < 0$.

The second property arises because all discrete probability density functions must sum to 1. We will make use of this when we have found the z-transform of a probability density except for a single unknown. We can easily solve for the single unknown, by using this relationship.

$$F^*(z) \bigg|_{z=1} = \sum_{k=-\infty}^{\infty} f_k z^k \bigg|_{z=1} = \sum_{k=-\infty}^{\infty} f_k = 1 \tag{3.9}$$

There is a similar relationship for the Laplace transform. This property follows directly from the fact that any value raised to the zero power is equal to 1 and continuous probability densities must integrate to 1.

$$F^*(s) \bigg|_{s=0} = \int_0^\infty f(t)e^{-st}\, dt \bigg|_{s=0} = \int_0^\infty f(t)\, dt = 1 \qquad (3.10)$$

These properties will prove useful in shortening our computations. We will use them often while manipulating transforms of probability densities.

3.4.2 Expectations

To obtain the moments of a random variable, we need to use two important properties of these transforms.

$$(-1)^n \frac{d^n}{ds^n} F^*(s) \Leftrightarrow t^n f(t) \qquad (3.11)$$

$$z \frac{d}{dz} F^*(z) \Leftrightarrow k f_k \qquad (3.12)$$

The idea behind these properties is very simple. For example, taking the derivative of the z-transform simply brings a factor equal to the exponent, k, out in front of each term and decreases the exponent by one. Therefore, multiplying each term by z again gives us the original function back, but with a multiplicative factor equal to its position in the series. Restating the definition of the z-transform, and following the above procedure, we can see how this property holds for the z-transform.

$$F^*(z) = \sum_{k=0}^\infty f_k z^k$$
$$= f_0 + f_1 z + f_2 z^2 + f_3 z^3 + \cdots$$
$$\frac{d}{dz} F^*(z) = f_1 + 2f_2 z + 3f_3 z^2 + \cdots$$
$$\frac{d}{dz} F^*(z) \bigg|_{z=1} = f_1 + 2f_2 + 3f_3 + \cdots = \sum_{k=0}^\infty k f_k \qquad (3.13)$$

This should look very familiar. This is precisely how we defined expectation (moments). So we can obtain the first moment of a discrete random variable simply by taking the derivative of the z-transform of its density and setting $z = 1$. Such functions are called *generating functions* since they can be used to generate any of the moments of the random variable.

$$E[K] = \frac{d}{dz} F^*(z) \Big|_{z=1}$$

$$E[K^2] = \frac{d^2}{dz^2} F^*(z) \Big|_{z=1} + E[K] \qquad (3.14)$$

Note that the higher moments are defined in terms of the derivative of the z-transform and the lower moments. This is due to the fact that the derivative decreases the exponent on successive applications.

A similar property holds for the Laplace transform. The Laplace transform has a simple form for higher moments since the exponent is never changed by taking the derivative.

$$E[T^n] = (-1)^n \frac{d^n}{ds^n} F^*(s) \Big|_{s=0} \qquad (3.15)$$

Example 3.11: Find the average value (first moment) for a continuous random variable T that has the probability density function $\lambda e^{-\lambda t}$.

$$f(t) = \lambda e^{-\lambda t}$$

$$F^*(s) = \frac{\lambda}{\lambda + s}$$

$$E[T] = \frac{d}{ds} F^*(s) \Big|_{s=0}$$

$$= -\lambda \frac{-1}{(\lambda + s)^2} \Big|_{s=0}$$

$$= \frac{\lambda}{\lambda^2} = \frac{1}{\lambda}$$

Example 3.12: Find the average value (first moment) for a random variable K that has the discrete probability density function $(1 - p) p^k$.

$$f_k = (1 - p)p^k$$

$$F^*(z) = \frac{1 - p}{1 - pz}$$

$$E[K] = -\frac{d}{dz} F^*(z) \Big|_{z=1}$$

$$= -\frac{-p(1 - p)}{(1 - pz)^2} \Big|_{z=1}$$

$$= \frac{p}{1 - p}$$

Exercise

3.6 Find the average value (first moment) of a discrete random variable K that has the Poisson probability density function, $[(\lambda\tau)^k/k!]e^{-\lambda\tau}$.

3.4.3 Sums of Independent Random Variables

When a random variable can be described as a sum of other random variables which are independent, we have a way of constructing the new probability density function from the probability density functions for each of the independent random variables. If you think about the problem carefully, it becomes clear that for every value of the new random variable, there are many combinations of the independent random variables summing up to that value. So our construction must take that fact into account. We integrate (or sum) over the entire range of the random variables, keeping the sum equal to the value in question:

$$U \triangleq V + W$$

$$\frac{d}{du} P[U \le u] = f(u)$$

$$\frac{d}{dv} P[V \le v] = g(v)$$

$$\frac{d}{dw} P[W \le w] = h(w)$$

$$f(u) = \int_{-\infty}^{\infty} g(v) \cdot h(u - v) \, dv \qquad (3.16)$$

and similarly for the discrete case:

$$U \triangleq V + W$$
$$P[U = u] = f_u$$
$$P[V = v] = g_v$$
$$P[W = w] = h_w$$

$$f_k = \sum_{n=-\infty}^{\infty} g_n h_{k-n} \qquad (3.17)$$

This operation is also a linear operator and is called *convolution*, usually denoted by the symbol ⊛. It turns out that transforms have a very intimate relationship to convolution. The relationship is usually referred to as the convolution theorem.

$$f(t) \circledast g(t) \Leftrightarrow F^*(s) \cdot G^*(s)$$
$$f_k \circledast g_k \Leftrightarrow F^*(z) \cdot G^*(z) \qquad (3.18)$$

This means that forming the transform of the probability density of a random variable which is defined as the sum of independent random variables is as simple as multiplying the transforms of the probability densities of the independent random variables.

Example 3.13: Find the probability density function for a random variable U, where $U = V + W$ and both V and W are independent and exponentially distributed with parameter λ.

$$F^*(s) = G^*(s) \cdot H^*(s)$$

$$G^*(s) = H^*(s) = \frac{\lambda}{\lambda + s}$$

$$F^*(s) = \frac{\lambda^2}{(\lambda + s)^2}$$

$$f(t) = \lambda^2 t e^{-\lambda t}$$

Exercise

3.7 Derive the probability density function for a random variable T which is the sum of r independent exponentially distributed random variables with parameter $r\mu$. (Note: This random variable is normally called an $r-$stage Erlang random variable.)

3.4.4 Unconditioning

In Chapter 2 we mentioned that unconditioning will prove to be a useful tool. However, inverting a transform, unconditioning, and transforming back is tedious. Luckily, that is not necessary. As we will show in this section, unconditioning a transform of a probability density function is the same as inverting the transform, unconditioning the probability density, and transforming the unconditioned probability density function.

$$f(t) = \int_0^\infty f(t \mid r) g(r) \, dr$$

$$F^*(s) = \int_0^\infty \int_0^\infty f(t \mid r) g(r) \, dr \, e^{-st} \, dt$$

$$= \int_0^\infty \int_0^\infty f(t \mid r) e^{-st} \, dt \, g(r) \, dr$$

$$= \int_0^\infty F^*(s \mid r) g(r) \, dr \tag{3.19}$$

In the process of interchanging the order of integration, you must be careful. In the example above, the range of integration is the positive quadrant of the plane. Interchanging the order of integration does not change the limits of integration. However, because the conditional density $f(t \mid r)$ may be restricted in some way by the range of r, you may have to perform the integration in pieces.

The same sort of derivation works for the z-transform. Again, it is important to note that interchanging the order of summation must be done carefully. A function that is defined only within some interval (although it could be evaluated outside the interval) would require careful determination of the limits on the interchanged summations.

$$f_k = \sum_{n=0}^{\infty} f_{k|n} g_n$$

$$F^*(z) = \sum_{k=0}^{\infty} \sum_{n=0}^{\infty} f_{k|n} g_n$$

$$= \sum_{n=0}^{\infty} \sum_{k=0}^{\infty} f_{k|n} g_n$$

$$= \sum_{n=0}^{\infty} F^*(z \mid n) g_n \qquad (3.20)$$

There is also no reason why a continuous random variable could not be conditioned on a discrete random variable, as long as both random variables are defined on the same sample space. This is common in our kinds of problems where time (a continuous random variable) and a count of events (a discrete random variable) are both defined on the same stochastic process.

3.5 Problems

3.1 Find the z-transform for the binomial probability density function for a given number of Bernoulli trials n with probability p.

$$b(k) = \begin{cases} \binom{n}{k} p^k (1 - p)^{n-k} & \text{for } 0 \leq k \leq n \\ \\ 0 & \text{elsewhere} \end{cases}$$

3.2 Solve for the function that has initial value $f_0 = 7/12$ and satisfies the difference equation $5f_n = 6f_{n+1} + f_{n-1}$.

3.3 Find the Laplace transform of $f(t) = [(\lambda t)^3/6] e^{-(\lambda + \mu)t}$, $t \geq 0$

3.4 Invert the following Laplace transform

$$F^*(s) = \frac{\mu^2 + 2s\mu}{s^4 + 2s^3\mu + s^2\mu^2}$$

3.5 Find the first and second moments of a discrete random variable K which has the binomial probability density function

$$b(k) = \begin{cases} \binom{n}{k} p^k(1 - p)^{n-k} & \text{for } 0 \le k \le n \\ 0 & \text{elsewhere} \end{cases}$$

3.6 Find the variance of a discrete random variable K that as the Poisson probability density function $[(\lambda\tau)^k/k!]e^{-\lambda\tau}$.

3.7 Derive the probability density functions for the interarrival time of the K processes created by randomly splitting a Poisson process. When an arrival occurs from the Poisson process with rate λ, one of K alternative paths is independently selected with probability p_k.

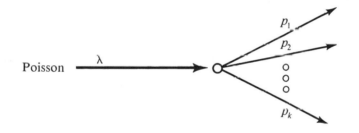

3.8 Compare the probability density functions of two random variables Y and Z, where $Y \triangleq 3X_1$ and $Z \triangleq X_1 + X_2 + X_3$. Assume that the random variables X_1, X_2, and X_3 are all independent and identically distributed with an exponential probability density function parameterized by λ.

Simulation

4

4.1 Introduction

In the previous chapters we have learned about an abstract mathematical model that can be used to represent systems whose outputs may be different, even though the inputs we see are the same. As we mentioned in Chapter 1, there is another way to model such systems. That method is called *simulation*.

In general, a simulation can be any action that mimics some reality. An example of such a technique has been used for centuries to train warriors. For a long time, board games have been used to simulate the strategies used in combat. Simulation models provided the opportunity for students to learn about possible situations and strategies without the horrible consequences of actual combat. Simulations are not limited to the military. Simulations of different kinds of processes can be created. *Monopoly* is an example of a board game used to simulate real estate investing.

When computers became more available, many people found an easy way to apply the rules in a simulation. They simply wrote a program to apply the rules repeatedly depending on the status of the "game" at the time. Such activities are still in extensive use. There are a number of societies devoted to the simple task of bringing together all the thousands of people who use computers to simulate some activity. Those activities may range from population growth and migrations to the mechanisms that control the expansion of the universe.

Simulation models are an important supplement to mathematical models because we can make the rules as complicated as we want. In the mathematical model, we found that certain models could be solved easily. (Remember the ease with which we used transforms to manipulate exponentially and geometrically distributed random variables.) But those same methods would fail to help us with many other distributions. Even if a mathematical model has been constructed, because it is an abstraction, comparing the mathematical model to a more detailed simulation adds confidence to the belief that the mathematical model is a good approximation to a real, as yet unrealized or untestable system.

Simulation models, although useful, are not a panacea either. Since simulations are complicated programs that will execute for a large number of iterations, they are very expensive to run on a computer system. In addition, simply because they are complex programs, it is difficult to prove that a simulation which is running is actually simulating the proposed system. So both mathematical models (for their compactness and simplicity) and simulations (for their complexity and flexibility) are important modeling tools.

For our purposes we will use the computer to execute a set of rules that simulate the execution of another computer. The level of detail of the rules will determine what name we apply to the simulation. If we restrict ourselves to the arrival and execution of jobs or tasks by a computer's central processing unit or some subsystems such as a disk or network, we will simply call it a simulation. If the level of detail becomes the smallest unit a user may specify, as in the case of machine code, we will call it an emulator. In this book, we are concerned only with the high-level models of the computer system. So our models will be simple simulations.

Since we are modeling the computer system at a level where the actual instructions in a job are not specified, we need to include a mechanism to determine the amount of space, execution time, and I/O resources required. Here we fall back on our concept of stochastic models. Oh, yes, we can have a simulation that is based on the theory of probability. (Remember how board games used a pair of dice to introduce behavior not modeled in the rules.)

4.2 Generating Random (?) Numbers

In order to have a computer program simulate a stochastic process, we need to be able to generate values that represent the various random variable values associated with outcomes. If we wish to simulate the roll of a pair of dice, we need to generate the numbers 2, 3, 4, 5, 6, 7, 8, 9, 10, 11, and 12 in an unpredictable order with the corresponding relative frequencies 1/36, 1/18, 1/12, 1/9, 5/36, 1/6, 5/36, 1/9, 1/12, 1/18, 1/36. This requirement would be satisfied if we could somehow find an algorithm to generate numbers randomly and independently based on some distribution. That is precisely the topic of this section.

To begin, let us limit our concern to generating numbers with a uniform distribution. Ideally, we would like to get a number (a value representing a random variable associated with an outcome) each time we execute some routine. We would like it to be independent so that the knowledge of the previous values would not change our distribution for the next value. This would indeed model what we consider to be the behavior of such actions as the rolling of a pair of dice.

Before discussing how we will generate such numbers, let me inform you that it is impossible. Since this random number generator is a program running on a computer, it is really a deterministic, not random, execution. In fact, if you generate numbers using any of the following techniques, you can rerun the program with the same initial values and get exactly the same sequence of "random" numbers. Therefore, what we are doing in reality is simply trying to generate numbers, which appear to be random when tested statistically. Some people emphasize this fact by calling these routines pseudorandom number generators.

The only source of truly random numbers is some physical process that is, itself, random. Such phenomena as rolling dice, counting cosmic particles, radio static, and the variation of capacitor decay times are all random processes. So if one "really" wants random numbers, some such device must be attached to the computer so that the program can input those numbers.

We will satisfy ourselves with using pseudorandom numbers and try to understand how to generate, transform, and use them safely. We will concentrate on three techniques for the generation of random numbers. The first one is discussed for historical perspective, while the second one will be the one we will normally use. The last one is presented for occasions when we need better statistical qualities. (A more complete discussion of these and other methods can be found in Law and Kelton's book *Simulation, Modeling, and Analysis* published by McGraw-Hill in 1982.)

4.2.1 Midsquares Method

This technique was used long before the properties of such routines were more clearly understood. The basic idea is simple. You start with a number (a seed) and you square it. You then take the middle digits of that result as your new number. So if I start with 12 and square it, the new number is 14 taken from the middle of 0144. The method has a serious flaw. It can get stuck. (Try the method starting with a value of 10.) Therefore we must be more careful about our design of a routine to generate pseudorandom numbers. (The actual midsquares method used larger numbers, but has the same problems.)

Example 4.1: Picking a value of 12 to start, we square it to get 0144. We then take 14 as our next number, squaring it to get 0196. We then take 19 and square it to get 0361. Continuing in this way gives us a sequence of numbers (12, 14, 19, 36, 29, 84, . . .).

4.2.2 Linear Congruential Method

If you have studied the areas in formal mathematics called abstract algebra or number theory, you are probably already aware of the reasons behind how this method works. However, since that kind of background is not a prerequisite of this book, let us define a few terms.

Definition 4.1: Arithmetic *modulo m* is the same as normal arithmetic except that the result is the remainder of the normal result divided by m. (Note that the values used in this arithmetic are all between 0 and $m - 1$.)

Example 4.2: The normal wall clock keeps track of time in arithmetic *modulo* 12 plus one. So its values are always between 1 and 12. If you talk about a time 4 hours past 11 o'clock, it would be 3 o'clock, not 15 o'clock.

Example 4.3: The value of 12 *modulo* 5 is 2. Therefore, $(4 + 4 + 4)$ *modulo* 5 is 2.

The linear congruential algorithm is actually quite simple. The new value, z_{n+1}, is created by multiplying the old value, z_n, times a constant a, adding it to another constant c (hence the name linear) and taking the result *modulo m*.

$$z_{n+1} = (a\, z_n + c)\ modulo\ m \tag{4.1}$$

This method will continue to generate a sequence of numbers until it has generated m of them, provided that the constants were selected properly. As we mentioned before, no generator can produce truly random numbers. All generators will produce a sequence and then repeat that sequence. Since the new number depends only on the last one generated, the sequence will cycle whenever a value is repeated. Since there are only m distinct values in *modulo m* arithmetic, the period (i.e. the length of the sequence) for this algorithm can be at most m values long.

The linear congruential method will produce a sequence of numbers of length m if and only if the following three conditions hold:

   (i) The constants m and c are relatively prime [i.e., $\gcd(m,c) = 1$].
  (ii) The constants m and a are selected such that all prime factors of m also divide $a - 1$.
 (iii) If the constant m is divisible by 4, then 4 also divides $a - 1$.

If you think about how a computer operates on integer values, you can see a particularly attractive value for m. Since most machines work in binary, selecting $m = 2^w$, where w is the word length of the machine, means that modulo arithmetic is automatically accomplished by the overflow of the arithmetic operations on integers. (We are not using any representation for negative numbers, such as one's or two's complement, strictly the integers 0 through $2^w - 1$.) This gives us some limits on the values of a and c. Since the only prime factor of 2^w is simply 2, we know that any value for c that was odd would satisfy condition (i). A good choice for the value is something in the middle of the range 0 through $2^w - 1$. In addition, since m is divisible by $4 = 2^2$, we must select the constant a so that 4 divides $a - 1$, which satisfies conditions (ii) and (iii). It is tempting to select $a = 2^k + 1$. Although the conditions are satisfied, they do not guarantee anything about the "randomness" of the sequence, only its length. It turns out, from some experimental work, that $a = 2^k + 1$ is not a good choice. It is better to choose a value for the constant a of the form $4p + 1$, where p is another prime. The best is a value p^k where p is a prime and $p^k - 1$ is divisible by 4. This is often difficult to find, but may be worth the effort if the simulation is to be used for a very important decision (such as whether or not to spend a trillion dollars, or launch atomic missiles).

Mixed Congruential

There are two special cases for the linear congruential method. The differences are based upon the values selected for the constants. The case where $c > 0$ is called the mixed congruential. This is, in fact, the most common type, and all the examples we have mentioned so far are of that type.

Example 4.4: Consider a small example of the mixed congruential method. We will use $m = 2^4 = 16$, $c = 7$, and $a = 5$. These values fit our criterion perfectly and are small enough to deal with in an example. We start with 0, which means that the next number generated is $5 \cdot 0 + 7$ *modulo* 16. That is 7. The next number will be $5 \cdot 7 + 7$ *modulo* 16, which is 42 *modulo* 16, which equals 10. The third number will be $5 \cdot 10 + 7$ *modulo* 16, which equals 9. Continuing in this way the sequence of numbers generated would be $(0, 7, 10, 9, 4, 11, 14, \ldots)$.

Exercise

4.1 Generate at least seven random numbers using the mixed congruential method with $m = 16$, $a = 13$, $c = 11$, and the seed 1.

Multiplicative Congruential

This method is the special case of the linear congruential when the constant c is not used. That is, c is set to 0. This would, of course, save some computation in the generation of pseudorandom numbers. However, the sequences generated cannot be of full period. In fact, they have a maximum period of $m/4$ if z_0 is odd and $a = 8k + 1$ for some k. Worse, we have no way of knowing which integers will not appear in the sequence. We may have large gaps in the sequence. It is best to use the mixed congruential method, if m is to be selected as a power of 2.

Example 4.5: For this case, let us use $m = 16$ and $a = 9$. If we again select the first number as 0, we see that we have a problem. Clearly, the multiplicative congruential cannot have 0 as a member of its sequence. Let us start with 3 instead. The next number will be 9·3 *modulo* 16, which is simply 5. The third number would be 9·5 *modulo* 16, which is 45 *modulo* 16, which is equal to 13. The fourth number would be 9·13 *modulo* 16, which is 117 *modulo* 16, which is equal to 5. The method has repeated already. So the sequence would look like (3, 5, 13, 5, 13, . . .). We could generate only three numbers since the period, the point where the sequence repeats, was at most of length 4. If we look at exactly which numbers were generated, we see another problem. Here we get two numbers in large frequencies, and no others. So we will never get the numbers in between them.

Exercise

4.2 Generate at least six random numbers using the multiplicative congruential method with $m = 16$, $a = 9$, and a seed of 7.

4.2.3 Additive Congruential

Many times we are faced with a problem for which random number generators with periods of 2^w are inadequate. One does not have to give up in despair; there is a technique to extend the period of a sequence of random numbers. The technique requires that a sequence of length k of random numbers has already been generated, somewhat like the seed in the other methods. We can then use the additive congruential method to extend the initial sequence.

Definition 4.2: Given a sequence of numbers of length k, a new number in the sequence may be generated by adding the last number generated to the kth previous number. (This is termed the *additive congruential method*.)

$$z_n = (z_{n-1} + z_{n-k})\ modulo\ m \qquad (4.2)$$

These random number generators can produce sequences with periods much greater than m. A special case of this generator is called the *Fibonacci generator* where k is set to 2. That case has a period greater than m, but has poor statistical properties. It is possible to get periods as large as $m^k - 1$ for a general case of the additive congruential method with the appropriate selection of weighting factors a_j.

$$z_n = \left(\sum_{j=1}^{k} a_j z_{n-j} \right) \ modulo \ m \tag{4.3}$$

Example 4.6: Let us generate numbers using the starting sequence from the mixed congruential example. The sequence of numbers generated 7, is (0, 7, 10, 9, 4, 11, 14). The additive congruential would begin with that sequence and a value for k equal to 6. The next number in the sequence would be 14 + 0 *modulo* 16 or 14. Then the next number after that would be 14 + 7 *modulo* 16 or 5. This could continue so that we get the following extension to the beginning sequence, (0, 7, 10, 9, 4, 11, 14, 14, 5, 15, 8, 12, 7, 5, . . .).

In a very interesting modification of this method, Tausworthe applied the additive congruential idea to bits rather than integers. By generating a bit sequence we can extract fixed-length groups of bits as integers to generate random numbers.

$$b_n = (b_{n-r} + b_{n-q}) \ modulo \ 2 = b_{n-r} \oplus b_{n-q} \tag{4.4}$$

There is some disagreement in the literature on how those fixed length groups should be extracted. However, the period of such generators is independent of the word size. Some periods in excess of 10^{156} have been described on 16-bit machines.

Exercise

4.3 Generate at least 12 random numbers using the additive congruential method with $k = 3$ and a starting sequence of (1, 7, 6, 9).

4.2.4 Validation Techniques

As we mentioned, random number generators do not generate truly random numbers. We said that we would accept a particular random number generator if it satisfied certain statistical tests. We may refer to this check as the validation of the random number generator. Hopefully, the previous discussion has helped convince you that using a random number generator found in a library of functions or built into a programming language is not necessarily a good idea. Before you begin to design and code a simulator, it is recommended that you validate the random number generator you intend to use.

There are two things to check in a sequence of numbers generated by a random number generator. First, the sequence should be independent. That means that no one value can be inferred from any of the others. Second, the numbers should be uniformly distributed. That means that the frequency plot of the numbers should be relatively flat. The independence is actually the more difficult of the two to check, so we will discuss it last. In actual use, you should check the independence requirement first.

Checking for a Uniform Distribution

In order to check to see if a random number generator generates a uniform distribution of numbers, we need to execute the random number generator a number of times to create a frequency plot. That means that we must divide up the range of the random numbers in groups or slots, and then count the number of occurrences of a random number in each of those groups or slots.

Example 4.7: Suppose that we wish to create a frequency plot with 10 subranges for a random number generator with a range of 0 through 1. Then we would form the subranges (slots) 0–0.1, 0.1–0.2, and so on. If we generate a number, say 0.382, it would fall in the subrange 0.3–0.4, so we would increment that subrange count. The result of this would be a frequency plot of 10 integer values.

The problem in verifying that a distribution is uniform is the same as verifying that flipping a coin 1000 times and getting heads 499 times does not invalidate our assumption that heads and tails are equally likely. We need to "measure" the amount of acceptable variation in the experimental values. Here we must turn to statistics. Statisticians have constructed a random variable that is a measure of the difference between the distributions for two random variables. This new random variable is called chi-squared, χ^2. It is a measure of the "sameness" of two discrete densities. If its value is low enough, we can say, with probability $1 - F(\chi^2)$, that the two random variables used to construct χ^2 have the same limiting distribution. That means, that if we could continue sampling the two discrete densities, they would become equal (i.e., $\chi^2 \rightarrow 0$).

Definition 4.3: The random variable χ^2 is defined in terms of two frequency plots (discrete densities multiplied by the number of repetitions). Given that the number of observed occurrences of experimental outcomes in a subrange n is O_n and the number of occurrences predicted by the assumed density for the same subrange n is E_n.

$$\chi^2 \triangleq \sum_{n=1}^{N} \frac{(O_n - E_n)^2}{E_n} \tag{4.5}$$

The actual cumulative distribution function for the χ^2 random variable is difficult to compute. Luckily for us, someone else has computed its values for us (See Appendix 4). This table is actually constructed a little differently from how we are used to discussing cumulative distribution functions. The table has row labels of degrees of freedom and column labels of probability values. The table entries are values of the random variable χ^2.

The values on the left are called the *degrees of freedom*. These values represent the number of different ways the two distributions may vary from each other. Clearly, if there are a large number of ways in which we may have small differences, we must make more allowance in the aggregate measure of the difference χ^2 before we can say that the distributions are "different."

The values on the top of the table are the actual probabilities of $\chi^2 \leq x$ from the cumulative distribution. So if you find a value x in the table for the degrees of freedom corresponding to the densities being matched, the probability that the actual value of χ^2 would fall below that value x is the value in the column heading where x was found. If you cannot find x (our benefactor only did some of the values), clearly a value $x' > x$ would include the range of interest.

To apply this statistical measure to our problem, let us look at the degrees of freedom for our densities, the construction of the χ^2 value x, and the meaning of the probability that $\chi^2 \leq x$.

1. The degrees of freedom for matching discrete densities is simply the number of subranges N in the density, minus the number of true differences in the density parameters R. (This is the so called "all parameters known" case.) For uniform distributions, R is simply 1, since if the range of a uniform distribution is given, you immediately know its height. This is also the case for the Poisson distribution. Since only the Poisson parameter is needed to fix the distribution, its number of density parameters, R, is also 1. There are other densities which require more than one parameter to fix their form. One such example is the Gaussian density (the bell-shaped curve). That density requires both a mean and a variance to fix its shape, so its R is 2.

2. The construction of the value x of the χ^2 random variable is easy. First we divide up the range into the number of slots N we decided on previously. We then run the random number generator for a sequence of M numbers, counting the number of occurrences of values in each subrange or slot. After the run we construct the value x by subtracting M/N from each count, squaring the result and adding them up. Finally, we multiply the result by N/M.

3. Now we look up that value in the row $N - R$ of the χ^2 table. If such a value is not listed, we pick the closest value $x' > x$. Now look up at the top of the column where x' was found. That value F is the probability that $\chi^2 < x'$. This means that with probability F, you cannot say that the two distributions you compared are different. That convoluted statement means that you must accept the hypothesis that the two densities are the same, with probability $1 - F$ since you cannot reject it with probability F. Alternatively, you can select the closest value $x' < x$ and look up at the top of the column with x' in it to reject the hypothesis with probability F. If you can reject it with a good-sized probability such as 25%, you will probably want another random number generator. If you can only reject it with probability 0.5% or 1%, you probably will consider it okay. *(Note:* You can always find a probability with which you can reject the hypothesis. It just may be quite small.)

To become more familiar with this technique, let us consider a simple example of a match between two densities, one observed and one hypothesized.

Example 4.8: A company has been shipping out truck loads of parts to its customers. Unfortunately, some of the parts are broken, either before they are packed or during shipment. In any case, the company wishes to be able to predict roughly how many parts will be broken in a shipment. To do this, it must have a model

Number of Broken Parts	Number of Shipments	Predicted Number of Shipments
0	10	14.3
1	41	40.5
2	57	57.5
3	55	54.4
4	43	38.6
5	27	21.9
6	11	10.4

Table 4.1

of the behavior. A consultant suggests that they use a Poisson distribution for their model. He says that he will validate the Poisson model using the χ^2 test. He starts to observe shipments and count the number of shipments that have 0, 1, 2, 3, 4, 5, and 6 broken parts in them. He then constructs Table 4.1, with the number of broken parts found, the number of such shipments, and the number predicted by the Poisson model he has suggested (using the average number of broken parts in a shipment, 2.84, for his Poisson parameter).

$$\chi^2 = \frac{(10 - 14.3)^2}{14.3} + \frac{(41 - 40.5)^2}{40.5} + \frac{(57 - 57.5)^2}{57.5} + \frac{(55 - 54.4)^2}{54.4}$$
$$+ \frac{(43 - 38.6)^2}{38.6} + \frac{(27 - 21.9)^2}{21.9} + \frac{(11 - 10.4)^2}{10.4}$$

The value of the random variable χ^2 is 3.034, and the degrees of freedom is $7 - 1 = 6$. So we find from the table in the appendix that we can reject the hypothesis that the distribution of broken parts is Poisson with probability 0.1 but we cannot reject it with probability 0.25. So we would accept his model with probability 0.75.

Exercise

4.4 Would you accept with 90% confidence, a RNG if it had the following histogram? $(0.0 - 0.1) = 21$, $(0.1 - 0.2) = 20$, $(0.2 - 0.3) = 19$, $(0.3 - 0.4) = 17$, $(0.4 - 0.5) = 22$, $(0.5 - 0.6) = 21$, $(0.6 - 0.7) = 20$, $(0.7 - 0.8) = 18$, $(0.8 - 0.9) = 21$, $(0.9 - 1.0) = 21$

Checking for Independence

As we mentioned previously, checking independence is much more difficult than simply checking for a match to the expected uniform distribution. There are several ways to approach this problem, but none of them ever "proves" independence. Each test we make can only prove that a sequence of random numbers is not independent. The whole idea of this testing is to improve your confidence in the random number generator, not to prove its correctness.

We will consider two techniques that attempt to test whether the sequence of numbers is truly independent with a uniform distribution. The first is an extension of the previous technique of distribution matching, the serial test. The second is a test of the independence alone, called the run-up test.

Definition 4.4: The *serial test* simply compares groups of random numbers in the sequence, rather than each one. If a sequence of numbers (Z_i) is truly independent and identically distributed with a uniform distribution, every nonoverlapping *n-tuple* will form an independent, identically distributed sequence of uniformly distributed vectors in the *n*-dimensional hypercube.

In the serial test, we construct ever increasingly large *n-tuples* and check to see whether those are still uniformly distributed by using the *n*-dimensional χ^2 test. This test deals with subareas rather than subranges of the possible values.

Example 4.9: Consider the sequence of random numbers that were generated by the additive congruential method. (0, 7, 10, 9, 4, 11, 14, 14, 5, 15, 8, 12, 7, 5, . . .). First we check the two-dimensional vectors (0,7), (10,9), (4,11), (14,14), (5,15), (8,12), (7,5). Since these vectors are supposed to be uniformly distributed within the square (0,0), (15,0), (15,15), (0,15), we would expect a vector to appear with probability 1/256 and to be in regions of area 16 with probability 1/16. So for our sample of seven vectors (which is really too small for a good test) we find, none fall in the area (0,0), (3,0), (3,3), (0,3), where we expected to see 7/16. We continue to calculate our χ^2 and finally check the value in the table.

For the other technique, we will look at the direction rather than specific location of subsequent values in the sequence. This technique is called the run-up test and is useful for nonuniform distributions as well.

Definition 4.5: The *run-up test* counts the number of sequences of lengths 1, 2, 3, 4, 5, or ≥ 6, where the values within those sequences are monotonically increasing.

This test looks only at the independence of the sequence, and it requires only a single pass through the sequence. Using r_k for the number of run-ups of length k, we can construct a random variable R whose distribution will tend, for large n (≥ 4000), toward the χ^2 distribution with 6 degrees of freedom.

$$R = \frac{1}{N} \sum_{j=1}^{6} \sum_{k=1}^{6} A_{jk}(r_j - N \cdot B_j)(r_k - N \cdot B_k) \qquad (4.6)$$

The constants A_{jk} and B_k have already been generated and may be found in Knuth.* The following values for those constants can be used for our purposes.

*These values are from Knuth, *The Art of Computer Programming,* vol. 2, (Reading, Mass.: Addison-Wesley, 1969), p.60

$$A = \begin{bmatrix} 4529 & 9045 & 13568 & 18091 & 22615 & 27892 \\ 9045 & 18097 & 27139 & 36187 & 45234 & 55789 \\ 13568 & 27139 & 40721 & 54281 & 67852 & 83685 \\ 18091 & 36187 & 54281 & 72414 & 90470 & 111580 \\ 22615 & 45234 & 67852 & 90470 & 113262 & 139476 \\ 27892 & 55789 & 83685 & 111580 & 139476 & 172860 \end{bmatrix} \quad (4.7)$$

$$B = \left(\frac{1}{6}, \frac{5}{24}, \frac{11}{120}, \frac{19}{720}, \frac{29}{5040}, \frac{1}{840} \right) \quad (4.8)$$

Example 4.10: Consider the sequence of numbers that were generated by the additive congruential method.

0	7	10	9	4	11	14	14	5	15	8	12	7	5
	3		1		3		1	2		2		1	1

From this we see that the number of run-ups of length 1, r_1, is 4, the number of run-ups of length 2, r_2 is 2, the number of run-ups of length 3, r_3, is 2, and there are no run-ups of length 4, 5, or 6 (i.e., r_4, r_5, $r_6 = 0$). We can compute R, which we find is 2.590272. Using the chi-squared table, we conclude with confidence 0.75 that this sequence is independent. This example is unfortunately too small to be accurate, but it is illustrative of the computation required.

4.2.5 Generating Nonuniform Distributions

Although it is useful to be able to generate sequences of numbers that appear to be random with a uniform distribution, we are often interested in generating sequences of numbers which still represent random variables, but have different distributions. We would like, given the cumulative distribution function and a uniformly distributed random number generator, to devise a method to generate nonuniformly distributed random numbers.

Inversion

Consider the cumulative distribution function, $F(y)$, for a random variable Y. Since it is a function on real values, we can use it to create a new random variable $Z \triangleq F(Y)$. What is the distribution of this new random variable?

$$G(z) \triangleq P[Z \le z] = P[F(Y) \le z]$$

Assuming that F^{-1} exists, the event $F(Y) \leq z$ is the same as the event $Y \leq F^{-1}(z)$, so

$$G(z) = P[Y \leq F^{-1}(z)]$$

But $P[Y \leq y] \triangleq F(y)$, so

$$G(z) = F(F^{-1}(z)) = z \qquad 0 \leq z \leq 1$$

Therefore, since Y is distributed according to $F(y)$, Z will be uniformly distributed on the interval [0,1]. That is precisely the distribution we can generate with our current techniques. Therefore, if we wish to generate random numbers with a distribution given by the cumulative distribution function $F(y)$, we need only generate uniformly distributed random numbers and apply the inverse function of $F(y)$, namely $F^{-1}(z)$, to those numbers.

However, not all nondecreasing functions $F(y)$ have an inverse. If any section of the curve $F(y)$ is flat (i.e., $dF/dy = 0$), then no inverse exists. This is always true for discrete random variables. We will see that we can avoid the problem of a lack of an inverse by using a slightly different rule which retains the intent of our method.

Example 4.11: In the case of exponentially distributed random numbers, a direct application of ideas for nonuniform distributions is appropriate. The cumulative distribution function for the exponential case is monotonically increasing, so the inverse exists.

$$F(y) = 1 - e^{-\lambda y}$$
$$z = 1 - e^{-\lambda y}$$
$$e^{-\lambda y} = 1 - z$$
$$-\lambda y = \ln (1 - z)$$
$$y = -\frac{1}{\lambda} \ln (1 - z) \qquad (4.9)$$

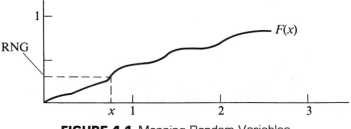

FIGURE 4.1 Mapping Random Variables

So we simply generate random numbers z with a uniform distribution between 0 and 1, and substitute into the equation (4.9) to obtain numbers whose distribution is exponential with parameter λ. If we note that $1 - z$ is again a different random variable that is uniformly distributed, we can save ourselves a step in the calculation by using the following instead.

$$y = -\frac{1}{\lambda} \ln(z) \qquad (4.10)$$

Example 4.12: The case of Bernoulli trials requires a slight modification of our ideas about generating nonuniform distributions. Since the Bernoulli trial has a discrete cumulative distribution with two steps, we cannot just invert the function. We can see, however, that by describing the function differently, with the vertical rather than the horizontal part of the steps (as shown in Figure 4.2), we can obtain an inverse function. Then we can generate a random number and apply the inverse function to it, to get the random variable, which is Bernoulli.

This procedure amounts to determining within which range the generated random number occurred, since the distribution of the generated random number is uniform. You simply compare the generated number to the value of the success probability. If it is less, you had a success; if not, you had a failure. You can then return the appropriate Bernoulli value. It is possible to generalize this using a vector of values to select a larger set of possibilities than just success or failure.

FIGURE 4.2 Inverse for the Bernoulli Distribution

```
PROCEDURE BERN ( PSUCCESS:REAL; VAR N:INTEGER );

VAR    Z : REAL;

BEGIN
       Z := RNG( SEED );
       IF ( Z < PSUCCESS ) THEN N := 1
                 ELSE N := 2
END;
```

Composition

In the composition method we simply take advantage of the fact that many random variables are defined in terms of other random variables. If we know how to generate the underlying random variables, we can use the definition to construct the "composite" random variable.

Example 4.13: Recall that a random variable which represents the count of the number of "successes" or "arrivals" for a Poisson process during a fixed period of time T has a Poisson distribution. We also know that the time between those "arrivals" is exponentially distributed. So we simply count the number of exponentially distributed random variables needed to add up to T. Then that number represents the number of arrivals that would have occurred during the fixed time interval T. Such a procedure is outlined below.

```
PROCEDURE POISSON( ARR,T:REAL; VAR N:INTEGER );
VAR    Y : REAL;

BEGIN
       N := 0;
       Y := -1 / ARR * LN( RNG( SEED ) );
       WHILE ( Y < T ) DO
         N := N + 1;
         Y := Y - 1 / ARR * LN( RNG( SEED ) )
         END
END;
```

This procedure works fine for generating numbers N that are Poisson distributed. However, by noting that adding up a lot of logarithms is the same as multiplying a series of values, we can save ourselves some computation.

```
PROCEDURE POISSON( ARR,T:REAL; VAR N:INTEGER );
VAR    Z : REAL;
       THRESHOLD : REAL;

BEGIN
       N := 0;
       THRESHOLD := 1 / EXP ( ARR * T );
       Z := RNG( SEED );
       WHILE ( Z >= THRESHOLD ) DO
              N := N + 1;
              Z := Z * RNG( SEED );
              END;
END;
```

Example 4.14: In the case of geometrically distributed random numbers, we find a case similar to that of the Poisson random number generator. First, they are both discrete. Second, they can be viewed as a series of independent actions. Recall that the geometric distribution represented the case where we counted the number of failures before the next success. Then we can simply generate a series of Bernoulli trials until a success is observed, and simply count the number of trials. The following procedure does precisely that.

```
PROCEDURE GEOM ( PSUCCESS:REAL; VAR N:INTEGER);

BEGIN
       N := 1;
       Z := RNG( SEED );
       WHILE ( Z > PSUCCESS ) DO
              N := N + 1;
              Z := RNG( SEED );
              END;
END;
```

Note that we have assumed that the number of steps until a success is relatively low. Otherwise, the execution of the loop may be more expensive computationally than inverting the cumulative distribution function, which requires logarithms. Alternatively, we could use the following for large N.

```
PROCEDURE GEOM ( PSUCCESS:REAL; VAR N:INTEGER);

BEGIN
N := TRUNC( LN( RNG( SEED ) ) / LN( 1 - PSUCCESS ) );
END;
```

Accept/Reject

There are many cases where inversion is impossible (such as when the cumulative distribution fuction is not in closed form) and composition cannot be used. In these cases, another method, called accept/reject, can often be used. The *accept/reject* method is based on the concept of conditional probability. We augment the problem of generating a random variable X whose density is $f(t)$ with another random variable Y whose density is $g(t)$. If we can generate a random variable whose density is $g(t)$ and that density majorizes the density $f(t)$ ($\forall t$, $c \cdot g(t) \geq f(t)$), then we can generate outcomes that are either inside (accept) or outside (reject) the conditional event ($X = Y$).

1. Generate Y with density $g(t)$ using a known RNG method.
2. Generate U with a uniform density independently of Y.
3. If $U \cdot g(Y) \leq f(Y)/c$, then accept (set $X = Y$); otherwise, reject (repeat the process).

This may seem complex, but it is actually easy to implement. If the random variable of interest X has finite range, it is trivial to find a majorizing density $g(t)$ since we can use a uniform density with c equal to the maximum value of the density $f(t)$. In cases where the range is infinite, other densities can usually be used.

4.3 Programming Simulations

Before getting too far into the complexities of constructing simulation programs, let us define several important concepts.

Definition 4.6: The *simulation time* is the value of the time that would have expired in the operation of the "real" system.

Definition 4.7: The *run time* is the value of the time that expired during the execution of the simulation. It is sometimes called the wall clock time.

Definition 4.8: *Events* are the particular operations of the system that cause a change of state in the model of the system.

The difference of simulation time and run time is important to the person actually using the simulation. If he or she wishes to execute the simulator for a simulated time of 24 hours, how much actual run time will expire? Does the individual have to wait (and pay for) several days of computer time, or just several minutes? Some people consider the ratio of the simulation time and the run time as the compression or expansion of time made by the simulator. Since the program only needs to keep track of simulation time, we will not concern ourselves with run time in the rest of this chapter except in discussions on efficiency.

The concept of events is critical to the operation of the simulation. The reason the simulation has been written is to follow the sequence of events. An event corresponds to the outcome in our mathematical model of stochastic systems. Any change to the state of the model, such as another person arriving, a person leaving, or a waiting person beginning service, will be events.

There are two basic structures for simulation programs which differ in what each execution of the main control loop represents. The first, the *time-based simulation* is the simplest and usually most inefficient control structure. The second, the *event-based simulation,* is more complex, but it is usually more efficient and accurate. The selection of which basic structure to use is driven by the application being simulated. The time-based simulation technique is very simple and is applicable to problems that have very few possible events at any moment. They are efficient if there is a very high probability of having an event occur at each clock "tick". Event-based simulation is applicable to a wide range of problems, so it tends to be the one selected most often. It can, unfortunately, be relatively complex and often requires complex data structures to maintain the state of the pending events.

4.3.1 Time-Based Simulations

In time-based simulation the program control loop is associated with time. For each execution of the main control loop, the simulation clock advances one "tick" of Δt. It is possible that many events may have occurred in that time interval, so each must be processed. (There is an underlying assumption that the order of events within a time interval is unimportant.) In time-based simulations, the clock advances on a regular basis, while the events are processed in differing groups. The basic, high-level flowchart in Figure 4.3, shows the basic structure of the time-based simulation model.

Example 4.15: Consider a model of the internal operation of a von Neumann computer. Fundamental to its operation is a procedure called the instruction fetch cycle. Suppose we have been given the task of determining the speed of execution, in instructions per second, of a new machine for different instruction set mixes. We have decided to model this new machine with a stochastic simulation. We will read in information on the frequency of instructions in the mix being one, two, or three words in length, the speed of memory, and the frequency of instructions of each

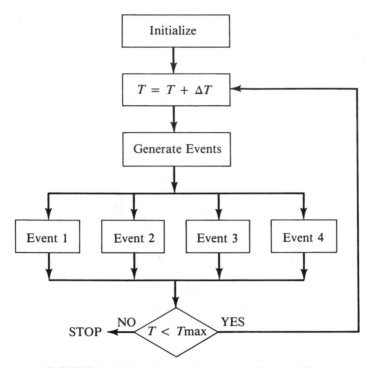

FIGURE 4.3 Time-Based Simulation Control Flow

length requiring access to memory for execution. We will assume that all register-to-register transfers take precisely one
cycle and that the length of an instruction is independent of the
lengths of the previous instructions. Since this system is
clocked, and since some action, memory access, or execution
must take place at each clock "tick", we have selected a time
based structure for our simulation. The actual program follows.

```
PROGRAM MIPS(INPUT,OUTPUT);

(* THIS PROGRAM IS A TIME BASED SIMULATION  *)
(* OF A VON NEUMANN COMPUTER INTSRUCTION    *)
(* FETCH CYCLE.  THREE INSTRUCTION SIZES ARE*)
(* MODELED.  MEMORY ACCESS FOR DATA DURING  *)
(* EXECUTION IS ALSO MODELED                *)

CONST  CLOCK  = 0.000001;(*CPU CYCLE SPEED *)
```

```
          MAXSTEP = 1000;    (*MAX STEPS IN SIM *)
          MEMSPEED= 1;       (*MEM SPEED-CYCLES *)
          SIZE    = 3;       (*MAX INSTR SIZE   *)
          K       = 49;

VAR       CNTR     : INTEGER;(* POS IN RNG SEQ  *)
          SEED     : INTEGER;(* PARAM FOR RNG   *)
          PROB     : REAL;   (* GEN RANDOM PROB *)
          MEMRD    : INTEGER;(* MEM ACCE REQ.   *)
          INSTR    : INTEGER;(* NO. INSTR WORDS *)

          PROBIN   : ARRAY [0..SIZE] OF REAL;
                             (* PROB OF WRD SIZE*)
          PROBMEM  : ARRAY [1..SIZE] OF REAL;
                             (* PROB OF MEM ACC.*)
          EXECI    : INTEGER;(* NO. OF INT EXEC *)
          STEP     : INTEGER;(* NO. OF CYCLES   *)
          KVALUES  : ARRAY[0..K] OF INTEGER;
(*********************************************)
BEGIN (* MAIN *)
    (* INITIALIZE VARIABLES *)
       PROBIN[0] := 0.0;
       SEED := 3;
       INSTR := 0;
       MEMRD := 0;
       EXECI := 0;

    (* INITIALIZE SEQUENCE OF RANDOM NUMBERS *)
    FOR CNTR := 0 TO K DO
       BEGIN
          RNG(SEED);
          KVALUES[CNTR] := SEED;
       END;
    CNTR := 0;

    (* PRINT HEADER FOR OUTPUT *)
    WRITELN;WRITELN;
    WRITELN(' STEP  INSTR  MEM ');
    WRITELN;

    FOR INSTR := 1 TO SIZE DO
    BEGIN
    READLN(PROBIN[INSTR],PROBMEM[INSTR]);
    PROBIN[INSTR] := PROBIN[INSTR] + PROBIN[INSTR-1];
    END;
```

```
   IF PROBIN[SIZE] <> 1.O THEN
                      PROBIN[SIZE] := 1.0;

   FOR STEP := 1 TO MAXSTEP DO
   BEGIN (* CLOCK LOOP *)
      IF INSTR = O THEN   (*INSTR FETCHED*)
         IF MEMRD = O THEN (*DATA FETCHED*)
            BEGIN   (* INSTR EXEC COMPLETE *)
            EXECI := EXECI + 1;
            ADDRNG( SEED, PROB );
            INSTR := 1;   (* GEN NEW INSTR *)
            WHILE PROBIN[ INSTR ] < PROB DO
                  INSTR := INSTR + 1;
            ADDRNG( SEED, PROB );
             (* SEE IF NEW INSTR NEEDS DATA *)
            IF PROBMEM[ INSTR ] < PROB
               THEN MEMRD := O
               ELSE MEMRD := MEMSPEED;
            END
         ELSE MEMRD := MEMRD - 1 (*GET DATA*)
      ELSE INSTR := INSTR - 1; (*FETCH NEW WORD*)
      WRITELN( STEP:5, INSTR:7, MEMRD:4);
      END; (* CLOCK LOOP *)

   WRITELN;
   WRITELN( EXECI/CLOCK/MAXSTEP:15:2,' INSTR/SEC');
END.  (* MAIN *)
```

4.3.2 Event-Based Simulations

In the case of event-based simulations, the execution of the main control loop represents a single event. The simulation time clock is simply advanced the amount of time since the last event, whatever that was. Thus no two events can be processed at any pass, making the high-level control structure simple. In addition, since execution of the loop does not occur when there is no event to process, it is efficient.

The difficulty in programming event-based simulations is maintaining the information necessary to determine which event is next. Care must be taken because an event could create several events in the future. Consider a person who arrives at a line waiting to be served. His arrival will precipitate the event of his own completion of service, in addition to the event of his entering service. The information about those events must be saved so that they can be properly scheduled. We will call this stored information the *event queue*. Although it is often maintained as a queue in time order, this is not necessary. Once scheduled,

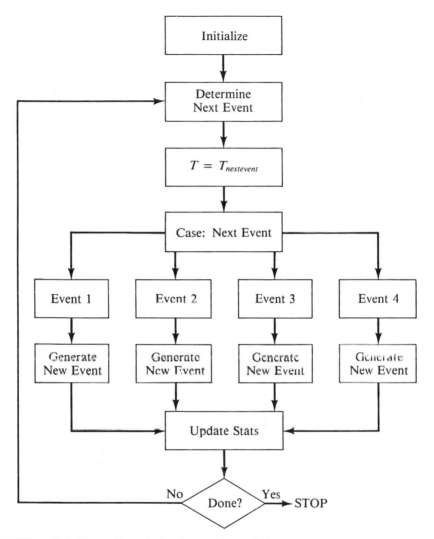

FIGURE 4.4 Event-Based Simulation Control Flow

events may still have to be rearranged, since as events are removed from this queue of pending events, they may again produce future events that interleave in time with the currently queued events. Also, newly generated events may require the removal of currently queued events. This can occur when unusual orderings are employed. In the case of a server taking the last customer to arrive, the previously scheduled customer is preempted by the newly arriving customer.

Example 4.16: Consider the actions of a floppy disk drive. The amount of time an access takes depends on the location of the head on a track relative to the destination track. In addition, a latency delay for the rotation of the disk is incurred to read a sector after the track has been reached. For normal 8 inch floppy drives, a standard track to track seek is roughly 6 ms. Since most drives use a stepper motor, multiple track seeks are simply multiples of 6 ms. The rotational speed of the floppy is 3600 rpm, which means that the average latency (assuming uniform access) is 83 ms. The number of tracks is 77 and the number of sectors is 26. This simulation will model the floppy disk drive to determine its performance under certain access request patterns. The basic pattern assumes that it is likely that a sector on the same track will be accessed again with probability P. If a different track is accessed, it is assumed that any of the other tracks are equally likely. The simulation maintains a state for the track and assumes a uniform access to the sectors in the track. The results are stored as an average delay for an access request. This model represents only the disk service time delay since there is no arrival time associated with a request. Because of this simplification, the event queue can have only one item, the next request. So there is no actual queue structure in the code, only a single variable containing the next request (i.e., an event queue of length 1).

```
PROGRAM DISKDRIVE(OUTPUT);

(* THIS PROGRAM IS AN EVENT BASED SIMULATION OF *)
(* A FLOPPY DISK DRIVE CREATED TO DETERMINE DISK*)
(* DRIVE PERFORMANCE UNDER RANDOM REQUEST       *)
(* PATTERNS.  THIS MODEL REPRESENTS THE DISK    *)
(* SERVICE TIME DELAY.                          *)

CONST  LATENCY = 0.085;  (* ROTATIONAL TIME       *)
       SEEK    = 0.006;  (* TRACK-TO-TRACK SEEK *)
       N       = 100;    (* NUMBER OF REQUESTS  *)
       P       = 0.50;   (* PROB. SAME TRACK    *)
       K       = 49;     (* SEQ. LEN. FOR RNG.  *)

VAR    CLOCK  : REAL;     (* SIMULATION CLOCK    *)
       CNTR   : INTEGER; (* POS. IN RNG SEQUENCE*)
       EVENT  : INTEGER; (* NUMBER OF EVENT     *)
       SEED   : INTEGER; (* PARAMETER FOR RNG   *)
       PROB   : REAL;     (* RANDOM VAR. GEN.    *)
       SOURCE : INTEGER; (* DISK HEAD POSITION  *)
```

```
         TRACKS  : INTEGER;(* NO. TRACKS TO SEEK  *)
         DELAY   : REAL;   (* TIME TO MOVE HEAD    *)
         DEST    : INTEGER;(* NEXT POS. OF HEAD    *)
         KVALUES : ARRAY[0..K] OF INTEGER;
                             (* RANDOM VALUES GEN.  *)
(*************************************************)


BEGIN (* MAIN *)
        (* INITIALIZE VARIABLES *)
        CLOCK  := 0;
        SEED   := 3;
        SOURCE := 38;

        (* INITIALIZE SEQUENCE OF RANDOM NUMBERS *)
        FOR CNTR := 0 TO K DO
           BEGIN
              RNG(SEED);
              KVALUES[CNTR] := SEED;
           END;
        CNTR := 0;

        (* PRINT HEADER FOR OUTPUT *)
        WRITELN(' FLOPPY DISK DRIVE ACCESS DELAY ');
        WRITELN;WRITELN;
        WRITELN('EVNT   REQUEST  AVERAGE ');
        WRITELN(' NO.  SRC  DEST  DELAY (SEC)');
        WRITELN;

        FOR EVENT := 1 TO N DO
            BEGIN (* FOR LOOP *)
               ADDRNG(SEED,PROB);
               (* DETERMINE WHETHER OR NOT WE*)
               (* STAY ON THE SAME TRACK *)
               IF (PROB < P) THEN
                   BEGIN
                      DEST := SOURCE;
                      DELAY:= LATENCY/2;
                   END
               ELSE
                   BEGIN
                      (* DETERMINE WHICH TRACK IS *)
                      (* THE NEXT TRACK *)
                      ADDRNG(SEED,PROB);
                      DEST   := TRUNC(PROB * 75) + 1;
                      (* RULE OUT THE SAME TRACK *)
                      IF ( DEST >= SOURCE ) THEN
                                   DEST := DEST + 1;
```

```
                    TRACKS := ABS( SOURCE - DEST );
                    DELAY  := TRACKS * SEEK + LATENCY/2;
                END;
            (* OUTPUT RESULTS *)
            WRITELN(EVENT:3,SOURCE:5,DEST:6,DELAY:14:3);

            (* UPDATE VARIABLÊS *)
            CLOCK := CLOCK + DELAY;
            SOURCE := DEST;
        END;  (* FOR LOOP *)

    (* OUTPUT STATISICS *)
    WRITELN;
    WRITELN(' TOTAL TIME = ',CLOCK:11:3, ' S');
    WRITELN(' AVG. DELAY = ',CLOCK/N:11:3,' S');
END.  (* MAIN *)
```

4.4 Accumulating Statistics

In any simulation, the purpose of the program is to acquire information about the execution of the model in the belief that the model represents some real system under study. One obvious method is to print out all the events and all the information about the state of the model at the time of each event. This list of information is called a *trace* and is very useful for debugging. The same technique occurs in the study of real systems. Measurements are often reported in traces and are useful in debugging the real system. Sometimes, these traces are called *logs,* such as a console log, or an error log. However, since traces are voluminous, it is important to provide summary statistics about a simulation. (Consider the problem of trying to decide if a model is predicting good performance for a system, given 100 pages of printout, listing all the events.)

We have already seen several examples of statistics that have been accumulated in our simple simulations. In this section we describe some basic concepts that are very useful in adding program segments for the accumulation of statistics in a simulation program. We begin by returning to the definitions for mean values (first moments) and standard deviations (second moments offset from the mean). For a discrete probability density function f_k, the mean $\bar{k}$ and standard deviation σ_k are defined by the following equations:

$$\bar{k} = E[k] = \sum_{k=-\infty}^{\infty} kf_k$$

$$E[k^2] = \sum_{k=-\infty}^{\infty} k^2 f_k$$

$$\sigma_k = \left(E[k^2] - E[k]^2 \right)^{1/2} \tag{4.11}$$

The objective of the simulation run is to obtain a set of experimental observations that are characteristic of the actual, underlying process. Any particular run can be considered as a representation of a particular sample path for the stochastic process being modeled. So we can collect a frequency plot (histogram) of the various values of the random variables of interest (continuous x or discrete k). After the simulation is complete, we can divide by the number of observations and we have an experimental probability density function. However, if we tried to acquire histograms for all variables of interest, we would need storage for a potentially infinite range of values. If we truncate the histogram, we are still faced with the trade-off of storage versus accuracy. So the question arises: Can we acquire these statistics without storing a histogram? The answer, of course, is yes.

If we visualize the execution of the program, it appears to the observer as a stochastic process (which is precisely how it was designed). So for each occurrence (observation) of a random variable, we can add its value to the contents of a program variable to maintain a running sum. When the simulation is complete, we simply divide by the number of observations to obtain the appropriate statistic. This is precisely the same as acquiring the histogram, except that we do not store the values. It is just adding up the values in a different order.

Example 4.17: Consider the following, very short sequence of observations of a random variable K at time t.

$$t = 0, 1, 2, 3, 4, 5, 6$$
$$k - 1, 3, 0, 2, 1, 4, 2$$

So we construct the histogram (one observation of 0, 3, and 4; two observations of 1 and 2) and divided by the total number of observations, 7, to get the experimental probability density function.

k	f_k
0	1/7
1	2/7
2	2/7
3	1/7
4	1/7

Table 4.2

To calculate the mean value, we perform the normal summation.

$$E[k] = 1 \cdot \frac{2}{7} + 2 \cdot \frac{2}{7} + 3 \cdot \frac{1}{7} + 4 \cdot \frac{1}{7} = \frac{13}{7}$$

However, if we are not interested, or find some difficulty in storing the entire histogram, we can do the same calculation "onthefly."

$$E[k] = \frac{1 + 3 + 0 + 2 + 1 + 4 + 2}{7} = \frac{13}{7}$$

In a similar fashion, we can get the experimental second moment by accumulating the sum of the squared value of the random variable.

$$E[k^2] = 1 \cdot \frac{2}{7} + 4 \cdot \frac{2}{7} + 9 \cdot \frac{1}{7} + 16 \cdot \frac{1}{7} = \frac{35}{7}$$

$$= \frac{1 + 9 + 0 + 4 + 1 + 16 + 4}{7} = \frac{35}{7}$$

There are still problems with these alternatives as well. For one, we are accumulating a specific statistic: the histogram was an approximation of the underlying probability density function which contains all the information about a random variable. We could always go back to the histogram and calculate an experimental third or fourth moment if we wished. We could not get the additional statistics with the running-sum method without rerunning the simulation. Furthermore, there are potential numerical problems with the running-sum techniques.

Since the values (or their squares) are being accumulated over a potentially large number of observations, the running sum or, worse, the running-sum of squares may overflow. A more subtle problem occurs because of the finite precision of the arithmetic used on computers. Even if the values do not overflow, when the sum of squares reaches a large value, the loss of precision means that the error range is also large (e.g., 1.314×10^{12} could be off by 5×10^8). When the standard deviation is calculated, $E[k^2] - E[k]^2$ may become negative. So in neither case is a foolproof approach possible.

In summary, there are two basic approaches to acquiring statistics during a simulation run. If the range of the random variable is small and known, a histogram may be built up by counting the actual observations. Alternatively, when the range is not known or it is too large, running sums may be maintained to calculate the statistics directly, hoping that numerical problems do not occur. It is often best to take both approaches for some particularly important parameters, as a cross check on the reported results.

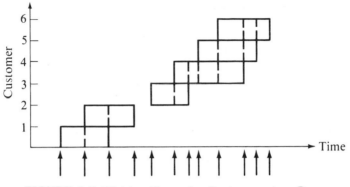

FIGURE 4.5 Waiting Times for Customers in a Queue

Another helpful hint is found by carefully examining the action of a running sum. It is not always easy to keep running sums for variables that are not observable at every event. An example of such a variable may be the waiting time for customers in a queue. Each customer has its own waiting time and its value is not known until the customer is no longer waiting. Consider Figure 4.5, a graph of a portion of the simulation of a queue (a waiting line). The graph is a plot of the waiting times (horizontal rectangles) for each customer.

Since each arrival and departure is an event (it changes the state of the system) during the simulation run, we see that a waiting time value is only known if the event is a departure and there are many values accruing at any particular moment in time. Clearly, keeping individual sums is possible, but complex. However, if we realize that our objective is to add up all the area of the rectangles and then divide by the number of customers, we see a simpler alternative. Instead of adding up the area in horizontal rectangles, add up the area in vertical rectangles. This amounts to keeping a running sum of the number of waiting customers multiplied by the amount of time between events. Then we again divide by the number of customers to get the average waiting time during this segment.

So we have seen how actually acquiring the statistics during a simulation run may take a little thought, but careful design can alleviate many of the complications in the simulation code.

4.5 Analyzing Simulation Results

We now know the basic control structure for simulations and how to accumulate statistics for reporting the results. However, we have not discussed how to determine the accuracy of the reported statistics, or how to determine the duration of the simulation.

4.5.1 Variability of Outputs

A simulation mimics a stochastic process in time so that the outputs of a simulation are themselves random variables. This can be an advantage or disadvantage, depending on your purpose in performing the simulation. It is an advantage if you wish to observe time-dependent behavior, since observing the simulation is just like observing the modeled process (if the model is a correct representation) except that you can observe the state of the simulation at any time. It is a disadvantage if you wish to make a statement about the modeled system's average behavior based on an observation of the simulation. This is the same problem as trying to deduce the probability of a head in a coin toss simply by observing one coin toss.

Startup Transients

When a simulation is actually executed, the simulation program starts in some state and continues to change state just as the modeled stochastic process might change state on a particular sample path. Just as in the case of the coin toss, during the initial steps of the simulation, no particular trend may appear. Consider the graph shown in Figure 4.6, which is the value of the average access delay for the floppy disk drive simulation plotted for each event in the simulation.

Notice how the value of the statistic varies over a large range during the initial portion of the simulation. If we had run the simulation for only a few events, we would have printed values that could have had significant error. This situation is due to the fact that the simulation, like the stochastic process it mimics, has not reached a steady state by that time. Even when we run the simulation for an extended period of time, the output values still demonstrate statistical fluctuations.

There are several approaches to dealing with the startup transient. The first

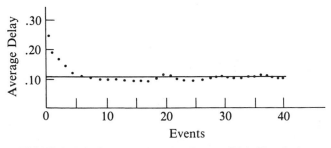

FIGURE 4.6 Startup for the Floppy Disk Simulation

is simply to run the simulation long enough to make any startup behavior negligible. That is expensive and it is difficult to determine how long is long enough. The second approach is to truncate the values at some point in time during the simulation. This is equivalent to starting the simulation (i.e., having the state variables set to some values) in a state approximating the steady state. The third approach, which is the best, is to start the simulation at a point that represents a renewal point for the stochastic process being modeled. We deal with this approach in more detail in Section 4.5.3.

Repeatability

Since the simulation relies on the random number generator as the source of the stochastic variation, repeated runs with same starting values for the variables (including the seed) will result in identical events and statistics. Again, this can be both an advantage or a disadvantage. The advantage is in the usefulness of repeatability for debugging and validation of the results by other users. The disadvantage is in our inability to determine whether the values reported are accurate or not. Clearly, just because rerunning the simulation results in the same outputs does not mean that they are representative. It only means that the computer is running correctly.

We know that any particular sample path for a process will not be the average behavior of the system. So the question remains about how to determine the average values for the underlying stochastic process from a simulation which represents a particular sample path. To understand the possible errors, consider the values observed in separate runs of the floppy disk drive simulation. Each run was made with 100 events and a different seed for the random number generator. The results are given in Table 4.3. As you can see, no two runs resulted in the same estimate for the average delay for a disk access. So what value should we use for the average delay? We can clearly average these results to get 0.1088 second for the delay, but since we have so much variation, what is the potential error in that estimate?

RNG Seed	Average Delay
3	0.108
5	0.112
17	0.111
51	0.115
227	0.098

Table 4.3

4.5.2 Confidence Intervals

To provide some error bounds on the estimate calculated from the collection of output values from a series of simulations, we must know something about the relationship between the individual simulations. If the collection of n output values x_k are independent and identically distributed with a normal (Gaussian) distribution, then an interval, $\pm \varepsilon$, within which the actual mean would fall with probability p is given by the student-t distribution normalized by the experimental variance, s.

$$\varepsilon = \mathbf{t}_{n-1,p} \cdot \left(\frac{s^2}{n}\right)^{1/2} \tag{4.12}$$

Example 4.18: For our five runs with different seeds in the floppy disk drive simulation, we can calculate the 90% confidence interval. We begin by calculating the experimental mean.

$$\bar{x}_n = \frac{1}{n} \sum_{k=1}^{n} x_k = 0.1088$$

From that we can calculate the unbiased experimental variance.

$$s_n^2 = \frac{1}{n-1} \sum_{k=1}^{n} (x_k - \bar{x}_n)^2 = 0.0000427$$

Now looking up the value of the Student-t random variable with degree of freedom 4 and probability 0.90, we find $\mathbf{t}_{4,0.90} = 2.132$. We can then report with confidence 90% that the delay for disk access is the following:

$$\text{delay} = 0.1088 \pm 0.00623$$

It is not always necessary to rerun the simulation. In the case of steady-state simulations, the outputs do not depend on the initial state, so we can break a long run up into n batches over which separate statistics are kept. We can then treat each of the n batches as independent simulation runs.

Unfortunately, the assumptions that the outputs are normally distributed random variables and that subsequent simulation runs or batches of a simulation run are independent are seldom correct. It is true that if the batches or simulation runs are long enough, they will tend to be uncorrelated. In addition, if the simulation runs or batches are long enough, the output variables will tend toward a normal distribution.

Exactly how long is enough is not easy to determine and depends on the application. The use of the Student-t distribution is valid only in the limit, and this could require a very large number of events to become a reasonable approximation.

4.5.3 Regenerative Simulation

If we know something special about the stochastic process the simulation represents, we can improve our analysis technique. Recall that a renewal process has points in time when the process probabilistically restarts (i.e., continues with the same distributions that it started with). At those points the process renews, or regenerates. Those intervals and any random variables defined over those intervals must be independent and identically distributed. Therefore, if we define our output statistics over those intervals (regenerative cycles) rather than over arbitrary batches, we are guaranteed independence regardless of the length of those intervals. If the number of intervals is large, the output variables will tend toward a normal distribution, so we can calculate confidence intervals as follows. For n regenerative cycles of average length N, the confidence interval $\pm\,\varepsilon$ of probability p for an output statistic whose experimental variance is s^2 is given by the following equation.

$$\varepsilon = \frac{t_{\infty,p}}{N} \left(\frac{s^2}{n}\right)^{1/2} \tag{4.13}$$

In practice, using regenerative simulation is more difficult because of the requirement of finding regeneration points. Although it removes one significant assumption on the simulation results (it still assumes that the output variables are normally distributed), actual improvements in the accuracy may not warrant the added complexity.

4.6 Problems

4.1 Write a random number generator using the linear congruential method. Normalize the values to the range (0,1), that is, divide by m. Make two runs, one with each of the two sets of parameters given below. Compare the results to the expected uniform distribution using a χ^2 analysis. You should use a 20 interval histogram and generate enough points so that each interval has at least five occurrences of a generated number.
   a. Set $m = 2^{16}$, $c = 256$, and $a = 2$.
   b. Set $m = 2^{16}$, $c = 255$, and $a = 2^{14} + 1$.

4.2 Run both versions of the geometric random number generators and compare the execution times for each of them. Use the following values for the probability of a success: 0.1, 0.01, 0.001, 0.0001.

4.3 Using the RNG in Problem 4.1(b), generate 1000 random numbers and apply the run-up test for independence.

4.4 Write a RNG using the additive congruential method with $k = 9$ to generate 1000 numbers. Validate the RNG by using a 20 interval χ^2 test and the run-up test.

4.5 Write a random number generator to produce numbers with an Erlangian distribution (see Exercise Ex 3.7). Use subroutine parameters for the rate of the stages and the number of stages.

4.6 Write a random number generator to produce numbers with a hyperexponential distribution (i.e., one that has the following density).

$$f(t) = p\,\lambda e^{-\lambda t} + (1 - p)\mu e^{-\mu t}$$

4.7 Write a simulation of the roll of a pair of dice. Execute the simulation for 100 events and compare the resulting relative frequencies with the theoretical values. Make 10 independent runs and provide 90% confidence intervals.

4.8 Rewrite the instruction fetch simulation example as an event-based simulation.

4.9 Code up and run the floppy disk drive simulation example. (Remove the debug print statement that prints each event.) Run the simulation for 1100 events, discarding the statistics from the first 100 events. Use 10 batches of 100 events each to calculate the 90% confidence interval.

4.10 Write a simulation of a street with a traffic light. The light is red for R minutes and green for G minutes. It alternates between red and green. Traffic arrives as a Poisson process at a rate of A cars per minute. You need only model the traffic in one direction and can assume that when the light is green, all waiting and any new traffic proceeds immediately. Calculate the average waiting time of a car at the light and the average number of cars waiting at the light as seen by a random observer. Be sure to provide 90% confidence intervals for your results. You may use values of $R = 2$, $G = 3$, and $A = 5$. Run the simulation for 1000 arrivals.

Markov Models   5

5.1 Introduction

We have seen how we can model simple systems with no "memory." How ever, clearly many of the systems that we wish to model do have dependencies from one instant to another instant in time. An example of such a system is a disk subsystem. Since programs are the initiators of the read/write requests, they tend to access certain sections (a file) on a disk. Therefore, some notion of locality is required in our model of a disk. We will now expand our capabilities to model systems with a special kind of dependency.

We can classify complex systems into two basic types. Some systems have states that can be any real value, such as a temperature or a position in a plane. These systems are called *continuous state space* (or real-valued) systems. Other systems can only occupy states which are discrete (possibly infinite), such as the winnings at the roulette table or the positions of a disk head. These systems are called *discrete state space* systems (or chains).

There are many examples in nature of each of these types. For example, we have already mentioned that the temperature in a room can be modeled as a stochastic process. It is, in fact, a continuous state space stochastic process. Another example is the static heard on a radio channel. The voltage values, which vary with time, can be any real value. In this book, we concentrate on discrete state space systems. Such things as a disk drive, a CPU job queue, or the commands in a time-sharing system are examples of discrete state space systems since we can "count" (enumerate) the possible states of the systems.

For a discrete state space system, if we call our states s_i (i.e., are denumerable), we can characterize the dependency of a possible state on the sequence of states S through which the system has previously passed (i.e. its history).

$$P[S_{n+1} = s_k \mid S_n = s_i, S_{n-1} = s_j, \ldots, S_1 = s_l] \tag{5.1}$$

Note that the states $\{s_i, s_j, s_k, \ldots s_l\}$ need not be unique. They could actually all be the same state. If we had assigned numbers, 1, 2, 3, . . . to the states, a sequence of states S may look like 1, 3, 2, 1, 1, 4, 2, . . . so the fourth state in the sequence was the state 1. Then, the probability that the state at position 8 in the sequence may depend upon the precise sequence of states up to that point.

To determine the probability of a particular state being the next state, we would need to know all of the previous states. It is, of course, possible to simulate such a process for a sufficiently small sequence. However, it should be clear that the complexity of the simulation program (model) is directly related to the amount of "history" required for determining the probability of the next state.

In addition to the distinction of whether a system has a discrete or continuous state space, we can distinguish how time is measured. Stochastic processes that are embedded at separate points in time are called *discrete-time* systems, whereas stochastic processes that change state (a new sample from a potentially different random variable distribution) at an arbitrary point in time, are called *continuous-time* systems. We consider both types of systems in this book.

For any stochastic process we can consider different levels of complexity depending on the dependencies between state changes. A general stochastic process could change states depending on its entire past history of state changes. However, if we restrict the dependencies, we can get different kinds of system models depending on what form the dependency takes.

If the dependency includes only the history of the process from the last state change, we have significantly reduced the complexity of the model. If we further restrict the dependency to be simply what the last state was, we have reduced the complexity even further. If we remove all dependencies on the history of the process, we are back to our well-known independent, memoryless processes, the Poisson and Bernoulli processes. Even when there is some dependency, the actual form of the dependency will define a type of process which may yield to a specific analysis technique.

We can categorize several different types of discrete state space processes which depend only on the history from the last state change.

1. Semi-Markov Process
   This stochastic process can have an arbitrary distribution of time between state changes and any new state is possible given the current state (i.e., the probability $P[S_k \mid S_j]$ is arbitrary).

2. Random Walk
   This stochastic process has an arbitrary distribution of time between

events. However, the next-state probabilities depend on the current position. The restriction can be described as $P[S_k \mid S_j] = P_{k-j}$. In other words, the transition probabilities depend only on the distance from the current position.

3. Markov Processes (Chains)
   This stochastic process restricts the time between events to be memoryless, but the next-state probabilities $P[S_k \mid S_j]$ are still arbitrary.

4. Birth-Death Processes
   This stochastic process restricts the time between events to be memoryless and further restricts the next-state probabilities to be nonzero for only the nearest-neighbor states (i.e., $|k - j| > 1 \Rightarrow P[S_k \mid S_j] = 0$).

Semi-Markov processes are beyond the scope of this book. The random walk is of some interest but does not usually model the kind of systems we are interested in studying. However, both Markov processes and the more restrictive case of birth-death processes prove to be of great interest to us. These two processes provide a good compromise between the complexity of systems they can represent and the difficulty of finding a solution.

The rest of this book is devoted to Markov chain models (queuing systems are a special case). We will deal with both the continuous time and discrete-time chains. We will exploit some special properties of birth-death systems to study queuing models more efficiently.

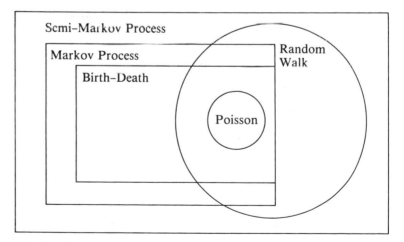

FIGURE 5.1 Different Types of Stochatic Processes
This figure was derived from Figure 2.4 in *Queueing Systems: Vol. I. Theory,* by Leonard Kleinrock, Copyright © 1975, John Wiley and Sons and is printed here with permission.

5.2 Discrete versus Continuous Time

As we have mentioned, Markov chains can have transitions (events of moving from one state to another) at separate moments in time (discrete) or at an arbitrary moment in time (continuous). If the Markov chain is discrete-time, we can speak of those points in time as steps. At those particular moments in time, some transition must occur, even if the transition is only from a state back to itself. We also know from the definition that this probability can depend only on the current state S_j, not on how long the system has occupied the state S_j. So the distribution of the amount of time the system spends in a state must be memoryless. We know from probability theory that the only such discrete distribution is the geometric distribution. Then the probability distribution for a transition at a step at some time $t_n + \Delta t$ is a simple Bernoulli trial with some probability $p_{jk}(t_n)$. When we consider all possible combinations of states S_j and S_k, we have a matrix $\mathbf{P}(t_n)$.

$$P[S_k(t_n + \Delta t)|S_j(t_n)] = p_{jk}(t_n)$$

$$\mathbf{P}(t_n) \triangleq [p_{jk}(t_n)] \tag{5.2}$$

If we have a finite state, discrete-time Markov chain, we can think of it as a game, where each state change occurs at the roll of some funny m sided die. At each throw, there is a different set of m different dice to choose from, one for each of the m possible states of the game. (So $p_{jk}(t_n)$ is the probability that the kth side will turn up on the jth die from the t_nth set.) The particular m sided die chosen for the roll, is the one corresponding to the current state of the game. After rolling the die, the game moves to the new state determined by the roll and a new set of dice are used.

If the Markov chain is a continuous time system, an event will not occur at a precise time $t_n + \Delta t$. However, we again know that the amount of time spent in a state must be memoryless by the definition of the Markov process. Since this is a continuous time system, the amount of time spent in a state must have an exponential distribution.

In the continuous time Markov chain, the process does not simply move from one state to another at discrete steps in time. So, it is not obvious how to separate the time that state changes occur and the probability of selecting the next state. However, realizing that we need not specify the probability of exactly which state is next, but only which state we are in at a particular moment in time, we can define a probability for going from state S_j at time t' to the state S_k at some later time t'', possibly going through other states along the way.

$$P[S_k(t'') \mid S_j(t')] \triangleq h_{jk}(t',t'') \tag{5.3}$$

Clearly this probability depends on states S_j, S_k and on $t'' - t'$. So $\mathbf{H}(t',t'') \triangleq [h_{jk}(t',t'')]$ is a matrix of cumulative distributions functions. This can be more difficult to deal with than the discrete-time case. However, we will see that we have an alternative to dealing directly with probabilities of events in continuous time Markov chains. Because it is easier to explain continuous time Markov chains once we understand discrete-time Markov chains, we defer this discussion until Section 5.6.

Now that we have defined the Markov chain and described the changes of state in terms of probabilities, we still have a very complex model. Note that the probabilities given in equations (5.2) and (5.3) are functions of time. The system may behave differently at 3 p.m. than it did at 10 a.m. This complicates the problem of solving the model for such a system. If the system parameters do not depend on the absolute value of time, but only on the state, we have reduced the complexity of the model. Such Markov systems are called *homogeneous*. Returning to the game analogy for the finite state, discrete-time Markov chain, a chain is homogeneous when the same set of dice are used over and over again. We will restrict our studies to homogeneous chains. This restriction does not mean that the model is not dynamic. It means only that the probability distributions do not depend on the absolute value of time. In this case, equations (5.2) and (5.3) reduce to the following equations.

$$\mathbf{P}(t_1) = \mathbf{P}(t_2) = \mathbf{P}$$
$$\mathbf{H}(t',t'') = \mathbf{H}(0,\, t'' - t') \tag{5.4}$$

5.3 Representations

There are many different ways to represent a homogeneous Markov chain. The first representation has already been introduced. It is simply a list of all the states and a list of probability distributions for the possible next states. A second representation is graphical and consists of a set of labeled states denoted by circles and arcs to the potential next states labeled with the probability of that next state. Finally, the last representation is a matrix whose rows correspond to a current state and whose columns correspond to a potential next state. This matrix is equivalent to the adjacency matrix for the arc weighted graph. The entry at row j and column k is the probability of the state k being the next state given that the current state is j. This representation will prove to be the easiest to manipulate mathematically.

As an example, consider a model of a processor that has certain tasks to perform. If we consider the possible states for such a system, we realize that it has the potential to be idle (no task to do), busy (working on a task), waiting (stopped for some resource), broken (no longer operational), and in repair (during the time it actually takes to fix the failure). Clearly, it can break down when the system is idle, busy, or waiting, but not when it is already broken. The system would also not wait unless there was still work to accomplish, so a state

Current State	Possible Next State	Possible Next State	Possible Next State
Idle	Busy	Broken	—
Busy	Idle	Waiting	Broken
Waiting	Busy	Broken	—
Broken	Repair	—	—
Repair	Idle	—	—

Table 5.1

change directly from waiting to idle is not allowed. In addition, the system would tend to fail more often when it is in use than when it is idle.

We can construct a Markov chain that exhibits behavior similar to that of the above system. As shown in Table 5.1, the Markov chain has five states and probabilities for the next state that depend on the current state. By using circles to denote states and arcs to denote state transitions, we can represent the Markov chain graphically, as shown in Figure 5.2, where the probabilities are given as arc weights.

The matrix representation which corresponds to the adjacency matrix of the previous graph is given below. Note that the rows sum to 1. This is simply because the set of next states given a particular state is the entire row, and the sum of the probabilities over all states is 1. Matrices of this form are called *stochastic matrices*.

$$
\begin{array}{cc}
\text{States} & \begin{array}{ccccc} \text{Idle} & \text{Busy} & \text{Wait} & \text{Broken} & \text{Repair} \end{array} \\
\begin{array}{c} \text{Idle} \\ \text{Busy} \\ \text{Waiting} \\ \text{Broken} \\ \text{Repair} \end{array} &
\begin{bmatrix}
0.20 & 0.75 & 0.00 & 0.05 & 0.00 \\
0.30 & 0.30 & 0.30 & 0.10 & 0.00 \\
0.00 & 0.55 & 0.40 & 0.05 & 0.00 \\
0.00 & 0.00 & 0.00 & 0.50 & 0.50 \\
0.60 & 0.00 & 0.00 & 0.00 & 0.40
\end{bmatrix}
\end{array}
\qquad (5.5)
$$

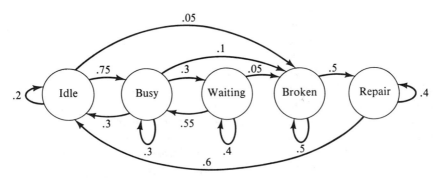

FIGURE 5.2 Graphical Representation of a Markov Chain

5.4 State Classification

Since, by definition, a Markov chain is characterized by a set of states and transitions, we can characterize a chain by considering some basic properties of the states for that chain. To begin, let us define some categories of states.

Definition 5.1: A state is *recurrent* if the system, once in that state, will return to that state through a series of transitions with probability 1.

Definition 5.2: A state is *transient* if it is not recurrent. (That is, the probability of returning to the state is strictly less than 1.)

Note that a state being transient does not mean that it cannot recur; it only means that the state is not guaranteed of recurring. Some states may recur as often as you like, but there is some possibility that they may not recur. These states are also considered transient. So states that cannot recur are clearly transient, but so are states that may not recur (i.e., are not guaranteed of recurring).

Even though all states are either recurrent or transient, we can further subdivide the recurrent class into two classes, depending on how much time it takes to return to it.

Definition 5.3: A recurrent state is *recurrent nonnull* if the mean time to return to the state is finite.

Definition 5.4 A recurrent state is *recurrent null* if the mean time to return to the state is infinite.

At this point, some confusion may arise when you consider how a system can be guaranteed to return to a state, yet take an infinite amount of time on the average. To begin with, the number of states in such a system must be infinite since it is impossible to spend an infinite amount of time in a finite number of states without spending an infinite amount of time in one of them. Consider a chain which meets the birth-death restriction so each transition can only go to the next higher state or the next lower state. So for a state j between states k and m, the system must pass through state j if it goes from state k to state m. Assume the probabilities are such that the probability the system is in each of the infinite number of states is the same. Therefore, the probability that the system is found in any particular state is infinitesimally small. However, the infinite sum of those infinitesimally small times must still be finite (the system has to spend time at the rate of 1 second per second). So, the average time to reach and the average time to return from a particular state are finite values. Since there are an infinite number of states, even though the time to return from each one is finite, the sum becomes infinite if the probability of reaching those states does not vanish. So because we assumed that the system spent an equal amount of time in each state, the mean time to return becomes infinite.

We can break down recurrent states even further. We can also classify recurrent states into two subcategories based upon exactly how they recur.

Definition 5.5: A recurrent state is *aperiodic* if for some number k, there is a way to return to the state in k, $k + 1$, $k + 2$, . . . , ∞ transitions.

Definition 5.6: A recurrent state is *periodic* if it is not aperiodic.

Because a periodic state does not have some number k, above which the system can return in k, $k+1$, $k+2$, . . . ∞ transitions, there must be "holes" in the sequence. Since the state is recurrent, the sequence still must have some values where the system can return to that state. The *period,* or cycle, of a periodic state is the minimum value $\gamma > 1$ such that the system can return to that state in γk, $k = 1, 2, 3, 4$ . . . transitions.

In summary, we can illustrate the categorization of a state in a Markov chain using Figure 5.3.

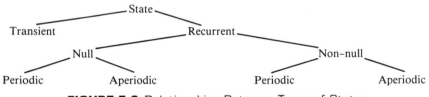

FIGURE 5.3 Relationships Between Types of States

Although periodic states do have a specific cycle, that does not mean that the sequence of states a system may go through is restricted to a single cycle. If the system can return to a state in 2, 4, 6, 8, . . . transitions or 4, 8, 12, . . . transitions, it could also have a sequence 2, 6, 8, 10, 14, ... The important distinction in this example is that it cannot return in an odd number of transitions. It is not aperiodic and therefore is periodic. Since the "holes" in the sequences are a minimum of two apart, the period for such a chain is 2. We will see several other ways to detect whether a system has periodic states.

Example 5.1: Consider the discrete-time Markov chain shown in Figure 5.4.

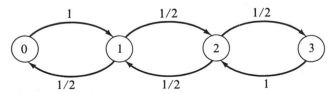

FIGURE 5.4 An Example Markov Chain with Periodic States

Is the state 0 recurrent or transient?

– It is recurrent since, given any other state, I can always get back. Therefore, there is nowhere to go from state 0 where it cannot return.

Is the state 0 recurrent null or recurrent nonnull?

– It is recurrent nonnull simply because there are only four states, a finite number.

Is the state 0 periodic or aperiodic?

– If it is aperiodic, then for some number of steps k, the system can return to state 0 in $k + 1$, $k + 2$, . . . steps. We can see, since for every step away a corresponding step back must be made, returning to state 0 in an odd number of steps is not possible. Therefore, there is no number k such that the system can return in $k + 1$ and $k + 2$ steps, since either $k + 1$ or $k + 2$ must be odd. Therefore, state 0 is periodic (with period 2).

There is a quick way to determine if a state in a Markov chain is aperiodic. If a state has a self-loop, it must be aperiodic. With a self-loop, if the system returns to the state at step k, it can obviously return at steps $k + 1$, $k + 2$, ... Therefore, self-loops always make a state aperiodic.

Example 5.2: Consider the previous discrete-time Markov chain with the addition of a self-loop at state 0, shown in Figure 5.5. Now the state 0 is aperiodic, recurrent nonnull. However, a state does not necessarily have to have a self-loop to be aperiodic. Consider state 2. Although the system cannot return to state 2 in 1 step, it can return in an odd number of steps for $k = 5$ and above. So state 2 is also aperiodic in this example.

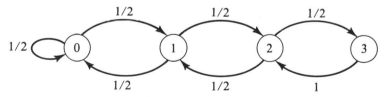

FIGURE 5.5 An Example Markov Chain with Aperiodic States

However, the absence of self-loops in the chain does not mean that a state is periodic.

Example 5.3: Consider state number 2 in the chains shown in Figure 5.6. In the first chain, after leaving state 2 the system can return to state 2 in 2, 4, 6, . . . steps, but not at any odd step.

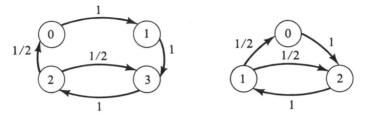

FIGURE 5.6 Periodic and Aperiodic Chains without Self-loops

In the second chain, leaving state 2 means that the system can return in 2, 3, 4, . . . steps. By having the option of a sequence of length 2 or 3, we can create sequences of any number of steps by combining 2's for all even numbers and a final 3 for an odd number of steps. Therefore, although we cannot return in 1 step (no self-loop) we can return in k, $k + 1$, $k + 2$, . . . , for $k = 2$, which satisfies the requirement for aperiodicity.

Now that we can characterize states, we can generalize the classification to entire chains.

Definition 5.7: A Markov chain is *transient* if all its states are transient, it is *recurrent nonnull* if all its states are recurrent nonnull, it is *recurrent null* if all its states are recurrent null, it is *periodic* if all its states are periodic, or it is *aperiodic* if all its states are aperiodic.

Definition 5.8: A Markov chain is *irreducible* if all states are reachable from all other states.

It should be clear that if a Markov chain has a transient state whose probability of recurring is 0, the chain must be reducible. Since the transient state is guaranteed to not recur after some point in time, then there is at least one state from which the transient state is not reachable. Therefore, there is a state that is not reachable from all others, and the condition for irreducibility is violated.

Example 5.4: Consider the Markov chain in Figure 5.7. What are the classifications of the states in this chain? Is the chain irreducible?

States 1, 2, 4, and 5 are recurrent, while state 3 is transient, since the probability of returning to state 3 after leaving is zero.

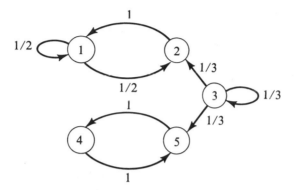

FIGURE 5.7 A Reducible Markov Chain with Periodic and Aperiodic States

Moreover, states 1 and 2 are aperiodic, since state 1 has a self-loop and state 2 is reachable from state 1. However, states 4 and 5 are periodic with period 2. Finally, since states 4 and 5 are not reachable from states 1 and 2, the system is reducible.

From the definitions above we can make the following conclusion.

Theorem 5.1: An irreducible Markov chain is either transient, recurrent non-null, or recurrent null. If it is recurrent, it is either periodic or aperiodic.

This is a direct result of the definitions. For a chain to be irreducible, all states are reachable from each other. So if a state is recurrent, you can always get from that state to any of the others, so they are also recurrent. Therefore transient and recurrent states cannot coexist in an irreducible Markov chain. Similarly, if a state is periodic, all states would have to be periodic. If not, then there would be some aperiodic and periodic states in the system. Since the system is irreducible by assumption, it is possible to get from a periodic state to an aperiodic state and back. To see that this is impossible, pick a sequence of transitions such that you go from the periodic state and through one of the aperiodic states and return to the periodic state in n steps. The aperiodic state has its own m such that you can return in $m, m + 1, \ldots$. Then there is a way to get to the periodic state in $k = n + m, k + 1 = n + m + 1, k + 2 = n + m + 2, \ldots$, which means that it is not periodic. This is a contradiction, so aperiodic and periodic states cannot coexist in an irreducible Markov chain. The remaining cases follow in a similar manner.

We have now seen various behavior that may be observed in a Markov chain. However, what is of interest to us as modelers is the long term, or limiting behavior of the system. In other words, can we obtain the probability that a random observer would find the system in a particular state? The answer is yes for a particular class of systems.

Definition 5.9: If the Markov chain is irreducible, recurrent nonnull, and aperiodic, it is called *ergodic*.

This class of stochastic processes will be the focus of our studies since we will discover that they have a well defined steady-state behavior. We will often have to raise the question of whether a particular process is within this class, since if it is not, its long-term behavior does not converge to some limiting behavior. We now quote, without proof, a theorem commonly referred to as the ergodic theorem.

Theorem 5.2: If a Markov chain is irreducible, recurrent nonnull, and aperiodic (i.e., it is ergodic), there exists a unique limiting distribution for the probability of being in a state k denoted as π_k, independent of the initial state. These probabilities are called the *steady-state* or *equilibrium* probabilities.

We now have a class of stochastic processes that have the desired properties of some limited dependency, a well defined steady-state behavior, and an efficient (depending on the size of the state space) solution technique. These properties will make it possible for us to model a wide range of system behavior with Markov processes.

In the following sections of this chapter we develop a methodology for solving such systems. This methodology is based on linear algebra, so the matrix representation will be our primary focus. We will note, in passing, how non-ergodic systems can be detected by their matrices.

Exercise

5.1 Classify the states in the following Markov chain.

$$
\begin{bmatrix}
0.50 & 0.50 & 0 & 0 & 0 & 0 & 0 \\
0.25 & 0.25 & 0.25 & 0 & 0 & 0.25 & 0 \\
0 & 0 & 0 & 1.00 & 0 & 0 & 0 \\
0 & 0 & 0.50 & 0 & 0.50 & 0 & 0 \\
0 & 0 & 0 & 1.00 & 0 & 0 & 0 \\
0 & 0 & 0 & 0 & 0 & 0 & 1.00 \\
0 & 0 & 0 & 0 & 0 & 0.50 & 0.50
\end{bmatrix}
$$

5.5 Discrete-Time Systems

In discrete-time systems we can speak of the system at a step rather than at a particular moment in time. So the system would start in some state, say j, at step 0, and proceed to change state (possibly to the same state) at each successive step. Therefore, the system simply "hops" from state to state at each step, occupying only one state at a time. Sometimes we will not be concerned with the entire sequence of transitions or hops but with the state of the system at some time in the future. We can then conceive of the system going from a particular state j at step m to another state k at step $m+n$.

5.5.1 State Probability Vector

When a system is modeled by a Markov chain, the model has a set of states and a set of transitions from each state to another state. The operation of the system is represented by a possibly infinite sequence of states. A subsequent operation of the same system could result in a different sequence of states. This sequence of states is the sample path of the Markov process. However, the purpose of all this work is to use the model to predict the behavior of the system Since we have a system that when allowed to operate (an experiment) may be in any state when we observe it, we represent the relative frequencies of the different outcomes by a probability.

We can describe the state of the system as a vector **p** whose elements are the probability of finding the system in that state. If we know the system is in state k, we will find it there with probability 1. Therefore, the state probability vector would be made up of all zeros, except for the kth entry, which would be a 1. If we do not know the state of the system, but we wish to represent the potential behavior of the system, we would have elements that represent the relative frequencies (i.e., the probabilities) of finding the system in each state.

Example 5.5: Consider a communication interface that is always left on and which has some light that indicates whether or not information is being sent out. We can describe two states for the system, busy or idle. We will represent the system state as a state probability vector $\mathbf{p} = [p_b, p_i]$. Then when the system is busy, the state probability vector is [1, 0] and when the system is idle, the state probability vector is [0, 1]. If we find out after many observations that the system is busy one-third of the time, we may represent our observation as the state probability vector [1/3, 2/3]. We have now replaced our observations with a model for the system that we can use to predict the next observation of the communication interface.

We can extend the concept of the state probability vector to be a function of the number of steps from some starting state. We then define $\mathbf{p}(n)$ to represent the predicted state of the system at step n given some starting state probability vector $\mathbf{p}(0)$.

5.5.2 Multistep State Probabilities

The first object of interest is the *single-step transition probability matrix* $\mathbf{P}$, which describes the probability p_{jk} that the system will go from one particular state j to another particular state k in one step. This is the same matrix as described previously, and contains all the information necessary to describe the behavior of a discrete-time Markov chain.

$$\mathbf{P} = [p_{jk}] = \begin{bmatrix} 0.20 & 0.75 & 0.00 & 0.05 & 0.00 \\ 0.30 & 0.30 & 0.30 & 0.10 & 0.00 \\ 0.00 & 0.55 & 0.40 & 0.05 & 0.00 \\ 0.00 & 0.00 & 0.00 & 0.50 & 0.50 \\ 0.60 & 0.00 & 0.00 & 0.00 & 0.40 \end{bmatrix} \tag{5.6}$$

We can describe the action of the system mathematically by constructing a state probability vector and applying the single-step transition probability matrix to obtain the probabilities for finding the system in any of the states after one step has occurred. If we start with the system in state 2, the state probability vector $\mathbf{p}(0)$ is [0, 1, 0, 0, 0], since the probability of the system being in state 1, 3, 4, 5 is 0 and the probability of the system being in state 2 is 1.

$$\mathbf{p}(0)\mathbf{P} = \mathbf{p}(1) \tag{5.7}$$

Example 5.6:

$$[0, 1, 0, 0, 0] \begin{bmatrix} 0.20 & 0.75 & 0.00 & 0.05 & 0.00 \\ 0.30 & 0.30 & 0.30 & 0.10 & 0.00 \\ 0.00 & 0.55 & 0.40 & 0.05 & 0.00 \\ 0.00 & 0.00 & 0.00 & 0.50 & 0.50 \\ 0.60 & 0.00 & 0.00 & 0.00 & 0.40 \end{bmatrix} = [0.3, 0.3, 0.3, 0.1, 0.0]$$

So even though for any one experiment the actual system would go to one and only one next state, we have a probability distribution describing the frequency of observations of each of the states as the next state over a sufficiently large number of repetitions of the experiment.

We can repeat the process as many times as we wish. We can produce the probability that the system will be found in any particular state after two steps simply by multiplying the one-step state probability vector $\mathbf{p}(1)$, [0.30, 0.30, 0.30, 0.10, 0.00], by the single-step transition probability matrix.

$$\mathbf{p}(1)\mathbf{P} = \mathbf{p}(2) \tag{5.8}$$

Example 5.7:

$$[0.3, 0.3, 0.3, 0.1, 0] \begin{bmatrix} 0.2 & 0.75 & 0.0 & 0.05 & 0.0 \\ 0.3 & 0.30 & 0.3 & 0.10 & 0.0 \\ 0.0 & 0.55 & 0.4 & 0.05 & 0.0 \\ 0.0 & 0.00 & 0.0 & 0.50 & 0.5 \\ 0.6 & 0.00 & 0.0 & 0.00 & 0.4 \end{bmatrix} = [0.15, 0.48, 0.21, 0.11, 0.05]$$

In Tables 5.2 and 5.3, we have listed the values of the zero-, one-, two-, three-, and four-step state probability vectors for two different starting states. It is useful to note that they are converging to the same values (remember the ergodic theorem).

p(0)	p(1)	p(2)	p(3)	p(4)	. . .	p(∞)
1	0.20	0.265	0.1805	0.20560	. . .	0.215554
0	0.75	0.375	0.4350	0.37725	. . .	0.380389
0	0.00	0.225	0.2025	0.21150	. . .	0.190194
0	0.05	0.110	0.1170	0.12115	. . .	0.116653
0	0.00	0.025	0.0650	0.08450	. . .	0.097210

Table 5.2

p(0)	p(1)	p(2)	p(3)	p(4)	. . .	p(∞)
0	0.30	0.15	0.204	0.1974	. . .	0.215554
1	0.30	0.48	0.372	0.3900	. . .	0.380389
0	0.30	0.21	0.228	0.2028	. . .	0.190194
0	0.10	0.11	0.121	0.1193	. . .	0.116653
0	0.00	0.05	0.075	0.0905	. . .	0.097210

Table 5.3

Since matrix multiplication is associative (although it is not commutative), we can also describe this same operation as follows.

$$\mathbf{p}(2) = \mathbf{p}(1)\mathbf{P} = \mathbf{p}(0)\mathbf{PP} = \mathbf{p}(0)\mathbf{P}^2 \qquad (5.9)$$

We can view the single-step matrix raised to a power n as the n-step transition probability matrix, since when multiplied by a state probability vector it results in the state probability vector after n steps. In fact, we can continue this indefinitely. For ergodic systems, we see the predicted convergence to the limiting distribution. Some Markovian software packages use precisely the same technique to converge on a solution. However, these packages can have convergence problems. The variation in the rate of convergence will be discussed in some detail in a later section.

Example 5.8:

$$\mathbf{P}^2 = \begin{bmatrix} 0.20 & 0.75 & 0.00 & 0.05 & 0.00 \\ 0.30 & 0.30 & 0.30 & 0.10 & 0.00 \\ 0.00 & 0.55 & 0.40 & 0.05 & 0.00 \\ 0.00 & 0.00 & 0.00 & 0.50 & 0.50 \\ 0.60 & 0.00 & 0.00 & 0.00 & 0.40 \end{bmatrix} \begin{bmatrix} 0.20 & 0.75 & 0.00 & 0.05 & 0.00 \\ 0.30 & 0.30 & 0.30 & 0.10 & 0.00 \\ 0.00 & 0.55 & 0.40 & 0.05 & 0.00 \\ 0.00 & 0.00 & 0.00 & 0.50 & 0.50 \\ 0.60 & 0.00 & 0.00 & 0.00 & 0.40 \end{bmatrix}$$

$$= \begin{bmatrix} 0.265 & 0.375 & 0.225 & 0.110 & 0.025 \\ 0.150 & 0.480 & 0.210 & 0.110 & 0.050 \\ 0.165 & 0.385 & 0.325 & 0.100 & 0.025 \\ 0.300 & 0.000 & 0.000 & 0.250 & 0.450 \\ 0.360 & 0.450 & 0.000 & 0.030 & 0.160 \end{bmatrix}$$

$$\mathbf{P}^3 = \begin{bmatrix} 0.265 & 0.375 & 0.225 & 0.110 & 0.025 \\ 0.150 & 0.480 & 0.210 & 0.110 & 0.050 \\ 0.165 & 0.385 & 0.325 & 0.100 & 0.025 \\ 0.300 & 0.000 & 0.000 & 0.250 & 0.450 \\ 0.360 & 0.450 & 0.000 & 0.030 & 0.160 \end{bmatrix} \begin{bmatrix} 0.20 & 0.75 & 0.00 & 0.05 & 0.00 \\ 0.30 & 0.30 & 0.30 & 0.10 & 0.00 \\ 0.00 & 0.55 & 0.40 & 0.05 & 0.00 \\ 0.00 & 0.00 & 0.00 & 0.50 & 0.50 \\ 0.60 & 0.00 & 0.00 & 0.00 & 0.40 \end{bmatrix}$$

$$= \begin{bmatrix} 0.1805 & 0.4350 & 0.2025 & 0.1170 & 0.0650 \\ 0.2040 & 0.3720 & 0.2280 & 0.1210 & 0.0750 \\ 0.1635 & 0.4180 & 0.2455 & 0.1130 & 0.0600 \\ 0.3300 & 0.2250 & 0.0000 & 0.1400 & 0.3050 \\ 0.3030 & 0.4050 & 0.1350 & 0.0780 & 0.0790 \end{bmatrix}$$

$$\mathbf{P}^\infty = \begin{bmatrix} 0.215554 & 0.380389 & 0.190194 & 0.116653 & 0.097210 \\ 0.215554 & 0.380389 & 0.190194 & 0.116653 & 0.097210 \\ 0.215554 & 0.380389 & 0.190194 & 0.116653 & 0.097210 \\ 0.215554 & 0.380389 & 0.190194 & 0.116653 & 0.097210 \\ 0.215554 & 0.380389 & 0.190194 & 0.116653 & 0.097210 \end{bmatrix}$$

Exercise

5.2 Starting the preceding example in state 3, what would the state probability vector be at step 1? at step 2?

5.5.3 Steady-State Probabilities

We have seen how the state probability vector changes at each step and converges to a limit value for ergodic systems. Clearly, successive multiplications of the single-step transition probability matrix is computationally complex. (Each step is of order m^3 for normal algorithms, where m is the number of rows or columns in the matrix.)

We now wish to use a more efficient computation if we are only interested in the limiting (steady-state) state probabilities. We adopt the notation $\pi \triangleq (\pi_1, \pi_2, \ldots, \pi_m)$ for this particular state probability vector to distinguish it from the normal n-step state probability vectors. [i.e., $\lim_{n \to \infty} \mathbf{p}(n) \triangleq \pi$].

How can we compute the values π_k more efficiently? We first observe what is happening as the number of steps increases. In other words, what does convergence itself imply?

$$\lim_{n \to \infty} \mathbf{p}(n)\mathbf{P} = \lim_{n \to \infty} \mathbf{p}(n + 1) \tag{5.10}$$

If the state probability vector $\mathbf{p}(n)$ is truly converging, there is a negligible difference between $\mathbf{p}(n)$ and $\mathbf{p}(n + 1)$ as $n \to \infty$. So the value of the limit vector, the steady-state probability vector would have to satisfy the equation

$$\pi\mathbf{P} = \pi \tag{5.11}$$

This equation can be solved quickly (it is also on the order of n^3). It is a special kind of equation in linear algebra. This vector π is called an *eigenvector* of the single-step transition probability matrix $\mathbf{P}$ for the *eigenvalue* 1.

Unfortunately, the set of simultaneous equations equivalent to $\pi \mathbf{P} = \pi$ are not linearly independent. Therefore, the equation $\pi \mathbf{P} = \pi$ does not uniquely determine the values of the steady-state probability vector π. This is clear when you note that if there is a solution π such that $\pi\mathbf{P} = \pi$, then $\alpha\pi \mathbf{P} = \alpha\pi$. So $\alpha\pi$ must also be a solution for the eigenvalue 1. In fact, there are an infinite number of such vectors since any value of α would suffice. In linear algebra we normally discussed these eigenvectors normalized with respect to some metric. But in our case, what is the metric for normalizing π?

Recall that π is a vector whose elements are the probabilities of the system being in any of its possible states. So if we sum the probability of all possible outcomes, that sum must equal 1. From that observation, we have a normalization equation that can give us the actual values of π, the steady-state probability vector.

$$\sum_{\forall k} \pi_k = 1 \tag{5.12}$$

Example 5.9:

$$[\pi_1, \pi_2, \pi_3, \pi_4, \pi_5] \begin{bmatrix} 0.20 & 0.75 & 0.00 & 0.05 & 0.00 \\ 0.30 & 0.30 & 0.30 & 0.10 & 0.00 \\ 0.00 & 0.55 & 0.40 & 0.05 & 0.00 \\ 0.00 & 0.00 & 0.00 & 0.50 & 0.50 \\ 0.60 & 0.00 & 0.00 & 0.00 & 0.40 \end{bmatrix} = [\pi_1, \pi_2, \pi_3, \pi_4, \pi_5]$$

$$\frac{1}{5}\pi_1 + \frac{3}{10}\pi_2 + \frac{3}{5}\pi_5 = \pi_1$$

$$\frac{3}{4}\pi_1 + \frac{3}{10}\pi_2 + \frac{11}{20}\pi_3 = \pi_2$$

$$\frac{3}{10}\pi_2 + \frac{2}{5}\pi_3 = \pi_3$$

$$\frac{1}{20}\pi_1 + \frac{1}{10}\pi_2 + \frac{1}{20}\pi_3 + \frac{1}{2}\pi_4 = \pi_4$$

$$\frac{1}{2}\pi_4 + \frac{2}{5}\pi_5 = \pi_5$$

We can then solve these simultaneous equations for all of the elements of π in terms of one of them. Since the equations are linearly dependent, we can omit one of them, and obtain the following solution.

$$\pi_1 = \frac{17}{30}\pi_2$$

$$\pi_3 = \frac{1}{2}\pi_2$$

$$\pi_4 = \frac{23}{75}\pi_2$$

$$\pi_4 = \frac{23}{90}\pi_2$$

We can now substitute back into our normalization equation to get the value of π_2.

$$\left(\frac{17}{30} + 1 + \frac{1}{2} + \frac{23}{75} + \frac{23}{90}\right)\pi_2 = 1$$

$$\pi_2 = \frac{450}{1183}$$

Finally, we substitute the value of π_2 back into the solutions from the simultaneous equations to get the remaining values of the vector π.

$$\left(\frac{255}{1183}, \frac{450}{1183}, \frac{225}{1183}, \frac{138}{1183}, \frac{115}{1183}\right)$$

$$[0.21554, 0.380389, 0.190194, 0.116653, 0.097210]$$

Exercise

5.3 Solve for the steady-state probabilities for the following Markov chain.

$$
\begin{bmatrix}
\frac{1}{4} & \frac{1}{2} & \frac{1}{4} & 0 \\
0 & \frac{1}{2} & 0 & \frac{1}{2} \\
\frac{1}{3} & \frac{1}{3} & \frac{1}{3} & 0 \\
\frac{1}{4} & 0 & \frac{1}{4} & \frac{1}{4}
\end{bmatrix}
$$

5.5.4 The General Multistep Transition Matrix

We have now seen how a Markov system can be represented by and manipulated as a matrix and how we can quickly determine what the state probability vector is in the limit as the number of steps that a system has made approaches infinity. For a small number of steps, we can also find the state probability vector by successive matrix multiplication. However, what if the number of steps is large but not infinite? In this section we take a different approach which will give us the n-step transition probability matrix directly.

Let us begin with our general matrix equation.

$$\mathbf{p}(n)\mathbf{P} = \mathbf{p}(n + 1) \tag{5.13}$$

Like any discrete system, we can take the z-transform of $\mathbf{p}(n)$.

$$\mathbf{p}^*(z) \triangleq \sum_{n=0}^{\infty} \mathbf{p}(n)z^n \tag{5.14}$$

So, let us take the z-transform of our general equation.

$$\sum_{n=0}^{\infty} \mathbf{p}(n)z^n\mathbf{P} = \sum_{n=0}^{\infty} \mathbf{p}(n+1)z^n$$

$$\mathbf{p}^*(z)\mathbf{P} = \frac{1}{z}\sum_{n=0}^{\infty} \mathbf{p}(n + 1)z^{n+1} = \frac{1}{z}[\mathbf{p}^*(z) - \mathbf{p}(0)]$$

$$z\mathbf{p}^*(z)\mathbf{P} = \mathbf{p}^*(z) - \mathbf{p}(0)$$

$$\mathbf{p}(0) = \mathbf{p}^*(z)[\mathbf{I} - z\mathbf{P}]$$

$$\mathbf{p}(0)[\mathbf{I} - z\mathbf{P}]^{-1} = \mathbf{p}^*(z) \tag{5.15}$$

Now we note that $\mathbf{p}(n) = \mathbf{p}(0)\mathbf{P}^n$, so taking the z-transform of that equation gives us $\mathbf{p}^*(z) = p(0)\mathbf{P}^*(z)$ where $\mathbf{P}^*(z)$ is the z-transform of $\mathbf{P}^n$. Therefore,

$[\mathbf{I} - z\mathbf{P}]^{-1}$ must be the z-transform of the n-step transition probability matrix $\mathbf{P}^n$. So "all" we need to do is to construct the matrix $[\mathbf{I} = z\mathbf{P}]^{-1}$ and invert the transform.

Example 5.10: As an example, consider the following* three state discrete-time Markov chain.

$$\mathbf{P} = \begin{bmatrix} \dfrac{3}{10} & \dfrac{1}{5} & \dfrac{1}{2} \\[2mm] \dfrac{1}{10} & \dfrac{4}{5} & \dfrac{1}{10} \\[2mm] \dfrac{2}{5} & \dfrac{2}{5} & \dfrac{1}{5} \end{bmatrix}$$

We can then construct the inverse of the z-transform of the n-step transition matrix directly.

$$[\mathbf{I} - z\mathbf{P}] = \begin{bmatrix} 1 - \dfrac{3z}{10} & \dfrac{-z}{5} & \dfrac{-z}{2} \\[2mm] \dfrac{-z}{10} & 1 - \dfrac{4z}{5} & \dfrac{-z}{10} \\[2mm] \dfrac{-2z}{5} & \dfrac{-2z}{5} & 1 - \dfrac{z}{5} \end{bmatrix}$$

To get the z-transform we must invert this matrix. We can invert this matrix in one of two ways. First, we can use the adjoint method, which is useful for human beings since each step is a decomposition step and can easily be checked. (Mistakes do not propagate through the computation.) Second, we can use the more computationally efficient techniques, such as Gaussian elimination. By using the adjoint method, the appearance of the characteristic equation is clearly shown, since it is simply the determinant of the matrix $[\mathbf{I} - z\mathbf{P}]$.

$$[\mathbf{I} - z\mathbf{P}]^{-1} = \frac{\text{adjoint}[\mathbf{I} - z\mathbf{P}]}{|\mathbf{I} - z\mathbf{P}|}$$

We can determine a great deal about the behavior of a Markov chain by studying the characteristic equation. The reason that this equation is so important (i.e., characteristic) to the

* The numerical values in this example are reprinted with permission from the Taxicab example in *Dynamic Probabilitic Systems: Vol I - Markov Models*, by Ronald Howard, Copyright © 1971, John Wiley and Sons.

Markov chain comes from some results in complex analysis. Since a z-transform is really defined in the complex domain (i.e., the values of z can be expressed as the combination of an imaginary term and a real term), the transform can be completely defined in terms of its poles and zeros. The poles are the roots of the characteristic equation (i.e. the determinant). The zeros are the values of z that make the adjoint become zero.

Let us evaluate the characteristic equation for this Markov chain by evaluating the determinant $|\mathbf{I} - z\mathbf{P}|$. First, we start by splitting up the determinant into smaller determinants, making use of cofactors.

$$|\mathbf{I} - z\mathbf{P}| = \frac{10 - 3z}{10} \begin{vmatrix} 1 - \dfrac{4z}{5} & \dfrac{-z}{10} \\[2mm] \dfrac{-2z}{5} & 1 - \dfrac{z}{5} \end{vmatrix} + \frac{z}{5} \begin{vmatrix} \dfrac{-z}{10} & \dfrac{-z}{10} \\[2mm] \dfrac{-2z}{5} & 1 - \dfrac{z}{5} \end{vmatrix}$$
$$- \frac{z}{2} \begin{vmatrix} \dfrac{-z}{10} & 1 - \dfrac{4z}{5} \\[2mm] \dfrac{-2z}{5} & \dfrac{-2z}{5} \end{vmatrix}$$

Finally, we can evaluate the 2×2 determinants directly.

$$|\mathbf{I} - z\mathbf{P}| = \frac{10 - 3z}{10} \frac{5 - 4z}{5} \frac{5 - z}{5} - \frac{10}{10} \frac{3z}{5} \frac{2z - 5}{10} \frac{z}{}$$
$$- \frac{z}{5} \frac{z}{10} \frac{5 - z}{5} - \frac{z}{5} \frac{2z}{5} \frac{z}{10} - \frac{z}{2} \frac{z}{10} \frac{2z}{5} - \frac{z}{2} \frac{2z}{5} \frac{5 - 4z}{5}$$
$$= 1 - \frac{13}{10} z + \frac{1}{5} z^2 + \frac{1}{10} z^3$$

This factors into three terms, each of degree 1.

$$|\mathbf{I} - z\mathbf{P}| = (1 - z) \left(1 - \frac{1}{2} z \right) \left(1 + \frac{5}{z} \right)$$

We can inspect a characteristic equation and determine several things about the corresponding Markov chain. First, if there is more than one root of magnitude 1, the chain is periodic. The reasons for this will become more clear as we proceed with this evaluation. Second, if the characteristic equation is a polynominal of degree j which is strictly less than the number of states K (which is equivalent to saying that the matrix **P** is singular), the system is reducible.

$$\mathbf{P}^*(z) = [\mathbf{I} - z\mathbf{P}]^{-1} = \frac{\begin{bmatrix} 1 - z - \dfrac{3z^2}{25} & \dfrac{z}{5} + \dfrac{4z^2}{25} & \dfrac{z}{2} - \dfrac{19z^2}{50} \\[2ex] \dfrac{z}{10} + \dfrac{z^2}{50} & 1 - \dfrac{z}{2} + \dfrac{7z^2}{50} & \dfrac{z}{10} + \dfrac{z^2}{50} \\[2ex] \dfrac{2z}{5} - \dfrac{7z^2}{25} & \dfrac{2z}{5} - \dfrac{z^2}{25} & 1 - \dfrac{11z}{10} + \dfrac{11z^2}{50} \end{bmatrix}}{(1 - z)(1 - z/2)(1 + z/5)}$$

Now that we have the z-transform of the n-step transition probability matrix, we need to invert the z-transform. We will need to perform a partial fraction expansion of the problem to get it into a form that appears in the table. We note that the fact that the numerator is a matrix has no effect on the expansion as long as the denominator is complete and factored.

$$\mathbf{P}^*(z) = \frac{1}{1 - z} \begin{bmatrix} \dfrac{1}{5} & \dfrac{3}{5} & \dfrac{1}{5} \\[1.5ex] \dfrac{1}{5} & \dfrac{3}{5} & \dfrac{1}{5} \\[1.5ex] \dfrac{1}{5} & \dfrac{3}{5} & \dfrac{1}{5} \end{bmatrix} - \frac{1}{1 - \dfrac{z}{2}} \begin{bmatrix} -\dfrac{13}{35} & \dfrac{26}{35} & -\dfrac{13}{35} \\[1.5ex] \dfrac{7}{35} & -\dfrac{14}{35} & \dfrac{7}{35} \\[1.5ex] -\dfrac{8}{35} & \dfrac{16}{35} & -\dfrac{8}{35} \end{bmatrix}$$

$$+ \frac{1}{1 + \dfrac{z}{5}} \begin{bmatrix} \dfrac{3}{7} & \dfrac{1}{7} & -\dfrac{4}{7} \\[1.5ex] 0 & 0 & 0 \\[1.5ex] -\dfrac{3}{7} & -\dfrac{1}{7} & \dfrac{4}{7} \end{bmatrix}$$

Note the form of the expanded transform. The number of factors is precisely the number of states in the system (because there is an eigenvector for each dimension of the matrix). All but the first matrix have denominators whose roots are less than 1, while the first has a root equal to 1. We also notice that each row in the matrix associated with the denominator $1 - z$ is the same and they sum to 1. In addition, note that the rows in all of the other matrices sum to zero. Now we can invert the transform by table look-up in Appendix 2.

$$\mathbf{P}^n = \begin{bmatrix} \dfrac{1}{5} & \dfrac{3}{5} & \dfrac{1}{5} \\[2mm] \dfrac{1}{5} & \dfrac{3}{5} & \dfrac{1}{5} \\[2mm] \dfrac{1}{5} & \dfrac{3}{5} & \dfrac{1}{5} \end{bmatrix} - \left(\dfrac{1}{2}\right)^n \begin{bmatrix} \dfrac{-13}{35} & \dfrac{26}{35} & \dfrac{-13}{35} \\[2mm] \dfrac{7}{35} & \dfrac{-14}{35} & \dfrac{7}{35} \\[2mm] \dfrac{-8}{35} & \dfrac{16}{35} & \dfrac{-8}{35} \end{bmatrix} + \left(\dfrac{-1}{5}\right)^n \begin{bmatrix} \dfrac{3}{7} & \dfrac{1}{7} & \dfrac{-4}{7} \\[2mm] 0 & 0 & 0 \\[2mm] \dfrac{-3}{7} & \dfrac{-1}{7} & \dfrac{4}{7} \end{bmatrix}$$

We now see the exact solution for the n-step transition probability matrix for an arbitrary value of n. We can also see that only the first term remains when $n \to \infty$. So the first matrix is simply the limiting matrix $\mathbf{P}^\infty$. If the system had been periodic, there would be two or more matrices that would not vanish. This could be detected directly from the characteristic equation by counting the number of roots with magnitude 1. If the number of such roots is greater than 1, then the corresponding Markov chain is periodic. This is clear when one sees that with a root of magnitude 1, no matter how large the power (i.e., number of steps), the terms will not vanish.

In a similar fashion we can locate transient states in finite Markov chains by examining the limiting matrix. (Note that for finite Markov chains, the probability of returning to a state is either 0 or 1.) If, in the limit, the probability of being in a state is zero, we will be guaranteed of leaving the state. That means that the states corresponding to zero columns in the limiting matrix $\mathbf{P}^\infty$ are transient. This deserves a note of caution. If a numerical technique is used to find $\mathbf{P}^\infty$, such as successive multiplication, the computation may underflow. In that case you cannot be sure if the state is truly transient or just very unlikely.

This technique is not really used in practice because of the requirement for a symbolic matrix inversion. In addition, by taking advantage of the sparseness of the matrix, successive multiplications can sometimes be used to get the n-step state probability vector, for a small value of n, with fewer actual computations than straight Gaussian elimination. However, the technique brings to light the critical features that determine the behavior of a Markov chain.

Exercise

5.4 Solve for the n-step transition probability matrix for the following Markov chain.

$$\begin{bmatrix} 0 & 1 \\ 1/2 & 1/2 \end{bmatrix}$$

5.5.5 Mean First Passage and Recurrence Times

One of the performance measures we may want to obtain is the average time until a system first reaches a state k after leaving another state j, the mean first passage time. In the case where $j = k$, it becomes the average time to return to a state, the mean recurrence time.

To begin, we need to introduce the probability, $f_{jk}(n)$, which is the probability that a system first reaches state k from state j on step n. This is different than the n-step transition probability $p_{jk}(n)$, which is the probability that the system went from state j to state k in n steps, but not necessarily for the first time. However, we can relate the first passage probabilities to the n-step transition probabilities by noting that to get to a state in n steps, you must have a first passage in $m \leq n$ steps. So we decompose the probability of reaching a state in n steps into the first passage in m steps and returning to the state in $n - m$ steps.

$$p_{jk}(n) = \sum_{m=1}^{n} f_{jk}(m) p_{kk}(n - m)$$

$$f_{jk}(n) = p_{jk}(n) - \sum_{m=1}^{n-1} f_{jk}(m) p_{kk}(n - m) \tag{5.16}$$

We can compute all of the probabilities by iteration using $p_{jk}(0) = 0$ for all $j \neq k$ and $p_{jj}(0) = 1$ as the starting values. However, since we are after mean values, this computation is really unnecessary. What we really want is the transform, $f_{jk}^{*}(z)$, of the discrete probability density, $f_{jk}(n)$, so we can obtain the mean, m_{jk}, by differentiating it and setting $z = 1$. To construct the transform we note that the previous equation is really a convolution equation, so the transform of $p_{jk}(n)$ is the product of the transforms where $p_{jk}^{*}(z)$ is the (j,k) entry of the $\mathbf{P}^*(z)$ matrix.

$$p_{jk}^{*}(z) = f_{jk}^{*}(z) \cdot p_{jj}^{*}(z) \quad \text{for } j \neq k$$

$$p_{jj}^{*}(z) = 1 + f_{jj}^{*}(z) \cdot p_{jj}^{*}(z) \tag{5.17}$$

In special case of $j = k$ we see that we only need $p_{jj}^{*}(z)$, to get $f_{jj}^{*}(z)$. Here we can take advantage of the special form of $\mathbf{P}^*(z)$ that we just investigated. The transform of the n-step transition matrix will always split up into the matrices we saw in the preceding section. So the form of the transform $p_{jj}^{*}(z)$ [the jth element on the diagonal of $\mathbf{P}^*(z)$] is simply the steady-state value with the term $1 - z$ and other terms denoted by $g^*(z)$.

$$p_{jj}^{*}(z) = \frac{\pi_j}{1 - z} + g^*(z) \tag{5.18}$$

Substituting that into equation (5.17), differentiating, and setting $z = 1$, we obtain the desired expected value, the mean recurrence time.

$$f_{jj}^*(z) = 1 - \frac{1 - z}{\pi_j + (1 - z)g^*(z)}$$

$$\left. \frac{d}{dz} f_{jj}(z) \right|_{z=1} = \frac{1}{\pi_j + (1 - z)g^*(z)}$$

$$+ (1 - z) \left. \frac{-g^*(z) + (1 - z) \frac{d}{dz} g^*(z)}{[\pi_j + (1 - z)g^*(z)]^2} \right|_{z=1}$$

$$m_{jj} = \frac{1}{\pi_j} \qquad (5.19)$$

So, surprisingly, the mean recurrence time turns out to be the inverse of the steady-state probability for that state. This c.n be understood intuitively if you recall that the steady-state probability can be viewed as the fraction of time the system is found in that state by a random observer.

In the case of the mean first passage time ($j \neq k$), we find that the ratio of the nondiagonal elements and the diagonal elements does not reduce to a form such that the differentiation results in the cancellation of the other terms with $g^*(z)$. We can construct a recurrence relationship for the mean time to first passage by noting that the system can either go directly from state j to state k or with probability p_{jn} take one additional step through some intermediate state n which has its own first passage time to state k.

$$m_{jk} = p_{jk} + \sum_{n \neq k} p_{jn}(1 + m_{nk}) \qquad (5.20)$$

This set of recurrence relationships can be solved by successive iterations from a first approximation of the mean first passage times. Unlike the mean recurrence time, there is no simple computation of mean first passage times. So any computation requires a functional iteration.

Example 5.11: As an example of a discrete-time Markov system, let us consider a modular program. The main section is a driver called A with two subroutines, B and C. We have counted instructions in the code and find that it takes roughly two time units to reach the first call of B from A. After the return from B it takes one additional time unit of execution to reach the call to C. After returning from C, the program completes execution in roughly one more time unit. Subroutine B is a simple subroutine that takes roughly one time unit to execute. Subroutine C, however,

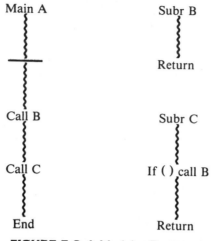

FIGURE 5.8 A Modular Program

takes one time unit to reach a conditional call to B. After B returns, C continues to execute for approximately one additional time unit. The outline of the code is shown in Figure 5.8.

How long does this code execute, on the average, for some distribution of input data? We can model this system at a high level by a discrete-time Markov chain. The states in the model represent the condition that the program is executing within some particular section of code. The duration of time in each state models the amount of time necessary to execute a certain number of instructions. To handle the fact that the code executes sequentially and that subroutines return to the calling position, we add states to "remember" the condition of the system. So the state B1 represents the condition where the program is executing subroutine B from the first call in the main body, while B2 represents the condition where the program is executing subroutine B from the call in subroutine C.

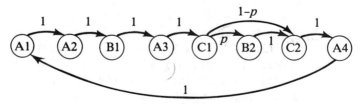

FIGURE 5.9 Markov Chain for a Modular Program

We assume that for the given input data, the conditional call to B occurs with probability p. So we now construct the eight state Markov chain.

This can be represented in matrix form by the following 8×8 matrix.

$$\begin{bmatrix} 0 & 1 & 0 & 0 & 0 & 0 & 0 & 0 \\ 0 & 0 & 1 & 0 & 0 & 0 & 0 & 0 \\ 0 & 0 & 0 & 1 & 0 & 0 & 0 & 0 \\ 0 & 0 & 0 & 0 & 1 & 0 & 0 & 0 \\ 0 & 0 & 0 & 0 & 0 & p & 1-p & 0 \\ 0 & 0 & 0 & 0 & 0 & 0 & 1 & 0 \\ 0 & 0 & 0 & 0 & 0 & 0 & 0 & 1 \\ 1 & 0 & 0 & 0 & 0 & 0 & 0 & 0 \end{bmatrix}$$

We can then solve this system for the steady-state probabilities and take $1/\pi_1$ to get the mean recurrence time which represents the amount of time spent in executing the code on the average for this system. For this simple system all the steady-state probabilities, except π_6, are equal. So π_1 is simply $(7 + p)^{-1}$ and the mean recurrence time is simply $7 + p$ time units.

5.6 Continuous Time Systems

For continuous time systems, we began with the definition of the matrix of cumulative distribution functions for going from state S_j at time t' to state S_k at time t''.

$$\mathbf{H}(t',t'') \triangleq [h_{jk}(t',t'')] = \left[P[S_k(t'')|S_j(t')] \right] \tag{5.21}$$

Consider the case where $t'' - t'$ is small, and we can define $t'' = t' + \Delta t$. The probability of some number of transitions (state changes) n in Δt is on the order of $(\Delta t)^n$. For $\Delta t = 0$, no transitions can take place. For values of $\Delta t > 0$ any number of transitions can occur. However, as Δt becomes very small, the probability of two or more transitions occurring during time Δt becomes negligible in comparison to the probability of a single transition. So, for a sufficiently small Δt, define the single-step transition matrix $\mathbf{P}(t,t + \Delta t)$ as the limiting matrix of $\mathbf{H}(t,t + \Delta t)$. Then since this is a single-step transition matrix, we can follow the same approach we used in discrete-time Markov chains. We can calculate the state probability vector at time $t + \Delta t$, $\mathbf{p}(t + \Delta t)$ from the state probability vector at time t, $\mathbf{p}(t)$.

$$\mathbf{p}(t)\mathbf{P}(t,t + \Delta t) = \mathbf{p}(t + \Delta t)$$

$$\mathbf{p}(t)\mathbf{P}(t,t + \Delta t) - \mathbf{p}(t) = \mathbf{p}(t + \Delta t) - \mathbf{p}(t)$$

$$\mathbf{p}(t) \frac{\mathbf{P}(t,t + \Delta t) - \mathbf{I}}{\Delta t} = \frac{\mathbf{p}(t + \Delta t) - \mathbf{p}(t)}{\Delta t} \tag{5.22}$$

When Δt is sufficiently small, we can define an infinitesimal matrix $\mathbf{Q}(t)$.

$$\mathbf{Q}(t) \overset{\Delta}{=} \lim_{\Delta t \to 0} \frac{\mathbf{P}(t,t + \Delta t) - \mathbf{I}}{\Delta t} \tag{5.23}$$

Now as $\Delta t \to 0$, the right-hand side of equation 5.22 becomes the familiar derivative, and the left-hand side is the $\mathbf{Q}(t)$ matrix.

$$\mathbf{p}(t)\mathbf{Q}(t) = \frac{d}{dt} \mathbf{p}(t) \tag{5.24}$$

5.6.1 The Transition Rate Matrix

What is the structure of this matrix $\mathbf{Q}(t)$? We know it is not a probability matrix, so its elements are not necessarily values between 0 and 1. In fact, if we return to the definition of $\mathbf{Q}(t)$, we see that it represents an instantaneous rate of change of probabilities.

$$q_{jk}(t) = \lim_{\Delta t \to 0} \frac{p_{jk}(t,t + \Delta t)}{\Delta t} \quad \text{for } j \neq k \tag{5.25}$$

Recall that probability density functions are rate of change functions (i.e. derivatives) of cumulative probability distribution functions. Therefore, this rate matrix must have something to do with the probability density function for the time between state transitions. We know that the time between transitions for a Markov chain must be memoryless, so the time to go from state j to state k must be exponentially distributed. So the nondiagonal elements of the matrix $\mathbf{Q}(t)$ are the parameters of the various exponential probability density functions for each state change.

However, we must remember that a state change to any one of a number of different states is possible, each with an exponentially distributed amount of time. Since the minimum of a set of independent exponentially distributed random variables is exponential with the sum of the rates as its parameter, the amount of time the system stays in the state j is also exponentially distributed but with a parameter equal to the sum of the rates of the transitions out of state j. So the diagonal elements of the matrix $\mathbf{Q}(t)$ are the sums of all the rates for changing from the current state to any other state, but with a negative sign because of the subtraction of the identity matrix $\mathbf{I}$. Therefore, the matrix $\mathbf{Q}(t)$ is the *transition rate matrix* for the continuous time Markov chain.

In this text we are restricting ourselves to homogeneous Markov chains, so there is no dependency on the value of time t in the rate matrix $\mathbf{Q}(t)$. Therefore the rate of change of state probabilities is constant with respect to time for homogeneous Markov chains and we can drop the (t) in our notation.

$$\mathbf{p}(t)\mathbf{Q} = \frac{d}{dt}\mathbf{p}(t) \tag{5.26}$$

Even though we can not compute the precise time the Markov chain will change to the next state, we can utilize the fact that we know the rate of change to compute the probability of which particular state is the next state. The probability that you go from state j to state k can be computed from the ratio of the exponential rates.

$$P[S_k|S_j] = \frac{q_{jk}}{\displaystyle\sum_{\forall l \neq j} q_{jl}} \tag{5.27}$$

Example 5.12: Consider a simple system where three people in an office share three phone lines. We assume that the people make phone calls in a Poisson fashion with a rate λ, and they stay on the phone an exponentially distributed time with the parameter μ. We further note that when none of the lines are busy, all three people are "thinking" about making a phone call. So the time until the next phone call is exponentially distributed with parameter 3λ because merging three independent Poisson processes with parameters λ is still Poisson with parameter 3λ. When one phone line is busy, only two people are thinking about making a phone call, so the time until the next phone call is exponentially distributed with parameter 2λ. In a similar fashion when two phones lines are busy, the time until the next call completion is exponentially distributed with parameter 2μ. So for this problem, we construct a continuous time Markov chain model with four states, each state being the number of busy phone lines (0, 1, 2, or 3).

$$\mathbf{Q} = \begin{bmatrix} -3\lambda & 3\lambda & 0 & 0 \\ \mu & -\mu - 2\lambda & 2\lambda & 0 \\ 0 & 2\mu & -2\mu - \lambda & \lambda \\ 0 & 0 & 3\mu & -3\mu \end{bmatrix}$$

5.6.2 Steady-State Probabilities

Before we can obtain the steady-state probabilities, we need to find a relationship between the steady-state probabilities and the transition rate matrix. Returning to our equation for state probabilities $\mathbf{p}(t)$, we recall the differential equation in $\mathbf{p}(t)$.

$$\mathbf{p}(t)\mathbf{Q} = \frac{d}{dt}\mathbf{p}(t)$$

If we are interested in the steady-state probability vector, $\pi \triangleq \lim_{t\to\infty}\mathbf{p}(t)$, we know that the rate of change of the steady-state probability vector must be zero. So if the vector π is the steady-state probability vector for the system, it must satisfy the following equation.

$$\pi\mathbf{Q} = 0 \tag{5.28}$$

Example 5.13: As an example, let us solve the previous example of a telephone system with three lines. We proceed in much the same fashion as in the case of the discrete-time Markov chain, except the right hand side is now zero.

$$[\pi_1, \pi_2, \pi_3, \pi_4] \begin{bmatrix} -3\lambda & 3\lambda & 0 & 0 \\ \mu & -\mu - 2\lambda & 2\lambda & 0 \\ 0 & 2\mu & -2\mu - \lambda & \lambda \\ 0 & 0 & 3\mu & -3\mu \end{bmatrix} = 0$$

$$-3\lambda\pi_1 + \mu\pi_2 = 0$$

$$3\lambda\pi_1 - (\mu + 2\lambda)\pi_2 + \mu\pi_3 = 0$$

$$2\lambda\pi_2 - (2\mu + \lambda)\pi_3 + 3\mu\pi_4 = 0$$

$$\lambda\pi_3 - 3\mu\pi_4 = 0$$

Solving these equations we obtain the following relationships.

$$\pi_2 = \frac{3\lambda}{\mu}\pi_1$$

$$\pi_3 = \frac{\lambda}{\mu}\pi_2$$

$$\pi_4 = \frac{\lambda}{3\mu}\pi_3$$

Using the fact that the probabilities must sum to 1 we obtain the final solution.

$$\pi_1 + \frac{3\lambda}{\mu}\pi_1 + \frac{\lambda}{\mu}\cdot\frac{3\lambda}{\mu}\pi_1 + \frac{\lambda}{3\mu}\cdot\frac{\lambda}{\mu}\cdot\frac{3\lambda}{\mu}\pi_1 = 1$$

$$\pi_1 = \frac{1}{1 + 3\dfrac{\lambda}{\mu} + 3\dfrac{\lambda^2}{\mu^2} + \dfrac{\lambda^3}{\mu^3}}$$

$$\pi_2 = \frac{3\lambda/\mu}{1 + 3\dfrac{\lambda}{\mu} + 3\dfrac{\lambda^2}{\mu^2} + \dfrac{\lambda^3}{\mu^3}}$$

$$\pi_3 = \frac{3\lambda^2/\mu^2}{1 + 3\dfrac{\lambda}{\mu} + 3\dfrac{\lambda^2}{\mu^2} + \dfrac{\lambda^3}{\mu^3}}$$

$$\pi_4 = \frac{\lambda^3/\mu^3}{1 + 3\dfrac{\lambda}{\mu} + 3\dfrac{\lambda^2}{\mu^2} + \dfrac{\lambda^3}{\mu^3}}$$

5.7 Simulation of Markovian Systems

The most straightforward way to write a simulation of a Markov chain model is simply to use an event-based simulation. However, if the Markov chain is discrete-time and the probability of remaining in a state is low, a time-based simulation may be used.

The structure of the simulation program can reflect the structure of the Markov chain. If the chain is finite, we have a simple finite-state machine that changes state based on the given probabilities. So the basic control loop is very simple. A table-driven program can use the current state to select the conditions for the next state and the transition time.

In one approach we simply generate a random variable which is used to select the next state and update our simulation clock. If the simulation is time-based, the clock update is trivial. If the simulation is event-based, we must generate a random variable to use as the time of the next event. In the case of continuous time Markov chains, that is an exponentially distributed random variable. In the case of discrete-time Markov chains, that is a geometrically distributed random variable.

In another approach, we generate the time for the next-state transition for each of the possible next states and take the smallest time as the actual clock update and the corresponding state as the next state. Since the system is Markovian, the time between state changes is memoryless, which means that we need not keep track of the previously generated values.

Example 5.14: As an example, let us simulate a more general case of the telephone switch. We assume that there are a number, PHONES, of telephones, each of which initiate calls as a Poisson process with parameter CALLRATE. In addition, we assume that there are a number, TRUNKS, of trunk lines out of the switch which can handle a call and that calls hold the trunk for an exponentially distributed amount of time with an average value of HOLDTIME. We wish to know the average number of calls in progress and the probability of having a call being blocked by the lack of a trunk (assuming PHONES > TRUNKS).

We will structure the simulation based upon our knowledge that this is a Markov process, so we can exploit the fact that the distributions of time are exponential. That allows us to decouple the probability of a particular event being the next event and the time for the next event. We could simply have generated the time until the next call being initiated and the time until the next hangup, compared them and taken the smallest to be the next event. (Note that we would still have to regenerate both of the times after the state change because the parameters of the distributions are state dependent.) Instead, what this program does is generate the time we stay in a state, and then selects the next state based on the probability that a particular exponential random variable was the smaller.

```
PROGRAM PHONES(INPUT,OUTPUT);

(* THIS PROGRAM IS AN EVENT BASED SIMULATION OF *)
(* A TELEPHONE PRIVATE BRANCH EXCHANGE (PBX)    *)
(*                                              *)
(* WE MODEL THE PBX AS A MARKOV CHAIN WITH THE  *)
(* STATE BEING THE NUMBER OF CURRENTLY ACTIVE   *)
(* CALLS.  CALLS ARRIVE AS A POISSON PROCESS    *)
(* FROM EACH OF THE INPUT PHONE LINES AND CALLS *)
(* LAST AN EXPONENTIALLY DISTRIBUTED AMOUNT OF  *)
(* OF TIME.  WE TAKE ADVANTAGE OF THE MEMORYLESS*)
(* PROPERTY IN THE CODE STRUCTURE, SO WE ALWAYS *)
(* REGENERATE TIMES UNTIL THE NEXT EVENT. WE    *)
(* ALSO TAKE ADVANTAGE OF THE STRUCTURE OF THE  *)
```

```
(* MATRIX BEING TRIDIAGONAL, SO WE CAN GENERATE *)
(* THE ELEMENTS EFFICIENTLY ON THE FLY AND NEVER*)
(* STORE THE MATRIX.                            *)

CONST   K       = 49;      (* LEN. OF SEQ. OF RNG *)

VAR     CLOCK   : REAL;    (* SIMULATION CLOCK    *)
        EVENT   : INTEGER; (* CURRENT EVENT NUM   *)
        LIMIT   : INTEGER; (* MAX NUM OF EVENTS   *)

        PHONES  : INTEGER; (* NUM OF INPUT PHONES *)
        TRUNKS  : INTEGER; (* NUM OF OUTPUT LINES *)
        HOLDTIME: REAL;    (* CALL DURATION       *)
        CALLRATE: REAL;    (* CALL INITIATION RATE*)
        AVGCALLS: REAL;    (* AVG NUM OF CALLS    *)
        VARCALLS: REAL;    (* VARIANCE OF # CALLS *)
        BLOCK   : REAL;    (* PROB OF BLOCKED CALL*)
        CALLS   : INTEGER; (* CURRENT # OF CALLS  *)
        TOTCALLS: INTEGER; (* TOT # CALLS IN SIM  *)

        PARM    : REAL;    (* EVENT RATE          *)
        NEWCALL : REAL;    (* RATE OF NEW CALLS   *)
        HANGUP  : REAL;    (* RATE OF HANGUPS     *)
        ETIME   : REAL;    (* TIME TIL NEXT EVENT *)

        PROB    : REAL;    (* RNG PROBABILITY     *)
        SEED    : INTEGER; (* PARAMETER FOR RNG   *)
        CNTR    : INTEGER; (* POS. IN RNG SEQ.    *)
        KVALUES : ARRAY[0..K] OF INTEGER;

(**************************************************)

BEGIN (* MAIN *)
    (* INITIALIZE VARIABLES *)
    CLOCK   : = 0;
    SEED    := 3;
    LIMIT   := 100;
    PHONES  := 24;
    TRUNKS  := 12;
    CALLRATE := 0.5; (* PER HOUR *)
    HOLDTIME := 0.25; (* 15 MINUTES *)

    (* INITIALIZE STATISTICS *)
    AVGCALLS := 0.0;
    VARCALLS := 0.0;
    BLOCK    := 0;
```

```
(* INITIALIZE SEQUENCE OF RANDOM NUMBERS *)
FOR CNTR := O TO K DO
   BEGIN
      RNG(SEED);
      KVALUES[CNTR] := SEED;
   END;
CNTR := O;

(* PRINT HEADER FOR OUTPUT *)
WRITELN('   PBX SIMULATION ');
WRITELN;WRITELN;
WRITELN;

CALLS  := O;  (* STARTING STATE *)

FOR EVENT := 1 TO LIMIT DO
   BEGIN (* EVENT LOOP *)
      ADDRNG ( SEED, PROB );

(* THE TIME UNTIL THE NEXT EVENT IS EXPON *)
(* DIST. WITH PARM EQUAL TO SUM OF ROW    *)
      NEWCALL := CALLRATE * (PHONES − CALLS);
      HANGUP  := CALLS / HOLDTIME;
      PARM :=  NEWCALL + HANGUP;

      ETIME := − 1 / PARM; (*CONV TO AVG TIME*)
      ETIME := ETIME * LN(PROB); (*RANDOMIZE*)

      (* UPDATE STATISTICS *)
      AVGCALLS := CALLS * ETIME + AVGCALLS;
      VARCALLS := CALLS * CALLS * ETIME + VARCALLS;

      (* UPDATE CLOCK *)
      CLOCK := CLOCK + ETIME;

   (* SELECT HANGUP OR NEW CALL EVENT *)
      ADDRNG ( SEED, PROB );
      IF PROB >= NEWCALL / PARM
         THEN CALLS := CALLS + 1 (* HANDUP *)
         ELSE BEGIN    (* NEW CALL *)
               TOTCALLS := TOTCALLS + 1;
               IF CALLS < TRUNKS
                  THEN CALLS := CALLS + 1
                  ELSE BLOCK := BLOCK + 1
               END;
```

```
        (* DEBUG OUTPUT *)
        WRITELN(EVENT:5,CALLS:8,ETIME:18:3);


END;  (* EVENT LOOP *)


(* COMPUTE STATISTICS *)
AVGCALLS := AVGCALLS / CLOCK;
VARCALLS := SQRT(VARCALLS/CLOCK-AVGCALLS*AVGCALLS);
BLOCK := BLOCK / TOTCALLS;


(* OUTPUT RESULTS *)
WRITELN;
WRITELN ( ' TOTAL TIME WITH TOTAL CALLS');
WRITELN ( CLOCK:10:3, TOTCALLS:16);
WRITELN;
WRITELN ( ' AVERAGE    STAND    PROB OF ');
WRITELN ( ' NUMBER     DEVIAT.   CALLS' );
WRITELN ( ' CALLS IN   # CALLS   BEING');
WRITELN ( ' PROGRESS   PROGRESS  BLOCKED');
WRITELN (AVGCALLS:8:3, VARCALLS:10:3, BLOCK:10:3);
WRITELN;

END.  (* MAIN *)
```

5.8 Problems

5.1 Which of the following are valid transition matrices of discrete-time Markov chains? If a representation is invalid, state why it is invalid.

a.
$$
\begin{bmatrix}
\dfrac{1}{6} & \dfrac{1}{4} & \dfrac{1}{3} & \dfrac{1}{4} \\[2mm]
\dfrac{1}{4} & \dfrac{1}{12} & \dfrac{1}{3} & \dfrac{1}{3} \\[2mm]
0 & \dfrac{1}{3} & \dfrac{1}{6} & \dfrac{1}{2} \\[2mm]
\dfrac{1}{4} & \dfrac{1}{4} & \dfrac{1}{4} & \dfrac{1}{4}
\end{bmatrix}
$$

b.
$$\begin{bmatrix} \dfrac{1}{3} & 0 & \dfrac{1}{6} & \dfrac{1}{2} \\[2mm] \dfrac{1}{4} & \dfrac{1}{6} & \dfrac{1}{4} & \dfrac{1}{3} \\[2mm] \dfrac{1}{3} & \dfrac{1}{3} & \dfrac{1}{3} & 0 \\[2mm] \dfrac{1}{4} & \dfrac{1}{12} & \dfrac{1}{3} & \dfrac{1}{4} \end{bmatrix}$$

c.
$$\begin{bmatrix} \dfrac{1}{4} & \dfrac{1}{3} & \dfrac{1}{12} & \dfrac{1}{3} \\[2mm] \dfrac{1}{3} & \dfrac{1}{3} & \dfrac{-1}{3} & \dfrac{2}{3} \\[2mm] \dfrac{1}{4} & \dfrac{1}{6} & \dfrac{1}{4} & \dfrac{1}{3} \\[2mm] \dfrac{1}{4} & \dfrac{1}{4} & \dfrac{1}{4} & \dfrac{1}{4} \end{bmatrix}$$

d.
$$\begin{bmatrix} \dfrac{1}{3} & \dfrac{1}{4} & \dfrac{1}{6} & \dfrac{1}{4} \\[2mm] \dfrac{1}{3} & \dfrac{1}{3} & \dfrac{1}{12} & \dfrac{1}{4} \\[2mm] 0 & \dfrac{1}{3} & \dfrac{2}{3} & \dfrac{1}{3} \\[2mm] \dfrac{1}{3} & 0 & \dfrac{1}{2} & \dfrac{1}{6} \end{bmatrix}$$

5.2 Classify the states in the following Markov chain.

$$\begin{bmatrix} 0.50 & 0 & 0 & 0 & 0.50 & 0 & 0 \\ 0 & 0 & 0 & 0 & 0 & 1.00 & 0 \\ 0 & 0 & 0 & 0 & 0 & 1.00 & 0 \\ 0 & 0 & 0 & 0.50 & 0 & 0 & 0.50 \\ 0.25 & 0.25 & 0 & 0 & 0.25 & 0 & 0.25 \\ 0 & 0.50 & 0.50 & 0 & 0 & 0 & 0 \\ 0 & 0 & 0 & 1.00 & 0 & 0 & 0 \end{bmatrix}$$

5.3 Solve for the steady-state probabilities for the following Markov chain.

$$\begin{bmatrix} \dfrac{1}{2} & \dfrac{1}{4} & 0 & \dfrac{1}{4} \\[2mm] \dfrac{1}{3} & \dfrac{1}{3} & \dfrac{1}{3} & 0 \\[2mm] 0 & \dfrac{1}{4} & \dfrac{1}{2} & \dfrac{1}{4} \\[2mm] \dfrac{1}{2} & 0 & \dfrac{1}{4} & \dfrac{1}{4} \end{bmatrix}$$

5.4 Solve for the steady-state probabilities for the following Markov chain.

$$\begin{bmatrix} \dfrac{1}{3} & \dfrac{1}{3} & 0 & \dfrac{1}{3} \\[2mm] \dfrac{1}{4} & \dfrac{1}{2} & \dfrac{1}{4} & 0 \\[2mm] 0 & \dfrac{1}{4} & \dfrac{1}{2} & \dfrac{1}{4} \\[2mm] \dfrac{1}{2} & 0 & \dfrac{1}{2} & 0 \end{bmatrix}$$

5.5 Solve for the n-step state probability vector for the Markov chain given below (the same as the example in Section 5.5.4). Assume that the system starts in state 1.

$$\mathbf{P} = \begin{bmatrix} \dfrac{3}{10} & \dfrac{1}{5} & \dfrac{1}{2} \\[2mm] \dfrac{1}{10} & \dfrac{4}{5} & \dfrac{1}{10} \\[2mm] \dfrac{2}{5} & \dfrac{2}{5} & \dfrac{1}{5} \end{bmatrix}$$

5.6 Solve for the n-step transition probability matrix for the following Markov chain.

$$\begin{bmatrix} 0 & 1 \\ 1/3 & 2/3 \end{bmatrix}$$

5.7 Solve for the n-step transition probability matrix for the following Markov chain.

$$\begin{bmatrix} 1/2 & 1/2 \\ 1/3 & 2/3 \end{bmatrix}$$

5.8 Which of the following are valid continuous time Markov chains? If a representation is not valid, state why it is not valid.

a.

$$\begin{bmatrix} -6 & 1 & 2 & 3 \\ 1 & -6 & 2 & 3 \\ 2 & 3 & -6 & 1 \\ 3 & 1 & 2 & -6 \end{bmatrix}$$

b.

$$\begin{bmatrix} -1 & \frac{1}{2} & \frac{1}{3} & \frac{1}{6} \\ \frac{1}{2} & -1 & 0 & \frac{1}{2} \\ \frac{1}{3} & \frac{1}{3} & -1 & \frac{1}{3} \\ \frac{1}{12} & \frac{7}{12} & \frac{1}{3} & -1 \end{bmatrix}$$

c.

$$\begin{bmatrix} -4 & 2 & 2 & 0 \\ 2 & -4 & 2 & 0 \\ 0 & -1 & -1 & 2 \\ 1 & 0 & 0 & -1 \end{bmatrix}$$

d.

$$\begin{bmatrix} -3 & 1 & 2 & 0 \\ 1 & -2 & 1 & 0 \\ 0 & 2 & -3 & 2 \\ 0 & 1 & 2 & -3 \end{bmatrix}$$

5.9 Solve for the steady-state probabilities for the following continuous time Markov chain.

$$\begin{bmatrix} -3 & 2 & 1 & 0 \\ 1 & -4 & 2 & 1 \\ 1 & 2 & -5 & 2 \\ 1 & 2 & 3 & -6 \end{bmatrix}$$

5.10 Solve for the steady-state probabilities for the following continuous time Markov chain.

$$\begin{bmatrix} -3 & 2 & 1 & 0 \\ 2 & -5 & 2 & 1 \\ 1 & 2 & -5 & 2 \\ 0 & 1 & 2 & -3 \end{bmatrix}$$

5.11 Write a simulation of the discrete-time Markov chain used as an example in Section 5.3 (the processor that could fail and be repaired). Compare your results with the steady-state values given in the text. Be sure to include confidence intervals with the results.

5.12 Consider a maintenance system for a group of K identical and independent machines. In this system, a single repairman fixes machines that have broken down. Each machine failure requires a different amount of time to fix, but most failures are repaired quickly, while a few may take a very long time. Machines are considered as running whenever they are not broken. A machine may fail at any time, but it tends to fail shortly after it has been repaired. Each machine fails at an equal rate λ, and the repairman fixes machines at the rate μ.

    a. Model this system as a Markov chain. Of course, we are assuming that the time to fail and the time to repair are exponentially distributed random variables. Construct the matrix that represents this Markov chain model.

    b. Solve for the steady-state behavior of this system given $K = 5$.

    c. Write a simulation program to model this system for an arbitrary K.

5.13 Write a simulation program for the following discrete-time Markov chain. Run the simulation for 10 independent runs of 5000 steps with different seeds for the random number generator and calculate the confidence intervals for each of the steady-state probabilities.

$$
P = \begin{bmatrix}
0.1 & 0.0 & 0.1 & 0.2 & 0.0 & 0.1 & 0.3 & 0.2 \\
0.1 & 0.2 & 0.0 & 0.0 & 0.3 & 0.0 & 0.1 & 0.3 \\
0.1 & 0.1 & 0.1 & 0.3 & 0.1 & 0.0 & 0.1 & 0.2 \\
0.3 & 0.1 & 0.2 & 0.0 & 0.1 & 0.1 & 0.2 & 0.0 \\
0.0 & 0.6 & 0.0 & 0.1 & 0.1 & 0.1 & 0.0 & 0.1 \\
0.2 & 0.1 & 0.0 & 0.2 & 0.2 & 0.1 & 0.1 & 0.1 \\
0.3 & 0.2 & 0.1 & 0.1 & 0.1 & 0.1 & 0.0 & 0.1 \\
0.1 & 0.3 & 0.1 & 0.0 & 0.3 & 0.0 & 0.0 & 0.2
\end{bmatrix}
$$

Compare the results of the simulation run (the averages of each steady-state probability) with the following steady-state vector using the χ^2 test.

$$
\begin{aligned}
p[1] &= 0.120818 \\
p[2] &= 0.245431 \\
p[3] &= 0.060446 \\
p[4] &= 0.079182 \\
p[5] &= 0.177575 \\
p[6] &= 0.051713 \\
p[7] &= 0.087841 \\
p[8] &= 0.176994
\end{aligned}
$$

Single Queues $\boxed{6}$

6.1 Introduction

In Chapter 5 we studied Markov chains that proved to be very useful models because of their ability to model state-dependent behavior. Unfortunately, we also found out that solving such models, although tractable for small finite models, was difficult in general. In fact, we dealt only with examples that were finite models, even though our definitions and theorems held for infinite state space Markov chains. We would like to deal with models of systems that have an infinite state space, like a queue (waiting line) of customers where any number of people may be waiting.

In this chapter we concentrate on models that represent individual queues. These models could be used to represent the line that forms at a bank where customers wait for a teller, or a job queue where programs are spooled to wait for the computer to start processing them. We will deal with two kinds of models. The first model will allow us to deal with a wide variety of state dependencies. For this model we will exploit the structure of a special subclass of Markov chains which have a restricted matrix form. The second model will allow us to deal with an arbitrary distribution of service time, not just the exponentially distributed service times required by Markov models. For this model we return to our study of renewal theory to derive an expression for the average waiting time spent by queued customers.

FIGURE 6.1 Queuing

157

6.2 Classifications of Queues

Queues are such a common phenomenon, that a special notation has been adopted to denote the precise type of queue being studied. The notation is based on five features of the queue.

1. The distribution of the time between arriving customers.
2. The distribution of the time to service a customer.
3. The number of servers available to handle customers in the queue (e.g., the number of parallel processors).
4. The number of customers that may actually wait in the queue (i.e., the storage size).
5. The number of customers that are available to enter the queue (i.e., the population size).

The distributions of time can be Markovian (memoryless), which is denoted by M, deterministic (denoted by D), r-stage Erlangian (denoted by E_r), k-stage hyperexponential (denoted by H_k), or general (denoted by G). The number of servers, customers, and storage are simply denoted by that number. So a queuing system with exponentially distributed interarrival times, exponentially distributed service times, a single server, infinite population, and infinite storage would be labeled as the $M/M/1/\infty/\infty$ queue. In cases where the number of customers and storage are infinite, we often drop the last two values. So such a system is often denoted as the $M/M/1$ system.

In addition to the structure of the arrival and service processes, we can consider the order of removal from the queue, sometimes called the queuing discipline. There are any number of ways to select customers for service, but several methods are standard enough to have names.

1. FCFS: first come, first served (sometimes called FIFO, for first in, first out).
2. LCFS: last come, first served (sometimes called LIFO, for last in, first out).
3. RR: round robin, where a small, fixed amount of service is given to each customer in a circular fashion.
4. PS: processor sharing, which is the limit, as round robin spends infinitesimally small amounts of time on each customer, infinitely often.
5. Random: random order of service, the next customer for service is selected at random.
6. Priority: here customers have some identification which distinguishes them, so that preference can be given to different types of customers.

There are other types of service disciplines used in real systems, such as shortest job first, longest job first, and so on. If you really want to see the variety of queuing disciplines possible, you can look at large operating systems, optimizing disk controllers, and data communication systems. We will not try to describe or model all these different types.

In the case where an arriving customer may have priority over other customers already in the system, such as in a priority or LCFS queue, we can also distinguish whether that priority scheme is for the waiting customer only or for all customers, including the ones in service.

1. *Nonpreemptive.* Here an arriving customer follows the queuing discipline for the waiting line, but the customer(s) in service are not affected.
2. *Preemptive-resume.* Here the queuing discipline extends to the customers in service. Therefore, if an arriving customer has priority over the customer in service, the current customer in service is "preempted" by the arriving customer. When the preempted customer begins service again, the service resumes where it left off.
3. *Preemptive-restart.* Here an arriving customer follows the queuing discipline for the waiting line and will preempt any customer of lower priority currently in service. However, when the preempted customer begins service again, the service must "restart" as if no service had been received.

Note that for exponentially distributed service times, preemptive-resume and preemptive-restart are identical because of the memoryless property.

6.3 System Utilization

One of the important performance measures of a system is its utilization. *Utilization* is defined as the fraction of time a system is busy (i.e., utilized). In a system with many components, increasing the load on the system will increase the utilization of the components. As the system reaches capacity, not all of the components will be utilized uniformly. The bottleneck in a system at capacity would be the component with a utilization close to 1 when the other components had utilizations significantly lower than 1. A system manager would like to keep all components utilized and utilized at a uniform level. In a system characterized by a single server queue, the utilization is the fraction of time a server is busy.

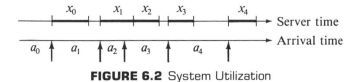

FIGURE 6.2 System Utilization

We can characterize the system utilization by recognizing that the fraction of time a server is busy is the sum of the times the system spends servicing customers, x_i, divided by the total amount of time. We can break up the total amount of time into pieces that are the interarrival intervals a_i. Since for each interarrival time, there is a corresponding service time, so we can add up precisely the same number of service and interarrival times.

$$P[\text{system is busy}] = \lim_{N \to \infty} \frac{\sum_{n=1}^{N} x_n}{\sum_{n=1}^{N} a_n}$$

We can divide the numerator and the denominator by N to form averages.

$$P[\text{system is busy}] = \lim_{N \to \infty} \frac{\sum_{n=1}^{N} x_n/N}{\sum_{n=1}^{N} a_n/N}$$

Replacing the averages with the average values, we can write down the average system utilization in terms of the average service time, $\bar{x}$, and the average arrival rate, λ.

$$P[\text{system is busy}] \triangleq \rho = \lambda\bar{x} \tag{6.1}$$

A multiserver situation is more complicated since the m servers may be working in parallel and the busy time is not just the sum of the amount of service. However, if we change our viewpoint slightly, we can consider separate time lines for each server and simply include all of the m time lines together. The number of customers is the same and the average time between customer arrivals is the same.

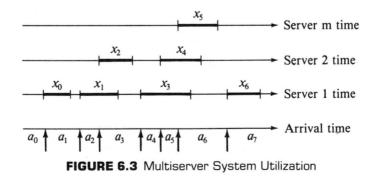

FIGURE 6.3 Multiserver System Utilization

So now when we add up the service times, we are really looking at all of those m time lines together. To compensate, we divide the computation by the number of those time lines. This now gives the fraction of time *each* of the m servers is busy.

$$P[\text{system is busy}] \triangleq \rho = \frac{\lambda \bar{x}}{m} \tag{6.2}$$

Exercises

6.1 For a queue with arrivals at a rate of λ and with service times that are exponentially distributed with the rate of service equal to μ, what is the utilization of the queue under the LCFS queuing discipline?

6.2 For a queue with two servers, each of which serves at a rate μ, what is the utilization of the queue if arrivals occur at a rate λ and are processed FCFS?

6.4 Little's Result

A very powerful result, which existed as a folk theorem for some time, was finally proved by J. D. C. Little in 1961. It is fundamental to many of the formulas and algorithms used in performance modeling and analysis. Although the complete proof of the theorem is beyond the scope of this book, a sketch of the proof is useful in understanding the result. To begin with, let us restrict ourselves to a first come, first serve queue (FCFS). The result is actually far more general, but it is easy to see what is happening in the case of a FCFS queue.

In general, for some queuing system, customers arrive, wait in a queue, receive some amount service, and then depart. If we look at the arrival and departure processes, we can see that the number of arrivals at time t, $a(t)$, and the count of the number of departures at time t, $d(t)$, can be used to calculate the number of customers in the system at time t, $n(t) = a(t) - d(t)$. If we graph arrival and departure functions, we see that the area between the curves represents the total accumulated customer-seconds for all the waiting customers over time. We can think of that total as adding up the time spent by each customer or as adding up the number of customers waiting at each time point.

Given some period of time τ, with $a(\tau)$ arrivals, and the time, t_k, each of the arrivals remains in the system, you can compute several averages for the system. Using these values, an average arrival rate λ, an average delay time T of a customer, and an average number N of customers waiting.

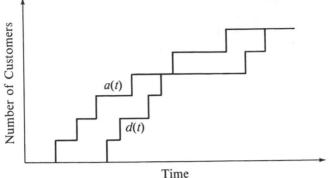

FIGURE 6.4 The Arrival and Departure Processes

$$\lambda = \frac{a(\tau)}{\tau}$$

$$T = \frac{1}{a(\tau)} \sum_{k=1}^{a(\tau)} t_k$$

$$N = \frac{1}{\tau} \int_0^\tau n(t) \, dt \qquad (6.3)$$

If the time begins and ends when the system is empty (i.e., $a(0) = d(0)$ and $a(\tau) = d(\tau)$), we can note the following. The area between the curves can be computed in two different ways which must yield the same result.

We can add up vertical rectangles as shown in Figure 6.5.

$$\int_0^\tau [a(t) - d(t)] \, dt \qquad (6.4)$$

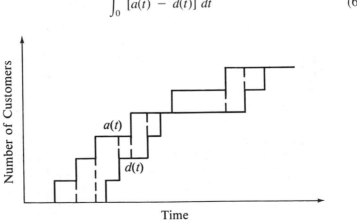

FIGURE 6.5 Delay Computed per Unit Time

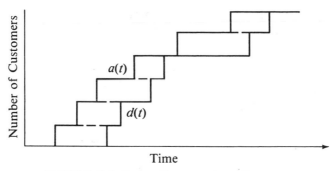

FIGURE 6.6 Delay Computed per Customer

Alternatively, we can add up horizontal rectangles as shown in Figure 6.6.

$$\sum_{k=1}^{a(\tau)} t_k \tag{6.5}$$

Equating these two calculations (they result in the same area) gives us the following relationship.

$$\int_0^\tau [a(t) - d(t)] \, dt = \sum_{k=1}^{a(\tau)} t_k$$

$$\int_0^\tau [n(t)] \, dt = a(\tau)T$$

$$\tau N = \lambda \tau T$$

$$N = \lambda T \tag{6.6}$$

This is known as *Little's result* (or *theorem*). Given that a system is *work conserving* this relationship holds. It says that the average number of customers in the system is equal to the average arrival rate times the average amount of time spent by the customers in the system.

Note that we have assumed nothing about the actual arrival or departure processes. We have only assumed that no work is created or destroyed within the system (i.e., the system is work conserving). In fact, this result holds for any queuing discipline.

We will make extensive use of this relationship. Since we usually know the average arrival rate to a queue (it is part of the load specification), we only need to find a means of determining the average number of customers in the system or the average time spent in the system. Little's result will immediately give us the other one.

Example 6.1: Consider the problem of a spy from Burger King trying to figure out how many people are at a McDonald's. He cannot sit inside and watch all day, so he must somehow calculate the number from information obtainable from outside observations. If he observes 32 customers per hour arriving on the average (over a long period of time) and notices that each customer exits after 12 minutes on the average, he can apply Little's result to obtain the mean queue length in the restaurant. The 32 customers per hour is simply 0.53333 customer per minute, multiplied by the 12 minutes per customer, which gives us the fact that 6.4 customers in the McDonald's, on the average.

Exercise

6.3 A simulation program of a complex multiprocessor system starts running with no jobs in the queue and ends with no jobs in the queue. The simulation program printed out the average number of jobs in the system over the simulation run as 12.356 and the average arrival rate as 25.6 jobs per minute. If the simulation program also printed that the average delay for a job was 7.34 minutes, was the simulation correct?

6.5 Birth-Death Systems

We noted, when we tried to solve for the steady-state behavior of a continuous time Markov chain, that we needed to solve the matrix equation $\pi Q = 0$. One such solution technique is Gaussian elimination. Normally, Gaussian elimination will tend to change zero entries to nonzero entries above the diagonal of a matrix when it eliminates the elements below the diagonal. However, if the matrix is of a special form, when we apply Gaussian elimination we see that the algorithm proceeds to eliminate an entire diagonal without adding elements to the matrix. This special form, tridiagonal, is a matrix whose elements p_{jk} are all zero except for $j = k, k + 1, k - 1$. If you will recall, such systems were called birth-death systems.

$$\pi Q = 0$$

$$\forall k \sum_{j=0}^{\infty} q_{jk} \pi_j = 0 \tag{6.7}$$

But for B-D systems, only $j = k - 1, k, k + 1$ are potentially nonzero.

$$\forall k \geq 1 \quad q_{k-1,k} \pi_{k-1} + q_{k,k} \pi_k + q_{k+1,k} \pi_{k+1} = 0$$

but $q_{k,k} = -q_{k,k-1} - q_{k,k+1}$

$$\forall_k \geq 1 \quad q_{k+1,k} \pi_{k+1} = (q_{k,k-1} + q_{k,k+1}) \pi_k - q_{k-1,k} \pi_{k-1} \tag{6.8}$$

We now have a series of equations to calculate the steady-state probability for a state in terms of the steady-state probabilities for the previous two states. If we also include the fact that, for $k = 0$, there are only two terms, $j = 0$ and 1, in the matrix operation, we can further reduce our computation.

$$-q_{1,0}\pi_1 + q_{0,1}\pi_0 = 0$$

$$\pi_1 = \frac{q_{0,1}}{q_{1,0}} \pi_0 \tag{6.9}$$

We can substitute for π_1 in the equation for π_2.

$$q_{2,1}\pi_2 = (q_{1,0} + q_{1,2})\pi_1 - q_{0,1}\pi_0$$

$$= (q_{1,0} + q_{1,2}) \frac{q_{0,1}}{q_{1,0}} \pi_0 - q_{0,1}\pi_0$$

$$\pi_2 = \frac{(q_{1,0} + q_{1,2})q_{0,1}}{q_{2,1}q_{1,0}} \pi_0 - \frac{q_{0,1}}{q_{2,1}} \pi_0$$

$$= \frac{q_{0,1}q_{1,2}}{q_{2,1}q_{1,0}} \pi_0$$

Continuing this process, we can solve for π_k in terms of π_0.

$$\pi_k = \frac{q_{0,1}q_{1,2} \cdots q_{k-1,k}}{q_{k,k-1}q_{k-1,k-2} \cdots q_{1,0}} \pi_0 \tag{6.10}$$

Note that all of the elements that appear in the numerator are of the form $q_{k-1,k}$ (i.e. going from the lower to the higher state, birth) and all the elements in the denominator are of the form $q_{k,k-1}$ (i.e. going from the higher to the lower state, death). A common notation is to set $q_{k,k+1} \stackrel{\Delta}{=} \lambda_k$ and $q_{k+1,k} \stackrel{\Delta}{=} \mu_{k+1}$.

$$\pi_k = \frac{\lambda_0 \cdot \lambda_1 \cdots \lambda_{k-1}}{\mu_k \cdot \mu_{k-1} \cdots \mu_1} \pi_0 \qquad k \geq 1$$

$$= \left(\prod_{j=0}^{k-1} \frac{\lambda_j}{\mu_{j+1}} \right) \pi_0 \qquad k \geq 1$$

Since $\sum_{k=0}^{\infty} \pi_k = 1$,

$$\pi_0 = \frac{1}{1 + \sum_{k=1}^{\infty} \prod_{j=0}^{k-1} \frac{\lambda_j}{\mu_{j+1}}}$$

$$\pi_k = \frac{\prod_{j=0}^{k-1} \frac{\lambda_j}{\mu_{j+1}}}{1 + \sum_{k=1}^{\infty} \prod_{j=0}^{k-1} \frac{\lambda_j}{\mu_{j+1}}} \tag{6.11}$$

As we noted in our study of general Markov systems, simply solving for a solution to these equations does not guarantee that the system will ever reach that steady-state. We may have used the product equation to obtain the values π_k, but we still have not determined whether or not the system is ergodic. In this section we introduce the conditions under which the system is ergodic and would therefore have a steady-state solution equal to the probabilities π_k.

One requirement for ergodicity is aperiodicity. Since birth-death systems are a special case of a continuous time Markov system, they are always aperiodic. Another requirement to check is whether the system is recurrent null, recurrent nonnull, or transient. We know that state can not be recurrent nonnull if the steady-state probability of a state is zero, Since π_k is calculated from the value of π_0, we know that if π_0 is zero, so are all the other states. (We restrict ourselves to finite birth, λ, and death, μ, rates.) So our first test is whether or not π_0 vanishes.

$$S_0 \triangleq \frac{1}{\pi_0} = 1 + \sum_{k=1}^{\infty} \prod_{j=0}^{k-1} \frac{\lambda_j}{\mu_{j+1}} \tag{6.12}$$

However, we are not sure that the steady-state probabilities are zero because the mean time to recur is infinite or because the state is not recurrent. If they vanish in just the right way, they may be recurrent null. So we now distinguish between the case where the probabilities vanish due to the mean recurrence time being infinite and where the probabilities actually become zero because they cannot recur infinitely often.

The second condition determines whether or not the probability of the states recurring is 1. This condition is a little more difficult to interpret. Basically, it is looking for a point, k, above which the birth rate is dominated by the death rate. If there is no such point, this sum must converge.

$$S_1 \triangleq \sum_{k=0}^{\infty} \frac{1}{\displaystyle\prod_{j=0}^{k-1} \frac{\lambda_j}{\mu_{j+1}}} \tag{6.13}$$

So if $S_0 < \infty$ and $S_1 = \infty$, the system is ergodic. If $S_0 = \infty$ and $S_1 = \infty$, the system is recurrent null. If $S_0 = \infty$ and $S_1 < \infty$, the system is transient.

In most cases, a simple restriction on the ratio of birth rates to death rates will guarantee ergodicity. The usual concept is that any ratio is acceptable up to some state k and after that the death rate always exceeds the birth rate for a state $> k$. This is sufficient to guarantee ergodicity. In an example like a bacteria colony, the birth rate can exceed the death rate for low populations, but after some population level the death rate must exceed the birth rate for the system to be ergodic.

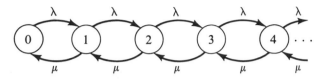

FIGURE 6.7 State Transition Diagram for the M/M/1 Queue

6.5.1 The M/M/1 Queue

One of the most commonly and heavily used models of a processing system is the M/M/1 queue. The M/M/1 queue is an example of a birth-death system. In the M/M/1 queue the birth rate is a constant value λ for all states. The death rate is also a constant, μ, for all states. Graphically, the systems can be viewed as the one-dimensional Markov chains shown in Figure 6.7.

Note that since the birth rate (arrival rate when viewed as a queue) is constant for all states (number of customers in the system), this model assumes an infinite population model for the arrival process. Otherwise, the rate would depend on how many customers were in the queue and not available for arrivals. Also note that since the death rate (service rate when viewed as a queue) is constant for all states (number of customers in the system) this model represents a single server. If it was not, the service rate would be different if more than one customer was in the queue.

To calculate the probability that the queue is in state k (i.e., has k customers waiting or in service), we use the general birth-death formulas with constant birth rates, $\lambda_i = \lambda$, and death rates, $\mu_i = \mu$.

$$
\begin{aligned}
\pi_k &= \left(\prod_{j=0}^{k-1} \frac{\lambda_j}{\mu_{j+1}} \right) \pi_0 \\
&= \left(\prod_{j=0}^{k-1} \frac{\lambda}{\mu} \right) \pi_0 \\
&= \left(\frac{\lambda}{\mu} \right)^k \pi_0
\end{aligned}
\tag{6.14}
$$

Using the fact that the sum of the probabilities must equal 1, we can solve for the steady-state probability of the system being empty.

$$
\pi_0 = \frac{1}{1 + \sum_{k=1}^{\infty} \left(\frac{\lambda}{\mu} \right)^k}
$$

For the case where the birth rate is less than the death rate (i.e. $\lambda < \mu$) this can be written in a closed form.

$$
\pi_0 = \cfrac{1}{1 + \cfrac{\lambda/\mu}{1 - \lambda/\mu}}
$$

$$
= 1 - \frac{\lambda}{\mu} \tag{6.15}
$$

Substituting back into the equation for the steady-state probabilities, we obtain the equation

$$
\pi_k = \left(1 - \frac{\lambda}{\mu}\right)\left(\frac{\lambda}{\mu}\right)^k \tag{6.16}
$$

Notice that the steady-state probability density for states is a geometric probability density function. In fact, if we modify the equation to use the system utilization $\rho \overset{\Delta}{=} P[k > 0]$, we find the familiar geometric form

$$
\rho \overset{\Delta}{=} 1 - \pi_0 = \frac{\lambda}{\mu}
$$

$$
\pi_k = (1 - \rho)\rho^k \tag{6.17}
$$

Once we have calculated the values of π_k, we must determine for what values of λ and μ the system is ergodic. Otherwise, those values will be meaningless since the system may not have a steady-state behavior. For the case of the M/M/1 queue where the birth rate and the death rate are constant, we can easily determine the values of the sums S_0 and S_1.

$$
S_0 = 1 + \sum_{k=1}^{\infty} \left(\frac{\lambda}{\mu}\right)^k \tag{6.18}
$$

We see that this sum will converge if $|\lambda/\mu| < 1$. Therefore, since λ and μ are nonnegative, if $\lambda < \mu$ we satisfy the first criterion.

$$
S_1 = \sum_{k=0}^{\infty} \frac{1}{\lambda \left(\dfrac{\lambda}{\mu}\right)^k}
$$

$$
= \frac{1}{\lambda} \sum_{k=0}^{\infty} \left(\frac{\mu}{\lambda}\right)^k \tag{6.19}
$$

We see that the sum S_1 will diverge for all values of $\lambda \leq \mu$, so a sufficient condition to satisfy both conditions is that $\lambda < \mu$. Therefore, $\lambda < \mu$ is a requirement for the M/M/1 queue to have a steady-state behavior.

Of special note is the condition where $\lambda = \mu$. We see that $S_0 = S_1 = \infty$ and so we have a recurrent null system. Intuitively, we have a system where arrivals balance departures such that, on the average, it takes an infinite amount of time for the system to return to any particular state (such as the empty queue π_0). However, the system is such that it will return to that state with probability 1.

In the case where $\lambda > \mu$, we have a transient system. Intuitively, we have a system where arrivals exceed departures on the average and the queue continues to grow. So for any finite queue size, k, the system cannot return to that state with probability 1.

Since we now have the steady-state probabilities, we can calculate various parameters of interest. First, since we know that the state k corresponds to the number of customers in the system, we can calculate the average number of customers in the system, N, in the usual way.

$$\pi_k = (1 - \rho)\rho^k$$

$$\Pi^*(z) = \sum_{k=0}^{\infty} \pi_k z^k = (1 - \rho) \sum_{k=0}^{\infty} (\rho z)^k$$

$$= \frac{1 - \rho}{1 - \rho z}$$

$$N = \frac{d}{dz} \Pi^*(z) \Big|_{z=1} = \frac{\rho(1 - \rho)}{(1 - \rho z)^2} \Big|_{z=1}$$

$$= \frac{\rho}{1 - \rho} \tag{6.20}$$

Given the average number of customers in the system, N, we can make an immediate application of Little's result to get the average delay.

$$N = \frac{\rho}{1 - \rho}$$

$$= \lambda T = \frac{\rho}{1 - \rho}$$

$$T = \frac{1/\mu}{1 - \rho} \tag{6.21}$$

Because this model represents a single server queue serving customers at a rate μ with an arrival rate of λ, when there are $k > 0$ customers in the system there is precisely one customer in service. We can define a new random variable C which can have two values, 1 or 0, depending on whether or not a customer is in service. So for the M/M/1 queue, we can calculate the average number of customers in service, $E[C]$, as follows.

$$P[c = 1] = \sum_{k=1}^{\infty} (1 - \rho)\rho^k = 1 - \pi_0 = \rho$$

$$E[C] = 0 \cdot P[c = 0] + 1 \cdot P[c = 1]$$

$$= \rho \tag{6.22}$$

Similarly, we know, since the amount of service time for a customer is exponentially distributed with parameter μ, the average time spent in service by a customer is $1/\mu$. So we can modify our equations for the average values to obtain the average waiting time and average number of customers waiting in the queue (excluding service).

$$E[\text{number in queue}] \triangleq N_q = \frac{\rho}{1 - \rho} - \rho = \frac{\rho^2}{1 - \rho}$$

$$E[\text{waiting time}] \triangleq W = \frac{1/\mu}{1 - \rho} - \frac{1}{\mu} = \frac{\lambda/\mu^2}{1 - \rho} \tag{6.23}$$

So far we have computed the probability density for the number of customers in the system, the average number in the system, and the average time spent in the system and the queue. But, we have not mentioned anything about the queuing discipline. However, when we are interested in finding more than an average time spent in the system or the queue, such as finding the probability density (or even just the second moment) of the time spent in the system or queue, we need to know the order in which customers are served. As an example, let us derive the probability density function for the waiting time in the case of the FCFS queuing discipline.

To begin, we need to recall an important feature of the Poisson arrival process to the queue. Poisson arrivals are uniformly distributed within an interval. Therefore, a Poisson arrival views a system in precisely the same way that a random observer views the system. The solutions we have obtained so far are for a random observer, but are equally valid for a Poisson arrival. So an arriving customer will also find the system with k customers with probability π_k.

To find the probability density of the time spent in the queue $w(t)$ (i.e., the waiting time), we will decompose the random variable into a function of random variables we do know. We recognize that the time spent in the queue can be expressed as a sum of random variables as follows. The time spent in the queue is the residual lifetime, R, of the service time for the customer currently in service, plus the service times X_i of the customers ahead of the new arrival, since the queuing discipline is FCFS.

$$W = R + \sum_{i=2}^{k} X_i \tag{6.24}$$

Since the service times are exponentially distributed we know that the residual lifetime of the customer in service has a distribution identical to the original. In addition, since the distribution of each of the customers service $s(t)$ is identical and independent of the previous customer's service time, we can write down a conditional probability density function for the waiting time.

$$w(t|k) = s_1(t) \circledast s_2(t) \circledast \cdots \circledast s_k(t) \tag{6.25}$$

Applying the convolution theorem of transform theory (see Section 3.18) we can immediately write down a transform for the conditional probability density in terms of the transform of the service time density $S^*(s)$. Since we know the probability of the system having precisely k customers in it, we can then proceed to remove the condition on the transform of the density and invert the unconditioned transform.

$$W^*(s|k) = [S^*(s)]^k$$

Substituting the transform of the service time probability density, we obtain the following

$$W^*(s|k) = \left[\frac{\mu}{\mu + s}\right]^k$$

$$W^*(s) = \sum_{k=0}^{\infty} \left[\frac{\mu}{\mu + s}\right]^k \pi_k$$

$$= \sum_{k=0}^{\infty} \left[\frac{\mu}{\mu + s}\right]^k (1 - \rho)\rho^k$$

$$= (1 - \rho) \sum_{k=0}^{\infty} \left[\frac{\mu\rho}{\mu + s}\right]^k$$

$$= (1 - \rho) \frac{\mu + s}{(1 - \rho)\mu + s} \tag{6.26}$$

We can then invert this transform as follows.

$$W^*(s) = (1 - \rho) + (1 - \rho)\frac{\rho\mu}{s + (1 - \rho)\mu} \tag{6.27}$$

$$w(t) = \begin{cases} (1 - \rho) & t = 0 \\ (1 - \rho)\rho\mu e^{-(1-\rho)\mu t} & t > 0 \end{cases} \tag{6.28}$$

Exercises

6.4 If an M/M/1 queue has arrivals at a rate of 2 per minute and serves at a rate of 4 per minute, how many customers are found in the system on the average? How many customers are found in service on the average?

6.5 What is the utilization of an M/M/1 that has four people in the queue (not service) on the average?

6.5.2 The M/M/∞ Queue

Another interesting queuing model is the infinite server model. It is a birth-death system with an infinite population whose arrival process is Poisson with parameter λ and the service process is exponentially distributed with parameter μ. However, now we have an infinite number of servers, so that every arrival can receive service immediately. Note that this implies that everyone in the system is in service and that there really is no "queue." If the number of customers in the system is k, the number of busy servers is also k, each with an exponential rate μ. So the service rate with k customers in the system is $\mu_k = k\mu$.

We now have $\lambda_k = \lambda$ and $\mu_k = k\mu$ for the infinite server queue, so we substitute into our general birth-death equations to obtain the steady-state probabilities.

$$\pi_k = \left(\prod_{j=0}^{k-1} \frac{\lambda}{(j+1)\mu}\right) \pi_0$$

$$= \frac{1}{k!} \left(\frac{\lambda}{\mu}\right)^k \pi_0 \tag{6.29}$$

Since the probabilities must sum to 1, we can obtain a value for π_0.

$$\pi_0 = \frac{1}{1 + \sum_{k=1}^{\infty} \frac{1}{k!} \left(\frac{\lambda}{\mu}\right)^k}$$

$$= \frac{1}{e^{\lambda/\mu}} = e^{-\lambda/\mu} \tag{6.30}$$

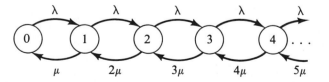

FIGURE 6.8 State Transition Diagram for the M/M/∞ Queue

Substituting back into our equation for the steady-state probabilities, we obtain the following.

$$\pi_k = \frac{(\lambda/\mu)^k}{k!} e^{-\lambda/\mu} \tag{6.31}$$

Recall that for the M/M/1 queue we found a geometric density for the steady-state probabilities. For the M/M/∞ queue we now find a Poisson density for the steady-state probabilities.

Before proceeding, we quickly check the ergodicity requirements of the M/M/∞ queue and find that the system is ergodic for any values of λ and μ such that $\lambda/\mu < \infty$.

$$S_0 = e^{\lambda/\mu} < \infty$$

$$S_1 = \frac{1}{\lambda} \sum_{k=0}^{\infty} \frac{k!}{(\lambda/\mu)^k} = \infty \tag{6.32}$$

To find the average number of customers in the system, N, we simply proceed as usual.

$$\pi_k = \frac{(\lambda/\mu)^k}{k!} e^{-\lambda/\mu}$$

$$\Pi^*(z) = e^{-\lambda/\mu} \sum_{k=0}^{\infty} \frac{\left(\frac{\lambda z}{\mu}\right)^k}{k!}$$

$$= e^{-\frac{\lambda}{\mu}} e^{\frac{\lambda z}{\mu}} = e^{\frac{\lambda(z-1)}{\mu}}$$

$$N = \frac{d}{dz} \Pi^*(z) \bigg|_{z=1} = \frac{\lambda}{\mu} e^{\frac{\lambda(z-1)}{\mu}} \bigg|_{z=1}$$

$$= \frac{\lambda}{\mu} \tag{6.33}$$

The average time spent in the system can be found immediately by Little's result.

$$N = \frac{\lambda}{\mu} = \lambda T$$

$$T = \frac{1}{\mu} \tag{6.34}$$

Alternatively, we could have recognized that since there is no queuing, the time spent in the system is only the service time, whose average was given as $1/\mu$.

Exercise

6.6 Consider the *m*-server loss queue, where there are *m* servers, but if an arrival occurs when all *m* servers are busy, it is not allowed into the system. Solve for the steady-state probability of *k* customers being in the system.

6.5.3 The M/M/1/L/M Queue

As a slightly more interesting example of a queuing model which is a birth-death system, consider the case of a queue with exponential interarrival times, exponential service times, a single server, a finite amount (L) of storage, and a finite population (M).

In the case of a finite population, we are assuming that each individual attempts to join the queue as an independent Poisson process with parameter λ. Therefore, when there are n individuals available in the population (i.e., not already in the system), the aggregate arrival rate is $n\lambda$. In the case of finite storage, it is assumed that if an arrival finds the system full, the arrival is simply lost and returns to the population.

We begin our analysis by assuming that $L < M$ since the case where $L \geq M$ is equivalent to a M/M/1/∞/M queue. This is clear when you recall that if there is more storage than the number of possible entries, the storage limit is not a constraint.

We proceed as usual with our analysis by applying the general birth-death equation. For the arrival process, since the population is finite, $\lambda_k = (M - k)\lambda$ for $k < L$, and since the storage is limited, $\lambda_k = 0$ for $k \geq L$. Since there is only one, state independent server, the service process has a constant rate and we use $\mu_k = \mu$ for all states. We note that since $\lambda_k = 0$ for $k \geq L$, it is impossible to reach states $k = L + 1, L + 2, \ldots$ so the steady-state probabilities $\pi_{L+1}, \pi_{L+2}, \ldots$ must all equal zero. This allows us to limit calculations to the range $k = 0$ to $k = L$.

$$\pi_k = \left(\prod_{j=0}^{k-1} \frac{(M - j)\lambda}{\mu} \right) \pi_0$$

$$= \frac{M!}{(M - k)!} \left(\frac{\lambda}{\mu} \right)^k \pi_0 \tag{6.35}$$

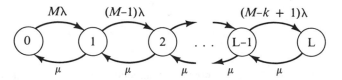

FIGURE 6.9 State Transition Diagram for the M/M/1/L/M queue

Again, since the probabilities must sum to 1 we obtain π_0. Unfortunately, in this case we cannot obtain a closed form.

$$\pi_0 = \frac{1}{1 + \sum\limits_{j=1}^{L} \dfrac{M!}{(M-j)!}\left(\dfrac{\lambda}{\mu}\right)^j} \tag{6.36}$$

Substituting back into our equation for the steady-state probability, we obtain the final equations.

$$\pi_k = \frac{\dfrac{M!}{(M-k)!}\left(\dfrac{\lambda}{\mu}\right)^k}{\sum\limits_{j=0}^{L} \dfrac{M!}{(M-j)!}\left(\dfrac{\lambda}{\mu}\right)^j} = \frac{\dfrac{(\lambda/\mu)^k}{(M-k)!}}{\sum\limits_{j=0}^{L} \dfrac{(\lambda/\mu)^j}{(M-j)!}} \tag{6.37}$$

$$N = \sum\limits_{k=1}^{L} \frac{\dfrac{k(\lambda/\mu)^k}{(M-k)!}}{\sum\limits_{j=0}^{L} \dfrac{(\lambda/\mu)^j}{(M-j)!}} \tag{6.38}$$

A special case of this model is when $L = M$. If you consider the case of M independent machines each of which fails as a Poisson process, then those machines can be viewed as queuing up for a single repairman who repairs machines in an exponentially distributed time with an average of $1/\mu$. This special case is referred to as the machine-repairman model. In realiability analysis, the probability that a random observer will find the system capable of doing some work is called the *availability* of the system. In this case the system is capable of doing some work when at least one machine is running. Therefore, the availability of this system is equal to $1 - \pi_M$.

Exercise

6.7 Consider the special case of the finite capacity, infinite population ($M/M/1/L/\infty$) queue where the aggregate arrival rate from the infinite population is λ. Find the probability of there being k customers in the system.

6.6 **Non-Birth-Death Systems**

Not all queuing models are birth-death systems. In some cases the Markov model will have transitions that are not nearest neighbor. However, they are

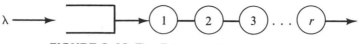

FIGURE 6.10 The Erlangian Service Queue

still Markovian and have a steady-state solution given by $\pi\mathbf{Q} = 0$. Even though the model may not be birth-death (i.e., $\mathbf{Q}$ is not tridiagonal), it still may have enough structure so that the steady-state equation will give rise to a small set of recurrence relationships, although they will not be as simple as the birth-death ones.

Given a set of recurrence relationships we can still attack the problem by using z-transforms techniques. So in such cases, we begin by drawing a transition diagram and write down the difference equations for the various states, corresponding to $\pi\mathbf{Q} = 0$. We then follow our steps for solving difference equations using z-transforms.

In the $M/E_r/1$ model, customers arrive as a Poisson process, but are serviced by a single server, which takes an r-stage Erlangian distributed amount of time. Since the Erlang distribution is not memoryless for $r > 1$, our normal description of the state of the queue results in a non-Markovian process.

However, the Erlangian distribution is the sum of identical and independent exponential distributions which are each memoryless. So if we change our concept of state, we can describe a Markov chain. The state is defined as the number of stages of service to be completed which are currently in the system. Under this interpretation each customer brings in r stages of service when it arrives. The state transition diagram is shown in Figure 6.11.

Note that the rate of decrease in the number of stages is always $r\mu$. Since no other customer may receive service until the current customer has completed all stages of service, precisely one stage of service is completed at a rate $r\mu$. Therefore, completing all r stages takes $1/\mu$ on the average, maintaining the average total service time of $1/\mu$.

Since we no longer have a birth-death system, we cannot simply apply our general birth-death equations. Instead, we return to the equation $\pi\mathbf{Q} = 0$. For

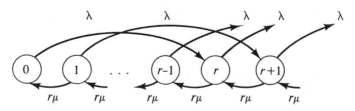

FIGURE 6.11 State Transition Diagram for the $M/E_r/1$ queue

our case we have two basic forms for the state equations from this balance equation.

$$\lambda \pi_0 = r\mu \pi_1$$
$$(\lambda + r\mu)\pi_k = r\mu \pi_{k+1} \qquad 0 < k < r$$
$$(\lambda + r\mu)\pi_k = r\mu \pi_{k+1} + \lambda \pi_{k-r} \qquad k \geq r \tag{6.39}$$

These equations form a set of difference equations that must be satisfied by the steady-state probability density for the state of the $M/E_r/1$ queue. We solve these difference equations with our established z-transform techniques (see Chapter 3).

$$\sum_{k=1}^{r-1} (\lambda + r\mu)\pi_k z^k = \sum_{k=1}^{r-1} r\mu \pi_{k+1} z^k$$
$$\sum_{k=r}^{\infty} (\lambda + r\mu)\pi_k z^k = \sum_{k=r}^{\infty} r\mu \pi_{k+1} z^k + \sum_{k=r}^{\infty} \lambda \pi_{k-r} z^k \tag{6.40}$$

Adding these two equations we can produce a single equation that we can solve for the z-transform of the steady-state probability density.

$$\sum_{k=1}^{\infty} \pi_k z^k = \sum_{k=1}^{\infty} r\mu \pi_{k+1} z^k + \sum_{k=r}^{\infty} \lambda \pi_{k-r} z^k$$
$$(\lambda + r\mu) \sum_{k=1}^{\infty} \pi_k z^k = \frac{r\mu}{z} \sum_{k=1}^{\infty} \pi_{k+1} z^{k+1} + \lambda z^r \sum_{k=r}^{\infty} \pi_{k-r} z^{k-r}$$
$$(\lambda + r\mu)[\Pi^*(z) - \pi_0] = \frac{r\mu}{z} [\Pi^*(z) - \pi_1 z - \pi_0] + \lambda z^r \Pi^*(z)$$
$$\Pi^*(z)[\lambda + r\mu - \frac{r\mu}{z} - \lambda z^r] = (\lambda + r\mu)\pi_0 - r\mu \pi_1 - \frac{r\mu}{z} \pi_0$$
$$\Pi^*(z) = \frac{(\lambda + r\mu)\pi_0 z - r\mu \pi_1 z - r\mu \pi_0}{(\lambda + r\mu)z - r\mu - \lambda z^{r+1}} \tag{6.41}$$

Substituting our initial equation, $\lambda \pi_0 = r\mu \pi_1$, we have $\Pi^*(z)$ in terms π_0.

$$\Pi^*(z) = \frac{(\lambda + r\mu)\pi_0 z - \lambda \pi_0 z - r\mu \pi_0}{(\lambda + r\mu)z - r\mu - \lambda z^{r+1}}$$
$$= \frac{(z - 1)r\mu \pi_0}{(\lambda + r\mu)z - r\mu - \lambda z^{r+1}} \tag{6.42}$$

Recall that all transforms of probability density functions have some special properties we can exploit. In this case we use the fact that $\Pi^*(1) = 1$ to find the value of π_0.

$$\lim_{z \to 1} \Pi^*(z) = \lim_{z \to 1} \frac{(z - 1)r\mu\pi_0}{(\lambda + r\mu)z - r\mu - \lambda z^{r+1}}$$

$$1 = \lim_{z \to 1} \frac{r\mu\pi_0}{(\lambda + r\mu) - (r + 1)\lambda z^r} = \frac{r\mu\pi_0}{r\mu - r\lambda}$$

$$\pi_0 = \frac{r\mu - r\lambda}{r\mu} = 1 - \frac{\lambda}{\mu}$$

$$\rho \triangleq 1 - \pi_0 = \frac{\lambda}{\mu} \tag{6.43}$$

Substituting back into our equation for the z-transform of the steady-state probability density, we obtain the following equation.

$$\Pi^*(z) = \frac{(z - 1)(r\mu - r\lambda)}{(\lambda + r\mu)z - r\mu - \lambda z^{r+1}} \tag{6.44}$$

If we substitute $z = 1$ into the denominator, we see that we obtain 0. Therefore, the denominator must also have a factor of $z - 1$, which we can divide out.

$$\Pi^*(z) = \frac{r\mu - r\lambda}{r\mu - \lambda \sum_{k=1}^{r} z^k}$$

$$= \frac{1 - \rho}{1 - \dfrac{\rho}{r} \sum_{k=1}^{r} z^k} \tag{6.45}$$

We can now generate the average number of customers in the system directly from the z-transform. We first calculate the average number of stages of service, $E[K]$, in the system.

$$E[K] = \frac{d}{dz} \Pi^*(z) \bigg|_{z=1} = \frac{d}{dz} \frac{1 - \rho}{1 - \dfrac{\rho}{r} \sum_{n=1}^{r} z^n} \bigg|_{z=1}$$

$$= \frac{1 - \rho}{\left[1 - \dfrac{\rho}{r} \sum_{n=1}^{r} z^n \right]^2} \left[\frac{\rho}{r} \sum_{n=1}^{r} n z^{n-1} \right] \bigg|_{z=1}$$

$$= \frac{1 - \rho}{(1 - \rho)^2} \frac{\rho}{r} \sum_{n=1}^{r} n = \frac{\rho}{r(1 - \rho)} \frac{r(r + 1)}{2}$$

$$= \frac{(r + 1)\rho}{2(1 - \rho)} \tag{6.46}$$

Now, ignore the state of the queue and consider only the stage of the server. If the system is busy, then the server is in one of r stages. Since the average time spent in each stage is the same and exponentially distributed, an observer will find the server in any one of those stages with equal probability ρ/r. or idle with probability $1 - \rho$. If we define a new random variable, C, as the number of the stage the server is in, we can obtain the average value of the number of stages left in service, $E[C]$.

$$E[C] = \sum_{c=1}^{r} C \frac{\rho}{r} = \rho \frac{r + 1}{2} \tag{6.47}$$

We now have the average number of stages of service in the system in steady-state and the average number of stages of service actually in service. So we can compute the average number of stages in the queue in steady-state. However, we also know that each customer enters with precisely r stages of service requirement. So if a random observer sees k stages of service in the queue, he is really seeing k/r customers in the queue since none of the stages of service have been completed for the queued customers. We can now compute, N_q the average number of customers in the queue from the average number of stages of service in the queue.

$$N_q = \frac{E[K] - E[C]}{r} = \frac{\rho^2(r + 1)}{2r(1 - \rho)} \tag{6.48}$$

Since this is a single server queue we know that the average number of customers in service is ρ. So we can calculate the average number of customers in the entire system in steady-state, N, and from Little's result, the average time spent in the system, T. Note that for $r = 1$, the system reduces to the case of an M/M/1 queue, and the equation for the average number of customers in system reduces to the expected result.

$$N = \rho + \frac{\rho^2(r + 1)}{2r(1 - \rho)} \tag{6.49}$$

$$T = \frac{N}{\lambda} = \frac{1}{\mu} + \frac{\rho(r + 1)}{2r\mu(1 - \rho)} \tag{6.50}$$

Although we have obtained formulas for the average number of customers in the system, we can not generate a closed-form for the transform of the steady-state probabilities for an arbitrary number of stages. However, since we could find the roots of that polynominal for a particular value of r, let us assume that we have found those values $z_1, z_2, \ldots, z_r$. Then following our usual approach of partial fraction expansion, we can find the inverse of this z-transform in terms of the roots z_n.

$$\Pi^*(z) = \frac{1 - \rho}{\left(1 - \dfrac{z}{z_1}\right)\left(1 - \dfrac{z}{z_2}\right) \cdots \left(1 - \dfrac{z}{z_r}\right)}$$

$$= (1 - \rho) \sum_{n=1}^{r} \frac{A_n}{1 - \dfrac{z}{z_n}} \quad \text{where } A_n = \prod_{\substack{m=1 \\ m \neq n}}^{r} \frac{1}{1 - \dfrac{z_n}{z_m}} \quad (6.51)$$

Finally, we can do a table lookup for the inverse of this transform.

$$\pi_k = (1 - \rho) \sum_{n=1}^{r} \frac{A_n}{z_n^k} \quad (6.52)$$

6.7 Non-Markovian Systems

Although all of the systems we have considered so far are Markovian (i.e., exponentially distributed times between events) many real systems are not. Even the "simple" system of Poisson arrivals and a deterministic service time is not Markovian. We found that we could get around the problem for the $M/E_r/1$ queue by using a different concept of state. There are general techniques that can be applied to non-Markovian systems, but they are beyond the scope of this book. However, we can derive formulas for average values in some cases using techniques that we have already studied.

We can take advantage of the fact that the average of a sum of random variables is the sum of the averages of the individual random variables even when there are dependencies. This allow us to use average values without checking the probability density functions for independence. Therefore, generating the probability density functions is unnecessary for deriving some average values. This avoids a difficult part of the analysis if all we are interested in are the average values.

6.7.1 The FCFS M/G/1 Queue

The M/G/1 queue has a Poisson arrival process and a single server whose service time has some general distribution independent of the arrival process. We will use the parameter λ for the arrival rate of the Poisson process but since the service process is general, we denote the random variable for the service time as X with a mean and second moment as $\bar{x}$ and $\overline{x^2}$, respectively.

In the case of Poisson arrivals to a queue, the arrivals view of the system is the same as the view of the system seen by a random observer. Therefore, we can determine the average waiting time in an M/G/1 queue by using average values from the viewpoint of an outside (i.e., random) observer.

To begin, we break down the problem of finding the average waiting time in the queue into two components. The first component, $N_q\bar{x}$, is the waiting time due to the required processing (a time of $\bar{x}$ on the average) of the customers (N_q on the average) already waiting in the queue before the arrival (i.e., FCFS). The second component is the waiting time due to the customer in service. This component is nonzero if the system is busy, but zero if the system is empty. Since this is a single server system, the second component of the waiting time is simply the residual lifetime of the customer currently in service if the system is busy. Since the probability that the system is busy is equal to ρ and the average residual lifetime is simply $\overline{x^2}/(2\bar{x})$, we can uncondition to obtain the average residual lifetime seen by an arriving customer. Combining these components, we can obtain the average waiting time W.

$$W = N_q\bar{x} + (1 - \rho)\cdot 0 + \rho\frac{\overline{x^2}}{2\bar{x}}$$

$$= N_q\bar{x} + \rho\frac{\overline{x^2}}{2\bar{x}} \tag{6.53}$$

We have described the waiting time seen by an arriving customer in terms of the average number of customers seen in the queue and the average residual lifetime of the customer in service as seen by an outside observer. Now we note that Little's result holds for the queue itself, and that the average number seen by an outside observer is $W\lambda$. Therefore, since the arrivals are Poisson, $N_q = W\lambda$, resulting in the following equation.

$$W = W\lambda\bar{x} + \rho\frac{\overline{x^2}}{2\bar{x}} \tag{6.54}$$

Solving that equation for the average waiting time W, we obtain the standard equation attributed to Pollaczek and Khinchin (sometimes called the P-K equation).

$$W - \bar{x}\lambda W = \rho\frac{\overline{x^2}}{2\bar{x}}$$

$$W(1 - \rho) = \lambda\bar{x}\frac{\overline{x^2}}{2\bar{x}}$$

$$W = \frac{\lambda\overline{x^2}}{2(1 - \rho)} \tag{6.55}$$

In addition, simply adding the average service time, $\bar{x}$, to the waiting time in the queue gives us the average time, T, spent in the entire system.

$$T = \bar{x} + \frac{\lambda \overline{x^2}}{2(1 - \rho)} \tag{6.56}$$

By simply applying Little's result we can obtain the average number in the queue (not including service) and the average number in the system.

$$N_q = W\lambda = \frac{\lambda^2 \overline{x^2}}{2(1 - \rho)} \tag{6.57}$$

$$N = \rho + N_q = \rho + \frac{\lambda^2 \overline{x^2}}{2(1 - \rho)} \tag{6.58}$$

So we have now derived equations for the average values we are usually interested in for the general case of the M/G/1 queue. However, since we have not found the actual steady-state probabilities, we can not say much about anything else (like the second moments of the number in the system). If we want to find out more about the system, we must construct the transform of the number of customers in the system. For that, more general techniques are needed.

Example 6.2: As an example, let us calculate the average values for the M/E_r/1 queue using these new equations. Since we have already derived the average values for this system by a more direct method, we can compare the answers. First, we need the first and second moments of the E_r service time distribution.

$$B^*(s) = \left(\frac{r\mu}{r\mu + s}\right)^r$$

$$\bar{x} = -\frac{d}{ds} B^*(s) \bigg|_{s=0}$$

$$= r(r\mu)^r (r\mu + s)^{-r-1} \bigg|_{s=0} = \frac{1}{\mu}$$

$$\overline{x^2} = \frac{d^2}{ds^2} B^*(s) \bigg|_{s=0}$$

$$= r(r + 1)(r\mu)^r (r\mu + s)^{-r-2} \bigg|_{s=0} = \frac{r + 1}{r\mu^2}$$

Now we can simply substitute into our equations for the M/G/1 queue.

$$N = \rho + \frac{\lambda^2(1 + r)}{\dfrac{r\mu^2}{2(1 - \rho)}} = \rho + \frac{\rho^2(1 + r)}{2r(1 - \rho)}$$

Example 6.3: As another example, consider the non-Markovian system of Poisson arrivals to a FCFS queue with a deterministic server, the M/D/1 queue. In this case the distribution for the service time is a constant C. Then the average value for the service time is C and the second moment is C^2.

$$N = \lambda C + \frac{\lambda^2 C^2}{2(1 - \lambda C)}$$

6.7.2 The Priority M/G/1 Queue

Not all systems treat every task or customer in the same way. Sometimes some customer will have priority over another customer. In these cases, customers are distinguished in some manner. This is the case in the LCFS queuing discipline and the head of the line (HOL) priority queue. In the LCFS queuing discipline any arriving customer has priority over the other customers in the system. In the head of the line priority queuing discipline, one can view the queue as a collection of separate queues for each priority class. The service is performed on all customers in the highest priority queue until there are no more customers of that class. Then service is performed on the next highest priority class in a similar fashion. When viewed as a single queue, higher priority class arrivals move to the head of the line formed by lower class customers.

We now have different average arrival rates for each class and different average service times for each class. However, since we are assuming Poisson arrivals, the merging of the different Poisson streams is still Poisson. We will denote the average service time for a class m as $\bar{x}_m$, and we will denote the average arrival rate for a class m as λ_m. The fraction of time the system is working on class m customers is $\rho_m = \lambda_m \bar{x}_m$.

As we did in the case of the FCFS M/G/1 queue, we will take advantage of the fact that Poisson arrivals see the same average behavior as an outside (i.e., random) observer. In addition, we again use the fact that the sum of averages is equal to the average of the sums regardless of the dependencies.

We begin by recognizing that customers of a priority m are not affected at all by lower priority customers in the queue. Therefore, for a preemptive system, the highest priority customers would simply see a M/G/1 queue. The next highest priority customers would see a system where service was available only

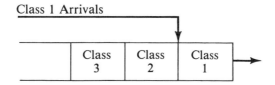

FIGURE 6.12 Head of the Line Priority Queue

$(1 - \rho_1)$ of the time. In a non-preemptive system, the highest priority class would see an M/G/1 queue with a residual lifetime of the current customer in service regardless of the priority of the customer in service.

Our approach is to break down the average waiting time into three components. The first component of delay due to the customer currently in service, W_0, will depend on whether or not the system is preemptive. The second term can be computed by noticing that an arriving customer must wait for the service completion of each customer of higher or equal priority already in the queue. By applying Little's result to the queue, the number of customers of each class seen by a Poisson arrival is simply $\lambda_m W_m$. The third term can be computed by noticing that a customer in the queue will have to wait an additional amount of time for any higher priority customers which arrive after him but before he enters service. This additional delay is equal to the number of higher priority class customers arriving during the waiting time of the current customer class, $\lambda_i W_m$, times the amount of time to service those customers.

$$W_m = W_0 + \sum_{i=1}^{m} \bar{x}_i(\lambda_i W_i) + \sum_{i=1}^{m-1} \bar{x}_i(\lambda_i W_m) \qquad (6.59)$$

We can then solve this equations recursively, starting with the highest priority class.

$$W_1 = W_0 + \rho_1 W_1$$

$$W_1(1 - \rho_1) = W_0$$

$$W_1 = \frac{W_0}{1 - \rho_1} \qquad (6.60)$$

$$W_2 = W_0 + \rho_1 W_1 + \rho_2 W_2 + \rho_1 W_2$$

$$W_2[1 - \rho_1 - \rho_2] = \frac{W_0}{1 - \rho_1}$$

$$W_2 = \frac{W_0}{(1 - \rho_1 - \rho_2)(1 - \rho_1)} \qquad (6.61)$$

Continuing this for all of the classes we get the following equation.

$$W_m = \frac{W_0}{\left(1 - \sum_{i=1}^{m} \rho_i\right)\left(1 - \sum_{i=1}^{m-1} \rho_i\right)} \qquad (6.62)$$

To simplify the notation we define a cumulative utilization value, σ_m, which represents the fraction of time the system spends on classes of equal or higher priority than class m.

$$\sigma_m = \sum_{i=1}^{m} \rho_i \qquad (6.63)$$

$$W_m = \frac{W_0}{(1 - \sigma_m)(1 - \sigma_{m-1})} \tag{6.64}$$

Now we can return to the computation of the term, W_0, representing the delay due to the customer currently in service. We know that an outside observer will see the system working on class i customers ρ_i of the time. Combining that with the residual lifetime of service for each class, we can uncondition the residual lifetime. By using the fact that the Poisson arrivals see the same averages as the outside observer, we can write down the final equations for W_0.

For the nonpreemptive case, the delay for the customer currently in service will be the same for all classes.

$$W_0 = \sum_{i=1}^{P} \rho_i \frac{\overline{x_i^2}}{2\overline{x_i}} \tag{6.65}$$

For the preemptive case, the delay for the customer currently in service will only be due to customers with higher priority. Specifically, for preemptive resume, no change in the service times occurs due to preemption, so we can compute W_0 as follows.

$$W_0 = \sum_{i=1}^{m} \rho_i \frac{\overline{x_i^2}}{2\overline{x_i}} \tag{6.66}$$

6.8 Simulation of the M/M/1 Queue

The following program is a simulation of the M/M/1 queue. The structure of the program is very similar to the Markov simulation program. In the case of the M/M/1 queue, the parameters of the arrival and service process are not state dependent, so we select the other option for Markov simulations, where all of the next events are generated and the earliest is selected as the next event. We will generate new events only when we process an event of that type.

```
PROGRAM MM1(INPUT,OUTPUT);

(* THIS PROGRAM IS AN EVENT BASED SIMULATION OF *)
(* AN M/M/1 QUEUE.                              *)
(*                                              *)
(* IN THIS PROGRAM WE STILL EXPLOIT THE MARKOV  *)
(* PROPERTY IN THE STRUCTURE OF THE PROGRAM     *)
(* SINCE THE ARRIVAL AND SERVICE PROCESSES DO   *)
(* NOT VARY WITH THE STATE, WE WILL USE THE IDEA*)
(* OF GENERATING ALL POSSIBLE NEXT EVENTS AND   *)
(* SELECT THE EARLIEST.  WE ARE USING THE FACT  *)
(* THAT THE SYSTEM IS BIRTH-DEATH SO WE ONLY    *)
(* WORRY ABOUT TWO POSSIBLE EVENTS AT EACH STEP *)
```

```
CONST   K       = 49;        (* LEN. OF SEQ. OF RNG *)
        INFINITY = 1.0E+64;

VAR     CLOCK   : REAL;   (* SIMULATION CLOCK     *)
        ETIME   : REAL;   (* EVENT INTERVAL TIME *)
        EVENT   : INTEGER;(* CURRENT EVENT NUM    *)
        LIMIT   : INTEGER;(* MAX NUM OF EVENTS    *)

        SERVTIME: REAL;   (* SERVICE DURATION     *)
        ARRVRATE: REAL;   (* CUST. ARRIVAL RATE  *)
        SERVPARM: REAL;   (* SERVICE PARM FOR RNG*)
        ARRVPARM: REAL;   (* ARRIVAL PARM FOR RNG*)

        AVGCUSTS: REAL;   (* AVG NUM OF CUSTOMERS*)
        AVGDELAY: REAL;   (* AVG TIME IN SYSTEM  *)
        CUST    : INTEGER;(* CURR. # OF CUSTOMERS*)
        TOTARRV : INTEGER;(* TOT# ARRIVALS IN SIM*)
        UTIL    : REAL;   (* UTILITY OF SYSTEM   *)
        BUSY    : REAL;   (* TOT TIME SYS IS BUSY*)

(* SINCE THERE ARE TWO POSSIBLE NEXT EVENTS THE  *)
(* EVENT QUEUE NEVER HAS MORE THAN TWO ENTRIES    *)
(* SO INSTEAD OF HAVE A TRUE QUEUE WE SIMPLY      *)
(* KEEP THE TWO FUTURE TIMES                      *)

        NEXTARR : REAL;   (* TIME TO NEXT ARRIVAL*)
        NEXTDEP : REAL;   (* TIME TO NEXT DEPART *)

        PROB    : REAL;   (* RNG PROBABILITY     *)
        SEED    : INTEGER;(* PARAMETER FOR RNG   *)
        CNTR    : INTEGER;(* POS. IN RNG SEQ.    *)
        KVALUES : ARRAY[0..K] OF INTEGER;

(*********************************************)
FUNCTION EXPON ( PARM : REAL ) : REAL;
    BEGIN
    ADDRNG ( SEED, PROB );
    EXPON := PARM * LN ( PROB )
END;  (* EXPON *)

(*********************************************)
BEGIN (* MAIN *)
    (* INITIALIZE VARIABLES *)
    CLOCK   := 0;
    SEED    := 3;
    LIMIT   := 100;
```

```
(* INITIALIZE STATISTICS*)
TOTARRV := 0;
AVGDELAY:= 0.0;
AVGCUSTS:= 0.0;
BUSY    := 0.0;


(* READ IN THE CONTROL VARIABLES *)
WRITELN (' PLEASE ENTER THE AVG SERVICE TIME ');
READLN ( SERVTIME );

WRITELN (' PLEASE ENTER THE AVG ARRIVAL RATE ');
READLN ( ARRVRATE );


WRITELN (' THANK YOU ');

(* CONVERT RATES TO NEGATIVE AVERAGE TIMES *)
SERVPARM := - SERVTIME;
ARRVPARM := - 1.0 / ARRVRATE;

(* INITIALIZE SEQUENCE OF RANDOM NUMBERS *)
FOR CNTR := 0 TO K DO
   BEGIN
      RNG(SEED);
      KVALUES[CNTR] := SEED;
   END;
CNTR := 0;


(* PRINT HEADER FOR OUTPUT *)
WRITELN('   MM1 SIMULATION ');
WRITELN;WRITELN;
WRITELN;

CUST := 0;  (* STARTING STATE *)

NEXTARR := EXPON ( ARRVPARM ) + CLOCK;
IF ( CUST AROUND > 0 )
   THEN NEXTDEP := EXPON ( SERVPARM ) + CLOCK
   ELSE NEXTDEP := INFINITY;

FOR EVENT := 1 TO LIMIT DO
   BEGIN (* EVENT LOOP *)

   IF ( NEXTARR < NEXTDEP )
      THEN ETIME := NEXTARR - CLOCK
      ELSE ETIME := NEXTDEP - CLOCK;
```

```
      (* UPDATE STATISTICS *)
      AVGCUSTS := CUST * ETIME + AVGCUSTS;
      AVGDELAY:= CUST * ETIME + AVGDELAY;
      IF ( CUST AROUND > O ) THEN BUSY := ETIME + BUSY;

      (* UPDATE CLOCK *)
   CLOCK := CLOCK + ETIME;

   (* SELECT NEXT EVENT *)
   IF ( NEXTARR < NEXTDEP )

     THEN BEGIN  (* AN ARRIVAL *)
        TOTARRV := TOTARRV + 1;
        CUST := CUST + 1;
        IF ( CUST = 1 )
         THEN NEXTDEP := EXPON ( SERVPARM ) + CLOCK;
        NEXTARR := EXPON ( ARRVPARM ) + CLOCK;
        END

     ELSE BEGIN  (* A DEPARTURE *)
        CUST := CUST - 1;
        IF ( CUST > O )
         THEN NEXTDEP := EXPON ( SERVPARM ) + CLOCK;
         ELSE NEXTDEP := INFINITY;
        END;

   (* DEBUG OUTPUT *)
   WRITELN (EVENT :5, CUST :8, ETIME : 18 : 3);

END;  (* EVENT LOOP *)

(* COMPUTE STATISTICS *)

AVGCUSTS := AVGCUSTS / CLOCK;
AVGDELAY := AVGDELAY/ TOTARRV;
UTIL := BUSY / CLOCK;

(* OUTPUT RESULTS *)
WRITELN;
WRITELN ( ' TOTAL TIME WITH TOTAL ARRIVALS');
WRITELN ( CLOCK:10:3, TOTARRV:16);
WRITELN;
WRITELN ( ' AVERAGE ARRIVAL RATE ' );
WRITELN ( ' EXPECTED       ACTUAL ' );
WRITELN ( ARRRATE:10:3, TOTARRV/CLOCK:12:3);
WRITELN ( ' AVERAGE SERVICE TIME ' );
```

```
WRITELN ( ' EXPECTED        ACTUAL ' );
WRITELN ( SERVTIME:10:3, BUSY/TOTARRV:12:3);
WRITELN ( ' AVG NUM OF QUEUED CUSTOMERS' );
WRITELN ( AVGCUSTS:10:3 );
WRITELN ( ' AVG TIME IN SYSTEM FOR A CUSTOMER' );
WRITELN ( AVGDELAY:10:3 );
WRITELN ( ' SYSTEM UTILITY ' );
WRITELN ( UTIL:9:4 );
WRITELN;

END.  (* MAIN *)
```

6.9 Problems

6.1 Compare the efficiency of two separate $M/M/1$ queues each with arrivals at a rate $\lambda/2$ and service rates of μ and a single $M/M/1$ queue with combined arrivals at a rate λ and service at a rate 2μ.

6.2 For the $M/M/m$ queue find the following.
  a. π_k
  b. N
  c. ρ

6.3 For the $M/M/m/L/M$ queue where $M > L$, find the following.
  a. π_k
  b. N
  c. ρ

6.4 For an $M/M/1$ queue with arrivals at a rate λ per second and service at a rate μ per second, what is the probability that a customer must wait for more than 2 seconds of time?

6.5 In many cases, arrivals can view the state of the queue and join only if they think it is short enough. We can model this by using a state-dependent arrival rate, $\lambda_k = \lambda/(1 + k)$, which will decrease with the increasing size of the queue. For this model, which is know as the discouraged arrivals model, find the following quantities.
  a. π_k
  b. N
  c. ρ

6.6 For a queue with exponential service times with parameter μ and a Poisson arrival process with parameter λ, but whose arrivals contain precisely n

customers, find the following. (This is an example of an M/M/1 queue with bulk arrivals.)

a. π_k
b. N
c. ρ

6.7 For a queue with a Poisson arrival process with an average interarrival time of $1/\lambda$ and a two-stage Erlangian service process with an average service time of $1/\mu$, find the following.

a. π_k
b. $E[K]$
c. ρ

6.8 For a single server queue with Poisson arrivals at a rate λ and a service time whose probability density function has the following transform, find the average number of customers in the system.

$$B^*(s) = \frac{\mu}{2\mu + s} + \frac{\mu/2}{\mu + s}$$

6.9 For a single server queue with Poisson arrivals at a rate λ and a service time whose probability density function has the following transform, find the average number of customers in the system.

$$B^*(s) = \left(\frac{8\mu/3}{4\mu + s} + \frac{\mu/3}{\mu + s}\right)\frac{2\mu}{2\mu + s}$$

6.10 Not all systems have a Poisson arrival process. A useful model is the r-stage Erlangian arrival queue with exponential service. The solution follows the same method as the r-stage Erlangian service queue. Solve the $E_r/M/1$ model for, $\Pi^*(z)$, the z-transform of the probability of finding k stages of work in the system.

6.11 Model the check-in counter at an airport as a nonpreemptive priority M/M/1 queue. First-class passengers arrive at a rate of three customers per hour and the service takes 10 minutes on the average. There are, in general, more second-class passengers, who arrive at a rate of six per hour, but they are treated with only minimum attention, so the service takes only 3 minutes.

1. What fraction of time is the server busy? busy with first-class? busy with second-class?
2. How long do first-class customers stay in the system (queue and service)?
3. How long do second-class customers stay in the system (queue and service)?

4. On the average, how many customers of each type are there in the system (queue and service)?

6.12 Modify the simulation program for the $M/M/1$ queue to model the $M/M/m$ queue. Note that the departure rate is now state-dependent, so you may consider the ideas given in the previous Markov simulation program.

6.13 Write a simulation program to model the $E_r/E_q/1$ queue. Structure your input to take a mean and variance for the arrival and service processes.

Networks of Queues

7

7.1 Introduction

In Chapter 6 we studied how a restricted Markov model could be used to model a single queue. We extended that idea to model more complicated processing systems (multiple servers, multiple stages of service, etc.) by changing the definition of the state of the Markov model. However, many processing systems are characterized by a series of stations, each with its own queue and servers. A customer will wait in a queue for some service at station 1, and after completing service at that station will proceed to station 2, where the customer may again queue for service. We may model such a system as a network of queues as shown in Figure 7.1.

In this chapter we study models and solution techniques based on multiple queues where the outputs of one queue may become the input to another queue (i.e., a network). These models represent the most widely used model for computer system performance analysis. We will show that the problem of finding solutions to such models is hard in general, but for a large subclass of queues, exact solutions are still obtainable using numerical techniques.

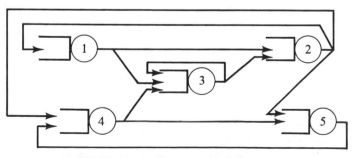

FIGURE 7.1 A Network of Queues

There are two basic types of queuing networks distinguished by the topology of network. If a system has no potential for arrivals from the outside and correspondingly, does not allow customers to leave, we say that the system is *closed*. If arrivals and departures are allowed, the system is called *open*. Clearly, the number of customers in a closed system is fixed, while the number of customers in an open system can be any value from zero to infinity. The example shown in Figure 7.1 is a closed queuing network.

7.2 The Routing Chain

Since we are now using a network of queues as a model, we must specify how customers determine the next queue they will visit when they have completed service at a particular queue. For all of the models described in this book, we assume that the selection is random and based on a discrete probability density function. We define these probabilities, p_{ij}, as the probability of a customer going from queue i to queue j. The probability measure gives a great deal of control on how the customers move about the network. For example, we can force a customer to follow a certain path, say from queue 1 to queue 2 to queue 3 and back to queue 1, by setting p_{12}, p_{23}, and p_{31} equal to 1.

For the complete network of M queues, these probabilities can be viewed as an $M \times M$ matrix $\mathbf{P} \triangleq [p_{ij}]$. Since a customer cannot disappear after leaving a queue, the rows of this matrix must sum to 1 (i.e., the matrix is stochastic), just as rows of the matrix describing a discrete time Markov chain. In fact, if you ignore the amount of time spent in each queue and simply assign a unit step to visiting a queue, we see that the movement of a customer is similar to the change of state in a Markov chain. Therefore, this description of the routing of customers in the network of queues is often called a *routing chain*. (We will return to this concept when we introduce multiple class systems).

Example 7.1: As an example, consider the closed network of queues that is shown in Figure 7.1. (For convenience, we will assume an equal split between alternative destinations.)

$$\mathbf{P} = \begin{bmatrix} 0 & 1/2 & 1/2 & 0 & 0 \\ 1/3 & 0 & 0 & 1/3 & 1/3 \\ 0 & 1/2 & 1/2 & 0 & 0 \\ 0 & 0 & 1/2 & 0 & 1/2 \\ 0 & 0 & 0 & 1 & 0 \end{bmatrix}$$

In an open network model, arrivals to a queue in the network may occur from the outside world and departures may leave the network. These models are called open queuing network models, since the network is "open" to arrivals from the outside. The number of customers in such a system is then unbounded and can be any possible combination of customers in each of the queues.

In general, we can have Poisson arrivals from the outside to any of the queues in the network. Similarly, we can have departures from any of the queues in the system that leave the system entirely. Recall the fact that Poisson arrivals are still Poisson when they are merged and still Poisson if they are split by random selection. We can take advantage of that fact to simplify our notation for open networks.

We will model the Poisson arrivals to each queue as a single Poisson process split into the specified individual processes. So if we have a specified arrival process of 5 customers per hour to queue 1, 3 customers per hour to queue 4, and 2 customers per hour to queue 5, we can model that as a single process with arrivals at 10 customers per hour with a probability of 0.5 of proceeding to queue 1, 0.3 of proceeding to queue 4, and 0.2 of proceeding to queue 5.

Example 7.2: To construct the matrix describing the routing chain in the network, it is convenient to represent the outside world as a special queue (usually numbered 0). This simply adds one row and one column to the matrix. Using this idea, we can construct the matrix for the open network shown in Figure 7.2 to get the following matrix.

$$\mathbf{P} = \begin{bmatrix} 0 & 1/2 & 0 & 0 & 3/10 & 1/5 \\ 0 & 0 & 1/2 & 1/2 & 0 & 0 \\ 1 & 0 & 0 & 0 & 0 & 0 \\ 0 & 0 & 1/2 & 0 & 0 & 1/2 \\ 0 & 0 & 0 & 1/2 & 1/2 & 0 \\ 1 & 0 & 0 & 0 & 0 & 0 \end{bmatrix}$$

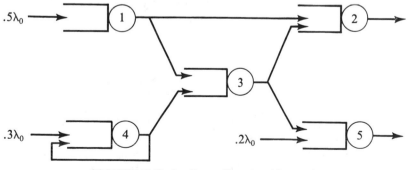

FIGURE 7.2 An Open Queuing Network

Exercise

7.1 Construct the routing matrix for the following closed network of queues. Note that the arc weights are probabilities.

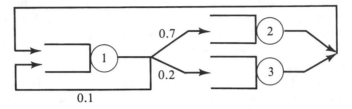

7.3 **Using the Routing Chain**

There are several things that can be computed from the routing chain. All of them incorporate the same basic information about the queuing network.

7.3.1 Relative Throughputs

If we consider the throughput (rate of customers passing through each queue), we can note that if the throughput of some queue i is λ_i, the rate of arrivals to another queue, j, from queue i is simply $\lambda_i \cdot p_{ij}$. Therefore, if the system does have a steady-state behavior, the throughputs for the queues λ must satisfy $\lambda \mathbf{P} = \lambda$.

Unfortunately, that equation is not sufficient to determine the throughputs since each row in the matrix $\mathbf{P}$ is dependent on the other $M - 1$ rows (or M rows in the case of an open network). So the equation $\lambda \mathbf{P} = \lambda$ can only be solved to within a multiplicative constant as in the case of the steady-state probabilities for the discrete time Markov chain. Since the throughputs do not have a simple normalization equation as the probabilities did for the steady-state solution to the discrete time Markov chain, we can find only *relative* throughputs r_i from that matrix equation. We often pick one queue and simply set the relative throughput for that queue to 1. This an artificial way of normalizing the relative throughputs.

Example 7.3: As an example, let us solve for the relative throughputs from the closed network example in Figure 7.1.

$$[r_1, r_2, r_3, r_4, r_5] \begin{bmatrix} 0 & 1/2 & 1/2 & 0 & 0 \\ 1/3 & 0 & 0 & 1/3 & 1/3 \\ 0 & 1/2 & 1/2 & 0 & 0 \\ 0 & 0 & 1/2 & 0 & 1/2 \\ 0 & 0 & 0 & 1 & 0 \end{bmatrix} = [r_1, r_2, r_3, r_4, r_5]$$

Which is equivalent to the following set of simultaneous equations.

$$\frac{1}{3} r_2 = r_1$$

$$\frac{1}{2} r_1 + \frac{1}{2} r_3 = r_2$$

$$\frac{1}{2} r_1 + \frac{1}{2} r_3 + \frac{1}{2} r_4 = r_3$$

$$\frac{1}{3} r_2 + r_5 = r_4$$

$$\frac{1}{3} r_2 + \frac{1}{2} r_4 = r_5$$

These equations can be solved for the throughput of each queue in terms of the throughput of queue 1.

$$r_2 = 3r_1$$
$$r_3 = 5r_1$$
$$r_4 = 4r_1$$
$$r_5 = 3r_1$$

So we can write down the throughput for the queuing network to within a multiplicative constant.

$$\lambda = (\alpha,\ 3\alpha,\ 5\alpha,\ 4\alpha,\ 3\alpha)$$

In the case of an open queuing network, where one of the throughputs is given as part of the problem specification, the multiplicative constant is known. Since the arrival rate from the outside world is given, we know one of the values a priori (i.e., λ_0). That knowledge gives us the normalization value so that we can solve $\lambda P = \lambda$ directly for the actual throughputs.

Example 7.4:

$$P = \begin{bmatrix} 0 & 1/2 & 0 & 0 & 3/10 & 1/5 \\ 0 & 0 & 1/2 & 1/2 & 0 & 0 \\ 1 & 0 & 0 & 0 & 0 & 0 \\ 0 & 0 & 1/2 & 0 & 0 & 1/2 \\ 0 & 0 & 0 & 1/2 & 1/2 & 0 \\ 1 & 0 & 0 & 0 & 0 & 0 \end{bmatrix}$$

This matrix equation is equivalent to the following simultaneous equations.

$$\frac{1}{2} \lambda_0 = \lambda_1$$

$$\frac{1}{2} \lambda_1 + \frac{1}{2} \lambda_3 = \lambda_2$$

$$\frac{1}{2} \lambda_1 + \frac{1}{2} \lambda_4 = \lambda_3$$

$$\frac{3}{10} \lambda_0 + \frac{1}{2} \lambda_4 = \lambda_4$$

$$\frac{1}{5} \lambda_0 + \frac{1}{2} \lambda_3 = \lambda_5$$

These can be solved for the throughputs of each queue in terms of the input rate λ_0 for the outside world.

$$\lambda = (0.5\lambda_0, 0.525\lambda_0, 0.55\lambda_0, 0.6\lambda_0, 0.475\lambda_0)$$

Exercise

7.2 Compute the relative throughputs for the closed network given in Exercise 7.1 normalized with respect to queue 1.

7.3.2 Visit Ratios

Another way of expressing the information about the routing chain is called the *visit ratio*. The visit ratio, V_i, of a queue, i, is simply the average number of times a queue is visited for each visit to a reference queue (usually, queue 1). This is precisely the same idea as picking a queue to normalize the relative throughputs. It has the advantage of being explicitly defined as a relative concept and has a more intuitive interpretation. Since the visit ratios are expressly relative, they are the same for the actual throughputs as well.

$$V_i \overset{\Delta}{=} \frac{\lambda_i}{\lambda_1} = \frac{r_i}{r_1} \tag{7.1}$$

where λ is the vector of the actual throughputs of each queue and r is any solution to the matrix equation $rP = r$. So the visit ratios are simply the solutions to the matrix problem $VP = V$, where $V_1 \overset{\Delta}{=} 1$.

Example 7.5: The visit ratios for the queuing network shown in Figure 7.1 are
$$V_1 = 1, \ V_2 = 3, \ V_3 = 5, \ V_4 = 4, \ \text{and} \ V_5 = 3.$$

7.3.3 Relative Utilities

We can also combine the information about the routing chain along with the information about the average service time for a queue. Recall that the utilization of a single server queue is defined as the product of the average throughput times the average service time. So if we replace the relative throughputs r_i with the product of the relative utilizations u_i times the average service rate μ_i, we can compute the relative utilizations.

$$\sum_{i=1}^{M} \mu_i u_i p_{ij} = \mu_j u_j \qquad \forall_j, \, 1 \leq j \leq M \tag{7.2}$$

which is the same as the matrix equation $(\mu \cdot \mathbf{u}) \, \mathbf{P} = (\mu \cdot \mathbf{u})$. Again, for closed systems, this set of equations can only be solved to within a scalar constant. In practice some queue is selected, and its relative utilization is set to 1. This does not mean that the queue is saturated, since other relative utilizations may be even greater than 1. It is simply picking some queue to normalize the relative utilizations.

7.4 The M ⇒ M Property

Before we begin a detailed study of the algorithms used to solve such systems we will begin by characterizing the problem itself. Recall that we always assumed some particular, well-behaved stochastic process (Poisson or Erlangian) completely described the input process to the queue. In a queuing network, the input process is often a merging of the output processes of other queues. So we begin our characterization by looking at the output process of a single queue.

The output process of a queue is just another stochastic process. The output process will depend, of course, on the input process, the queuing discipline, and the service process. So when we study the output process of a queue (i.e., a particular service process and queuing discipline) we must assume a particular input process. If we assume that the input process to a queue is Poisson and determine that the output process is again Poisson, we say that the queue has the M ⇒ M property.

Since the queue will delay arrivals, it will clearly change the timing and possibly the order of the arrivals. Therefore, the output process is not the same process as the input process. However, if the input process to a queue having the M ⇒ M property is Poisson, the output process will be another Poisson process with the same parameter.

7.4.1 The FCFS M/M/1 Queue

The first queue we studied was the single server queue with Poisson arrivals and exponential service. To find out if the M/M/1 queue has the M $\Rightarrow$ M property, let us derive the probability density function $d(t)$ of the interdeparture time for the output process. We begin by decomposing the problem into two cases. First, if the queue is busy, the departure of a customer will be the next service completion. Second, if the queue is idle, the departure of a customer will occur at the time of the service completion of the next arrival.

In Figure 7.3, customer 1 departs with an interdeparture time d_1 equal to x_1 the service time for customer 1, since the system is busy. Customer 3 departs with an interdeparture time d_3 equal to the residual lifetime of its arrival, r_3, plus its service time, x_3, since the system was idle.

For the M/M/1 queue, the interarrival times of all arrivals are identically distributed with an exponential probability density function. In addition, all service times are also identically distributed with an exponential probability density function. Therefore, we can write down the Laplace transform of the interdeparture times $D^*(s)$ in the case that the system is busy. It is simply the transform of the service time probability density function.

$$D^*(s \mid \text{busy}) = \frac{\mu}{\mu + s} \qquad (7.3)$$

In the case of the system being idle, the interdeparture time is the sum of the residual lifetime, r, of the interarrival time and the service time, x. Since the interarrival distribution is exponential, the residual lifetime distribution is simply the original exponential distribution. In addition, since those random variables are independent, we can use the convolution theorem to write down the transform of the interdeparture time for the case when the system is idle.

$$D^*(s \mid \text{idle}) = \frac{\mu}{\mu + s} \cdot \frac{\lambda}{\lambda + s} \qquad (7.4)$$

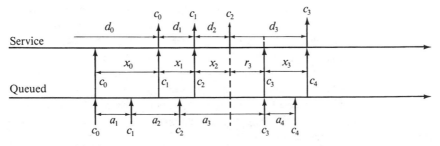

FIGURE 7.3 A Timing Diagram of the M/M/1 Queue

We can remove the conditioning by noting that the probability of the queue being busy is simply ρ.

$$D^*(s) = \rho \frac{\mu}{\mu + s} + (1 - \rho)\left[\frac{\mu}{\mu + s} \cdot \frac{\lambda}{\lambda + s}\right] \qquad (7.5)$$

Since ρ is simply λ/μ for the M/M/1 queue, we can reduce the equation for the transform.

$$\begin{aligned}
D^*(s) &= \frac{\lambda}{\mu + s} + (\mu - \lambda) \cdot \frac{\lambda}{(\lambda + s)(\mu + s)} \\
&= \frac{\lambda^2 + \lambda s + \lambda \mu - \lambda^2}{(\lambda + s)(\mu + s)} \\
&= \frac{\lambda}{\lambda + s} \qquad (7.6)
\end{aligned}$$

So we find that the interdeparture time for the output process is also exponentially distributed with precisely the same parameter as the input process. Therefore, the M/M/1 queue does have the M ⇒ M property.

7.4.2 Checking for the M ⇒ M Property

We saw that the M/M/1 queue had the M ⇒ M property, but we had to derive the output process completely to determine that fact. However, we need not completely derive the output process for a queue to check to see if the queue has the M ⇒ M property.

Consider what is needed for the M ⇒ M property to hold. Since the departure process is state dependent, we need to consider the rate of departures R for all possible states of the queue, times the steady-state probabilities π for each of those states. (Since there is no distinction between customers, the state of the queue can be denoted by n the number of customers in the queue and service.) Finally, since there can be no memory in the output process, departure rates from one state which are higher than the input rate cannot be compensated for by lower departure rates in another state. In other words, the departure rates must balance the input rates for each transition pair if the M ⇒ M property is going to hold.

$$\frac{\pi_{n+1}R(n + 1 \to n)}{\pi_n} = \lambda \qquad \forall_n \qquad (7.7)$$

So the check for the M ⇒ M property amounts to a check to see if the steady-state solution for the queue is in the birth-death form. Clearly we do not want to solve for the steady-state probabilities of each queue to check to see if it satisfies the M ⇒ M property. Therefore, to check to see if a queue has the

$M \Rightarrow M$ property that we assume it does, use the criterion above to get a relationship on the steady-state probabilities and substitute that back into the state balance equations for that queue to see if the solution derived from the $M \Rightarrow M$ property requirement is the steady-state solution for the queue.

Example 7.6: As an example, let us show that the infinite server queue with exponential service $(M/M/\infty)$ also has the $M \Rightarrow M$ property. We begin by assuming that the queue does have the $M \Rightarrow M$ property.

$$R(n + 1 \rightarrow n) = (n + 1)\mu$$

$$\frac{\pi_{n+1}(n + 1)\mu}{\pi_n} = \lambda$$

$$\pi_{n+1} = \frac{\lambda}{(n + 1)\mu} \pi_n$$

Since this must be true for all states, $0 \leq n \leq \infty$ if the $M \Rightarrow M$ property holds, we can solve this recursively to obtain a possible solution.

$$\pi_n = \left(\frac{\lambda}{\mu}\right)^n \frac{1}{n!} \pi_0$$

However, this may not actually be a valid solution. To check the validity of this expression we need to see if it satisfies the state balance equation.

$$(\lambda + n\mu)\pi_n = (n + 1)\mu\pi_{n+1} + \lambda\pi_{n-1}$$

Substituting the potential solution into the state balance equation for the $M/M/\infty$ queue, we see that it indeed is the solution for the steady-state behavior of the queue.

$$(\lambda + n\mu)\left(\frac{\lambda}{\mu}\right)^n \frac{1}{n!} \pi_0 = (n + 1)\mu \left(\frac{\lambda}{\mu}\right)^{n+1} \frac{1}{(n + 1)!} \pi_0$$

$$+ \lambda \left(\frac{\lambda}{\mu}\right)^{n-1} \frac{1}{(n - 1)!} \pi_0$$

$$= \lambda \left(\frac{\lambda}{\mu}\right)^n \frac{1}{n!} \pi_0 + n\mu \left(\frac{\lambda}{\mu}\right)^n \frac{1}{n!} \pi_0$$

$$= (\lambda + n\mu)\left(\frac{\lambda}{\mu}\right)^n \frac{1}{n!} \pi_0$$

So far we have considered only exponential service distributions. However, it is possible to expand the state description to include stages, both parallel and serial, to consider more complex service distributions. Any distribution that has a rational Laplace transform falls into this class of distributions, called *phase* or *Coxian-* type distributions, after the researcher who first developed the class. As you can see in the M ⇒ M property check, only the proper correspondence of states and rates was checked, so an expanded state space can be used to evaluate queues with nonexponential service times. There are many such queues that have the M ⇒ M property, including some that have the more general Coxian-type distribution for the service time.

7.4.3 Feedforward versus Feedback

We now know that there are queues that preserve the Poisson nature of their inputs. One such queue was the M/M/1 queue. So if the inputs of a M/M/1 queue are the outputs of another M/M/1 whose inputs are Poisson, then we can solve the system. Since a M/M/1 queue has the M ⇒ M property, a network of such queues could be solved by solving for the distribution of each queue independently as long as the network is only feedforward. Unfortunately, if feedback occurs, we violate one of our assumptions.

If there is feedback, we can no long assume that the input to the queue is Poisson. Although it is true that merging independent Poisson processes results in a Poisson process, if we allow feedback, the input process is no longer Poisson. To illustrate, consider the simplest feedback system in Figure 7.4.

To understand that the two processes feeding the queue (the Poisson process from the outside world and the feedback process) result in a non-Poisson process, consider the residual lifetime of an arrival. If the input process was Poisson, it would be memoryless, but clearly the input process will depend on the state of the queue because of the feedback. The state of the queue has memory of the most recent arrivals, so the feedback process has memory of the previous arrivals. Therefore, it cannot be Poisson. (It is, in fact, hyperexponential.) The distribution of time between arrivals will have a wide variance, depending on whether or not the queue empties (turning off the feedback) in between arrivals.

This is more clearly seen when you assume that the probability of returning to the queue is close to 1 and therefore (to maintain ergodicity) the service rate is much larger than the arrival rate. As the system runs, the input process is dominated by the feedback (looking much like the service process) until the queue empties, at which point the input process is simply the slow, outside arrival process.

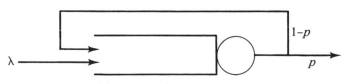

FIGURE 7.4 A Queue with Feedback

7.5 Local Balance

By now, the complexity of an arbitrary network of queues should be clearly understood. So far, we have concentrated on individual queues and the way the outputs of one queue will become the input to another queue. Now let us view the state of the network in its entirety. We can define the state of the system as the collection of the states of each of the individual queues in the system.

If we restrict ourselves to service centers with exponential service times, it is true that the entire system is still Markovian. In fact, even if we allow more arbitrary service distributions, as long as the Laplace transform is rational, we can use a state space expansion similar to our method of stages to show that the system is still Markovian with this expanded state space. However, finding a solution to such a large complex problem, even a Markovian one, is not tractable.

In a well known 1963 study, James Jackson constructed models of systems called job shops using a network of M/M/m queues, and studied the corresponding Markov system. In a surprising result, Jackson noted that even though the input processes to these queues were not Poisson, the steady-state probability density function for the entire Markov system was the product of the steady-state probability density functions for the individual queues. More formally, the joint probability density of the number of customers in each queue in the network in steady-state is the product of the marginal probability density functions. Therefore, even though the arrival processes are not Poisson, the random variables for the number of customers in each queue in steady-state are independent. This result, later known as *Jackson's theorem*, paved the way to our understanding of exactly why this product form should exist. This result meant that even large networks of such queues could be solved simply by multiplying the results for each queue together. (Closed queuing networks, studied by Gordon and Newell, will require a conditioning step that can be computationally expensive.)

This class of systems, of which the network of M/M/m queues is an example, is the class of systems that satisfy a property called "local balance." This property immediately gives rise to the product form of the solution and guarantees a tractable solution methodology. To understand local balance properly, let us consider a small example network in some detail. Consider a cyclic network of three queues with only two customers circulating with service rates of μ_1, μ_2, and μ_3, respectively.

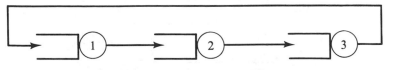

FIGURE 7.5 A Cyclic Network of Queues

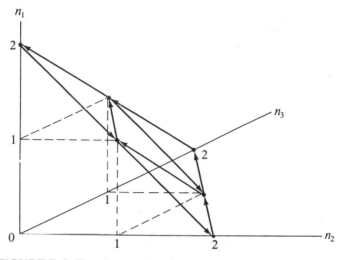

FIGURE 7.6 The Three-Dimensional State Transition Diagram

The state space for the system contains six different states, depending on precisely which queue (1, 2, or 3) each of the two customers is located. We note that not all transitions are possible since an increase in the number of customers at queue 3 (an arrival) requires a departure from queue 2, which is possible only if queue 2 is nonempty. Figure 7.6 shows the complex state transition diagram in 3-space, where each state is denoted by a point in space.

Since this is a closed system, the sum of the customers in all of the queues must be the same for all states. That restriction reduces the degrees of freedom in the system so that the actual state space is of dimension 2 rather than the full 3. So the legal states and state transitions all lie in one plane. We can therefore draw the state transition diagram in 2-space using the state coordinates (a triple n_1, n_2, n_3, where n_i is the number of customers in queue i) to denote the proper state information.

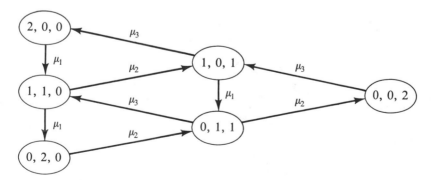

FIGURE 7.7 The Two-Dimensional State Transition Diagram

We know that any steady-state solution to this Markov chain must satisfy balance (i.e., the rate of change of probability of leaving each state must balance the rate of change of probability of entering it from all other states). We will call this requirement global balance. It is simply the equivalent of the matrix equation $\pi Q = 0$ for the entire system. Global balance is simply a requirement of the system being Markovian and having a steady-state solution. The following equations are the global balance equations equivalent to $\pi Q = 0$ for this example.

$$\mu_1 \pi_{2,0,0} = \mu_3 \pi_{1,0,1}$$
$$(\mu_1 + \mu_2)\pi_{1,1,0} = \mu_1 \pi_{2,0,0} + \mu_3 \pi_{0,1,1}$$
$$(\mu_1 + \mu_3)\pi_{1,0,1} = \mu_2 \pi_{1,1,0} + \mu_3 \pi_{0,0,2}$$
$$(\mu_2 + \mu_3)\pi_{0,1,1} = \mu_1 \pi_{1,0,1} + \mu_2 \pi_{0,2,0}$$
$$\mu_2 \pi_{0,2,0} = \mu_1 \pi_{1,1,0}$$
$$u_3 \pi_{0,0,2} = \mu_2 \pi_{0,1,1}$$

Consider the same diagram with all the transitions paired together. Each pair is marked with a bar across them. If we had balance across these pairs of transitions, we would have to have balance with all of the states. Note that this is a stronger requirement than simple global balance since states like (0,1,1) have two transitions in and two transitions out, which could balance as a group but not as pairs. If we do have this balance in subsets of transitions, we have what is termed "local balance."

The set of pairs shown in Figure 7.8 is not the only set of pairs that would determine local balance. We could just as easily have picked a different set of pairs as long as the pairs completely isolate the states. Another set of local balance pairs is shown in Figure 7.9. It is not necessary to select all the possible pairs since balance of one set implies balance holds for the other set. Balance

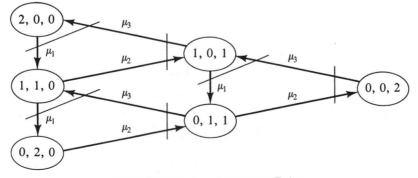

FIGURE 7.8 Local Balance Pairs

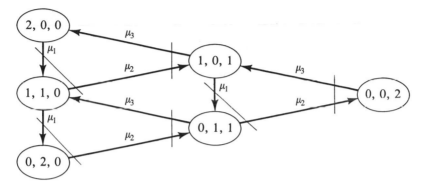

FIGURE 7.9 Different Local Balance Pairs

across any set of transition pairs will guarantee global balance as long as the pairs isolate all the states.

One way to determine whether or not a system satisfies local balance is to assume that it does, solve for a steady-state using local balance equations (it is much easier), and then check to see if that solution satisfies global balance. Since, if a steady solution exists, it is a unique solution to the global balance equation, the solution obtained by the local balance equations is the solution if it satisfies global balance. To illustrate this, consider the current system with three queues and two customers. The local balance equations are given below (they correspond to the pairing of transitions shown in the Figure 7.8).

$$\mu_1 \pi_{2,0,0} = \mu_3 \pi_{1,0,1}$$
$$\mu_1 \pi_{1,0,1} = \mu_3 \pi_{0,0,2}$$
$$\mu_1 \pi_{1,1,0} = \mu_3 \pi_{0,1,1}$$
$$\mu_3 \pi_{0,1,1} = \mu_2 \pi_{0,2,0}$$
$$\mu_3 \pi_{1,0,1} = \mu_2 \pi_{1,1,0}$$
$$\mu_3 \pi_{0,0,2} = \mu_2 \pi_{0,1,1}$$

These equations can then be solved (in a method similar to the solution technique for the birth-death systems) to give a possible steady-state solution.

$$\pi_{1,0,1} = \frac{\mu_1}{\mu_3} \pi_{2,0,0}$$

$$\pi_{0,0,2} = \frac{\mu_1^2}{\mu_3^2} \pi_{2,0,0}$$

$$\pi_{1,1,0} = \frac{\mu_1}{\mu_2} \pi_{2,0,0}$$

$$\pi_{0,1,1} = \frac{\mu_1^2}{\mu_2 \mu_3} \pi_{2,0,0}$$

$$\pi_{0,2,0} = \frac{\mu_1^2}{\mu_2^2} \pi_{2,0,0}$$

$$\pi_{2,0,0} = \left[1 + \frac{\mu_1}{\mu_3} + \frac{\mu_1}{\mu_2} + \frac{\mu_1^2}{\mu_2 \mu_3} + \frac{\mu_1^2}{\mu_3^2} + \frac{\mu_1^2}{\mu_2^2} \right]^{-1}$$

$$\pi_{2,0,0} = \frac{\dfrac{1}{\mu_1^2}}{\dfrac{1}{\mu_1^2} + \dfrac{1}{\mu_1 \mu_3} + \dfrac{1}{\mu_1 \mu_2} + \dfrac{1}{\mu_2 \mu_3} + \dfrac{1}{\mu_2^2} + \dfrac{1}{\mu_3^2}}$$

To simplify the notation we replace the denominator with a constant. Clearly, this denominator, although constant for this problem would depend on the number of customers circulating within the network of queues, so we will denote it as $G(2)$.

$$G(2) \triangleq \frac{1}{\mu_1^2} + \frac{1}{\mu_1 \mu_3} + \frac{1}{\mu_1 \mu_2} + \frac{1}{\mu_2 \mu_3} + \frac{1}{\mu_2^2} + \frac{1}{\mu_3^2}$$

Using that notation for the denominator we can back-substitute into the previous equations to get all of the steady-state probabilities in terms of the constants μ_1, μ_2, and μ_3.

$$\pi_{2,0,0} = \left(\frac{1}{\mu_1} \right)^2 G^{-1}(2)$$

$$\pi_{1,1,0} = \left(\frac{1}{\mu_1} \right)\left(\frac{1}{\mu_2} \right) G^{-1}(2)$$

$$\pi_{1,0,1} = \left(\frac{1}{\mu_1} \right)\left(\frac{1}{\mu_3} \right) G^{-1}(2)$$

$$\pi_{0,1,1} = \left(\frac{1}{\mu_2} \right)\left(\frac{1}{\mu_3} \right) G^{-1}(2)$$

$$\pi_{0,2,0} = \left(\frac{1}{\mu_2} \right)^2 G^{-1}(2)$$

$$\pi_{0,0,2} = \left(\frac{1}{\mu_3} \right)^2 G^{-1}(2)$$

We can combine these solutions into one notation by noting that anything raised to the zero power is equal to 1. In addition, we note that the solution is restricted to the cases where the sum of the number of customers in each queue is equal to 2.

$$\pi^{n_1, n_2, n_3} = \left(\frac{1}{\mu_1}\right)^{n_1} \left(\frac{1}{\mu_2}\right)^{n_2} \left(\frac{1}{\mu_3}\right)^{n_3} G^{-1}(2)$$

If you substitute this solution into the global balance equations, you will find that this is the solution to the system.

7.5.1 The Product Form Solution

The fact that the solution technique for the local balance equations was similar to the solution technique for birth-death systems was not a mere coincidence. Note how we started at the state (2,0,0) and followed the pairs in each direction [toward (0,2,0) and (0,0,2)] solving recursively. Because of this, the solutions for systems that satisfy local balance will have a product form solution similar to what we found for the birth-death systems. For closed systems, not all states are possible, so the actual probabilities are conditioned on there being precisely N customers in the system. The denominator (or normalization constant) is simply the sum of the products for each possible state in the open system with that number of customers.

In general, all networks of single server queues that satisfy local balance will have steady-state solutions of the following product form.

$$\pi_{n_1, n_2, \ldots, n_M} = \frac{\rho_1^{n_1} \rho_2^{n_2} \cdots \rho_M^{n_M}}{C} \tag{7.8}$$

where ρ_m is the actual utilization of the mth queue in the network and C is the normalization constant to make π a discrete probability density function. In an open queuing network, the normalization constant will simply be the inverse of the probability of the network being empty (i.e., $1/\pi_{0,0,\ldots,0}$). In a closed queuing network, the normalization constant will be the probability that the network contains precisely N customers.

So for an open network of M/M/1 queues, we can write down the steady-state solution for the entire network as the product of the steady-state solutions for the queues in isolation with the utilizations calculated from the routing chain ($\rho_m = \lambda_m / \mu_m$).

$$\pi_{n_1 n_2, \ldots, n_M} = (1 - \rho_1)\rho_1^{n_1} \cdot (1 - \rho_2)\rho_2^{n_2} \cdot \cdots \cdot (1 - \rho_M)\rho_M^{n_M} \tag{7.9}$$

In the case of networks of queues that have multiple servers, we note that the utilization of such queues is divided by the number of servers to normalize it. If there are s_i servers in queue i and n_i customers in that queue and $n_i < s_i$, then the state probability is divided by $n_i!/s_i^{n_i}$. If $n_i \geq s_i$, the state probability is divided by $s_i!/s_i^{s_i}$. So we add a function $f_i(n_i)$ to the denominator to handle the cases where there are multiple servers in some queues in the network.

$$f_i(n_i) = \begin{cases} \dfrac{n_i!}{s_i^{n_i}} & n_i < s_i \\ \dfrac{s_i!}{s_i^{s_i}} & n_i \geq s_i \end{cases} \qquad (7.10)$$

Note that this function reduces to 1 in the single server case. We can now write down the product form solution for networks of queues that satisfy local balance, including queues with multiple servers.

$$\pi_{n_1,n_2,\ldots,n_M} = \frac{\rho_1^{n_1}\rho_2^{n_2} \cdots \rho_M^{n_M}}{f_1(n_1)f_2(n_2) \cdots f_M(n_M)C} \qquad (7.11)$$

7.5.2 Systems That Satisfy Local Balance

We now have found a shortcut for finding the steady-state behavior in a certain class of systems. However, if we must always check to see if the solution satisfies global balance, we have not gained much. However, it is possible to determine, in advance, whether a system will satisfy local balance.

In an important result Muntz showed that any network made up of queues which individually satisfy the $M \Rightarrow M$ property will satisfy local balance when connected together. So by constructing models using networks of queues that have the $M \Rightarrow M$ property, we know that the solution must be product form. From this result, it is possible to select from a large set of queues that will satisfy local balance when placed in a network. This allows the analyst simply to pick from a preselected group of queue types to construct a model that can be solved easily due to its product form. The following list includes some of the more commonly used queue types for constructing product form networks.

1. FCFS with exponentially distributed service times
2. LCFS preemptive-resume with service times having a Coxian distribution
3. Processor sharing (PS) with service times having a Coxian distribution
4. Infinite server (IS) with service times having a Coxian distribution

It is important to note that since all of these queues satisfy the $M \Rightarrow M$ property and therefore have a product form solution to the network of queues, the solution depends only on the mean values of each of the service disciplines, not on the higher moments.

7.6 Solving Open Networks

Solving for the steady-state probabilities for open queuing networks is quite straightforward. First, we solve for the throughputs and resulting utilizations for each queue. We can then substitute directly into the product form solution. Second, we can use the steady-state solution (or the marginal probability density functions for each queue) to calculate any of the performance measures we are interested in obtaining.

If we consider our example of the M/M/1 queue with feedback shown in Figure 7.4, we can calculate the throughput for the queue in terms on the arrival rate, λ, from the outside world.

$$\lambda_1 = \rho\lambda_1 + \lambda$$
$$= \frac{\lambda}{1 - p}$$

So the utilization, ρ_1, of the queue is simply λ_1/μ_1 and the probability of a random observer seeing n customers in the queue is $(1 - \rho_1)\rho_1^n$. The average number of customers in the queue and the average time spent in the queue are calculated with our usual formulas.

$$E[n] = \frac{\rho_1}{1 - \rho_1} = \frac{\lambda}{\mu(1 - p) - \lambda}$$
$$T_1 = \frac{E[n]}{\lambda_1} = \frac{1 - p}{\mu(1 - p) - \lambda}$$

If we are interested in how long a customer cycles in the system before leaving (which is different from the amount of time spent in the queue on each pass), we use Little's result on the system as seen from the outside.

$$E[n] = \frac{\rho_1}{1 - \rho_1} - \frac{\lambda}{\mu(1 - p) - \lambda}$$
$$T = \frac{E[n]}{\lambda} = \frac{1}{\mu(1 - p) - \lambda}$$

Example 7.7: As a more complete example, let us model the motor vehicle registration process at some state bureau. The basic process has four stations.

1. *Reception.* A person looks at the application and directs the applicant to one of two clerks, who specialize in different aspects of the process.
2. *Clerk 1.* A person who handles out-of-state and new licenses and special application details.
3. *Clerk 2.* A person who handles the normal applications, renewals, and the standard parts of the form.

4. *Cashier.* A person who collects the payment and issues the plates.

Unfortunately, like most bureaucracies, nothing is straight-forward. So it is often the case that after seeing either clerk 1 or clerk 2, he or she will direct you to see the other clerk. This can, in some cases, cycle for some time, to the detriment of the customer's good humor. For our example we assume some particular values have been obtained by a systems analyst who actually looked at the paperwork and the way the clerks worked.

1. Arrivals are Poisson at some rate λ. The review and routing take about 20 seconds on the average and tends to be quick but may take some time. We will model the time as exponentially distributed. The receptionist will route the customer to clerk 1 with probability 0.3 and to clerk 2 with probability 0.7.
2. Clerk 1 spends about 10 minutes asking questions and processing a portion of the application. With probability 0.2, the clerk will send the applicant to clerk 2 for further processing.
3. Clerk 2 spends about 5 minutes asking questions and processing a portion of the application. With probability 0.1, the clerk will send the applicant to clerk 1 for further processing.
4. The Cashier spends about 1 minute accepting payment, filling in the license number of the plates issued, and giving the plates, change, and receipt to the customer.

We construct an open network of queues assuming that the queues are all FCFS with exponentially distributed service times. Therefore, the model satisfies local balance and has a product form solution. We begin by solving for the actual utilizations of each of the queues in the network.

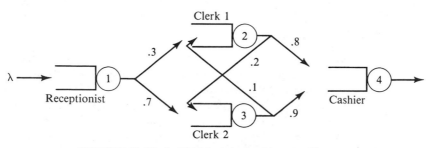

FIGURE 7.10 A QN Model of a License Bureau

Queue one represents the receptionist.

$$\lambda_1 = \lambda$$

$$\rho_1 = \frac{\lambda}{\mu_1} = 20\lambda$$

Queue two represents clerk 1 and queue three represents clerk 2.

$$\lambda_2 = 0.3\lambda + 0.1\lambda_3$$
$$\lambda_3 = 0.7\lambda + 0.2\lambda_2$$
$$\lambda_2 = 0.38\lambda \qquad \lambda_3 = 0.78\lambda$$
$$\rho_2 = 228\lambda \qquad \rho_3 = 234\lambda$$
$$\lambda_4 = 0.8\lambda_2 + 0.9\lambda_3 = \lambda$$
$$\rho_4 = 60\lambda$$

Substituting these values into the product form solution for M/M/1 queues, we obtain the joint probability density for the number of customers in each queue. Note that the input rate, λ, must be below 0.00427 customer per second (15.38 customers per hour) for the system to be ergodic since all of the utilizations must be less than 1.

$$\pi_{n_1,n_2,n_3,n_4} = (1 - 20\lambda)(20\lambda)^{n_1}(1 - 228\lambda)(228\lambda)^{n_2}(1 - 234\lambda)$$
$$\times (234\lambda)^{n_3}(1 - 60\lambda)(60\lambda)^{n_4}$$

More interesting to us are the values of several averages for the system. We can bound the average number of customers in each queue by using the bound on λ.

$$E[n_1] = \frac{20\lambda}{1 - 20\lambda} \leq 0.093$$

$$E[n_2] = \frac{228\lambda}{1 - 228\lambda} \leq 36.82$$

$$E[n_2] = \frac{234\lambda}{1 - 234\lambda} \leq \infty$$

$$E[n_4] = \frac{60\lambda}{1 - 60\lambda} \leq 0.34$$

So we see that the receptionist can never have much of a queue at all, and even the cashier can not become backed up. This is even clearer when you consider the utilizations, $\rho_1 \leq 0.0854$ and $\rho_4 \leq 0.2562$. Therefore, the receptionist is busy only a maximum of 8.5% of the time, while the cashier is busy a more normal 25.6%. To improve the system, the activities and number of individuals need to be changed to distribute the work more equitably. This would be optimal when all utilizations are the same for a given input rate.

We can apply Little's result to the entire network to get the average amount of time a customer spends in the system. Note that this is not the same as adding up the delays in each queue. Just adding up the delays in each queue would not be correct unless you weighted the delay by the average number of visits a customer makes to each queue before leaving the system. Using Little's result is simpler than multiplying each of the delays by the average number of visits.

$$T = \frac{E[n_1] + E[n_2] + E[n_3] + E[n_4]}{\lambda}$$

$$= \frac{20}{1 - 20\lambda} + \frac{228}{1 - 228\lambda} + \frac{234}{1 - 234\lambda} + \frac{60}{1 - 60\lambda}$$

We can get an estimate of how long the renewal customer will take by noting that renewals only visit clerk 2 and go directly to the cashier after filling out the paperwork. So in our model, we simply add up the individual delays in queues 1, 3, and 4 to see how long the renewals will take on the average. We can compute those delays by applying Little's result to each of the queues individually.

$$T_R = \frac{E[n_1]}{\lambda_1} + \frac{E[n_3]}{\lambda_3} + \frac{E[n_4]}{\lambda_4}$$

$$= \frac{20}{1 - 20\lambda} + \frac{300}{1 - 234\lambda} + \frac{60}{1 - 60\lambda}$$

7.7 Solving Closed Networks

At first glance, the closed network problem seems impossible to solve because we have to find the utilizations and the normalization constant. We know that solving the routing chain can only give us visit ratios or relative utilizations, so we cannot get the exact utilization directly. We also formulated the normalization constant as the sum over all possible states of the product of the actual utilizations.

This is not really a problem for the following reason. Note that we could solve the routing chain for relative utilizations which are within a scalar constant of the actual utilizations. Also note that when we calculate the normalization constant and use it to construct the steady-state probability density function, we could use those same relative utilizations. Therefore, if we use the relative utilizations instead of the actual utilizations, both the numerator and the normalization constant are off by precisely the same scalar constant so the error cancels out.

We can now reformulate our calculation of the normalization constant ignoring scalar constants (i.e., anything like α^{n_i}) in the relative utilization and the multiple server adjustment. That new normalization constant is given below.

$$G(N) = \sum_{\forall n, \sum_{i=1}^{M} n_i = N} \prod_{i=1}^{M} \frac{u_i^{n_i}}{\beta_i(n_i)} \tag{7.12}$$

where $\beta_i(n_i)$ is the function for multiple servers. If there are s_i servers at queue i, then $\beta_i(n_i)$ is defined as follows.

$$\beta_i(n_i) = \begin{cases} n_i! & n_i \leq s_i \\ s_i! s_i^{n_i - s_i} & n_i \geq s_i \end{cases} \tag{7.13}$$

Of course, for the single server case, $\beta_i(n_i)$ reduces to 1 for all n_i.

Once the normalization constant has been computed, we can get the actual utilizations, throughputs, and steady-state probabilities. The steady-state probabilities come directly from the definition, but the actual utilizations and throughputs take a little more thought.

Consider the form of the normalization constant. If we wanted to compute the probability that a queue m contained greater than n customers, we would sum over all states that had that condition. But that sum is just the same as computing the normalization constant for $N - n$ customers times u_m^n. So the probability that a queue m has n or more customers can be computed by taking the ratio of the normalization constants.

$$P[n_m \geq n] = u_m^n \frac{G(N - n)}{G(N)} \tag{7.14}$$

Now, recalling that the utilization of a single server queue is simply the probability that the queue is nonempty (i.e., $P[n_m \geq 1]$), we can immediately write down the computation for the actual utilization of queue m.

$$\rho_m = u_m \frac{G(N - 1)}{G(N)} \tag{7.15}$$

We can see that the correction factor to change the relative values used in the computation into the actual values is simply the ratio of the normalization constant for the population size, N, and the normalization constant for the population with one less customer. We can also use this ratio to get the actual throughputs of the queues from the relative throughputs.

$$\lambda_m = r_m \frac{G(N-1)}{G(N)} = u_m \mu_m \frac{G(N-1)}{G(N)} \tag{7.16}$$

Now we can also make use of the trick that computing an expected value (average) can be done but summing up discrete probabilities weighted by the value or by repeating the values in successive sums.

$$E[n] = \sum_{n=1}^{\infty} nP[n] = \sum_{n=1}^{\infty} \sum_{k=n}^{\infty} P[k] = \sum_{n=1}^{\infty} P[k \geq n]$$

$$E[n_m] = \sum_{n=1}^{N} u_m^n \frac{G(N-n)}{G(N)} \tag{7.17}$$

These calculations are very straightforward and can be completed very easily if only we had the normalization constant. We do have a way of computing the normalization constant which is just as straightforward, if not as computationally simple.

7.7.1 Convolution

The calculation of the normalization constant runs through all possible combinations of states with exactly N customers in the system. Precisely how it runs through those states does not affect the correctness of the result, but can significantly affect the algorithm. In addition, precisely how we accumulate sums of products cannot affect the correctness of the results as long as it is consistent with the distribution law. A very useful observation was made by Buzen which can significantly improve the algorithm. (Note that this does not improve the efficiency of the algorithm, but it does simplify the code and allows one calculation to prove normalization constants for all smaller populations.)

We begin by defining a partial sum that includes the terms for $n \leq N$ customers in $m \leq M$ of the queues.

$$g(n, m) = \sum_{\substack{\sum_{i=1}^{m} n_i = n}} \prod_{i=1}^{m} u_i^{n_i}$$

$$g(n, m) = (u_1^n + u_1^{n-1}u_2 + \cdots + u_1^{n-1}u_m + u_1^{n-2}u_2^2$$
$$+ \cdots + u_m^n) \tag{7.18}$$

Consider what the previous values of this partial sum look like.

$$g(n-1, m) = (u_1^{n-1} + u_1^{n-2}u_2 + \cdots + u_1^{n-2}u_m$$
$$+ u_1^{n-3}u_2^2 + \cdots + u_m^{n-1})$$

$$g(n, m - 1) = (u_1^n + u_1^{n-1}u_2 + \cdots + u_1^{n-1}u_{m-1}$$
$$+ u_1^{n-2}u_2^2 + \cdots + u_{m-1}^{n-1})$$

We can see from this that many of the terms in $g(n, m)$ are found in $g(n, m - 1)$ and the other terms divided by u_m are found in $g(n - 1, m)$. From this observation we can write down the following recurrence relationship between these partial sums.

$$g(n, m) = g(n, m - 1) + u_m g(n - 1, m) \tag{7.19}$$

Recognizing that only one state is possible for no customers circulating in any number of queues, we get a starting value for $n = 0$.

$$g(0, m) = 1 \tag{7.20}$$

Furthermore, we can see that the normalization constant for only one queue will have only one term since all the customers must reside in that queue.

$$g(n, 1) = u_1^n \tag{7.21}$$

Using the recursion equation with these starting values will give the normalization constants for the whole system.

$$G(N) = g(N, M) \tag{7.22}$$

The computation can be visualized as filling a table with the values computed from the elements one row above and one column to the left.

There are several advantages to calculating the normalization constant in this fashion. First, we note that the entire right column contains the normalization constants for 1 to N customers circulating in the network of queues. This means that once the algorithm has been run for N customers, the values for fewer

	u_1	u_2	$\cdots$	u_m	$\cdots$	u_M
0	1	1	$\cdots$	1	$\cdots$	1
1	u_1					$G(1)$
.	.			.		.
.	.			.		.
$n - 1$	u_1^{n-1}		$\cdots$	$g(n - 1, m)$	$\cdots$	$G(N - n - 1)$
n	u_1^n	$\cdots$	$g(n, m - 1)$	$g(n, m)$	$\cdots$	$G(N - n)$
.	.		.			.
.	.		.			.
N	u_1^N		$g(N, m - 1)$		$\cdots$	$G(N)$

Table 7.1

customers have also been computed. Second, since the values needed for computing the (n,m) entry are simply the $(n - 1, m)$ and $(n, m - 1)$ entries, we need only use a one-dimensional array to accumulate the intermediate values.

Example 7.8: As an example, consider a model of a small computer system. The system has two disk drives: an 8-inch floppy drive (with an average access time of 280 ms, including head load, settling, seek, and latency times) and a Winchester hard disk drive (with an average access time of 40 ms). The system processes a task for some variable amount of time (28 ms on the average). The task will then either perform some I/O (with probability 0.9) or it will complete its current required processing and return to restart execution on some new data. The ready queue is processed in a round-robin fashion with a time slice of 1 ms. Since this is small in comparison to the average amount of processing required, we approximate the round-robin by processor sharing. Both of the disk drive controllers are simple and the processing of I/O requests is FCFS. Since the duration of I/O is variable, we approximate the distribution of I/O service time by an exponential distribution.

First, we solve for the relative utilizations.

$$\frac{1}{40} u_2 = 0.7 \frac{1}{28} u_1$$

$$u_2 = u_1$$

$$\frac{1}{280} u_3 = 0.2 \frac{1}{28} u_1$$

$$u_3 = 2u_1$$

Next, we use the convolution algorithm to fill in the table.

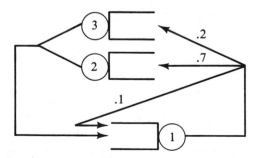

FIGURE 7.11 A QN Model of a Multitasking System

	u_1	u_2	u_3
0	1	1	1
1	1	2	4
2	1	3	11
3	1	4	26
4	1	5	57
5	1	6	120
6	1	7	247
7	1	8	502

Table 7.2

We can now write down the joint probability density function for the number of customers in each queue given the fact that there are precisely 6 customers in the network.

$$\pi_{n_1,n_2,6-n_1-n_2} = \frac{1}{247} 1^{n_1} 1^{n_2} 2^{6-n_1-n_2} = \frac{2^{6-n_1-n_2}}{247}$$

Given the values of the normalization constant in the table (we have all of the values for populations $0-7$ in the right-hand column) we can compute the various performance measures that we are interested in obtaining.

First, we can calculate the actual utilizations for the various queues.

$$\rho_1 = \rho_2 = 1 \cdot \frac{120}{247} = 0.4858 \qquad N = 6$$

$$\rho_3 = 2 \cdot \frac{120}{247} = 0.9717 \qquad N = 6$$

Next, we can calculate the actual throughputs for the various queues, in customers per second.

$$\lambda_1 = \rho_1 \cdot \mu_1 = \frac{0.4858}{0.028} = 17.35$$

$$\lambda_2 = \rho_2 \cdot \mu_2 = \frac{0.4858}{0.040} = 12.145$$

$$\lambda_3 = \rho_3 \cdot \mu_3 = \frac{0.9717}{0.280} = 3.47$$

Now we can calculate the average number of customers in each queue. Note that we are not using the M/M/1 formula for the average number in each queue. Since the system is closed, the number of customers is bounded so the assumptions in the M/M/1 derivation are violated. Therefore, we must use the normalization constant to compute the average.

$$E[n_1] = E[n_2] = \frac{1 + 4 + 11 + 26 + 57 + 120}{247} = 0.8866$$

$$E[n_3] = \frac{2^6 \cdot 1 + 2^5 \cdot 4 + 2^4 \cdot 11 + 2^3 \cdot 26}{247}$$

$$+ \frac{2^2 \cdot 57 + 2 \cdot 120}{247} = 4.2267$$

As a check, we note that $E[n_1] + E[n_2] + E[n_3] = 6$.

Finally, we can compute delays for customers in various parts of the system using Little's result.

$$T_1 = \frac{E[n_1]}{\lambda_1} = \frac{0.8866}{17.35} = 0.0511 \text{ second}$$

$$T_2 = \frac{E[n_2]}{\lambda_2} = \frac{0.8866}{12.145} = 0.073 \text{ second}$$

$$T_3 = \frac{E[n_3]}{\lambda_3} = \frac{4.2267}{3.47} = 1.218 \text{ second}$$

Exercises

7.3 What is the utilization of queue 1 in Example 7.8 for a population of $N = 4$?

7.4 What is the utilization of queue 3 in Example 7.8 for a population of $N = 4$?

7.5 What is the normalization constant in Example 7.8 for a population of $N = 8$?

7.6 What is the utilization of queue 1 in Example 7.8 for a population of $N = 8$?

7.7.2 Mean Value Analysis

There is a significant, if not obvious, problem with convolution (or any technique that calculates the normalization constant). Since we could not know the actual utilizations of the queues before the computation was accomplished, we needed to use the relative utilizations. Unfortunately, as you may have noted in the example problem, if the relative utilizations are larger than the actual utilizations, the normalization constant is larger than 1, and may become very large. On the other hand, if the actual utilizations are larger than the relative utilizations used in the computation, the normalization constant may become very small. This can cause a numerical overflow or underflow during the calculation.

This is a serious problem in practice since there is no way to predict how large or small the actual utilizations will be. One method tries to deal with this problem by rescaling the relative utilizations as the computation progresses. Since the rate of growth (or shrinking) or the normalization constant is proportional to the error in the relative utilization, you can rescale the computation on the fly.

However, another method was developed which never computes the normalization constant, but simply uses the average values of the various parameters we normally compute. (Note that we got the average values by taking ratios of the normalization constants.) This method, called mean value analysis (MVA), totally avoids the problem of underflow or overflow, since it effectively does its computations with the ratios of the normalization constants.

Mean value analysis also has the advantage of directly computing all the performance measures for each population in the network of queues. Mean value analysis has the disadvantage of computing only the average values, so it is impossible to construct the complete state steady probability density (and therefore get other measures on the system) directly from the results of mean value analysis. Therefore, such questions as "What is the probability of queue 3 having two or more customers?" cannot be answered using normal mean value analysis. (You can extend the algorithm to compute the probability densities as shown in the load-dependent version of the algorithm.)

Before we begin to describe the algorithm, we note that mean value analysis is based on two fundamental theorems. First, it uses Little's result applied to each queue in the network and to the network as a whole. Second, it uses the mean value theorem formulated by Lavenberg and Reiser, which states that a customer arriving to a queue in a product form queuing network sees precisely the same distribution of customers as an outside observer would see if one less customer was circulating in the network.

The mean value theorem gives us the ability to compute what the waiting time for a new customer would be in terms of what was computed for the network with one less customer. This is the recurrence relationship we need to form the iteration loop in the algorithm. The algorithm can be broken down into three parts, which are repeated for each additional customer in the system until we reach the target population.

1. Calculate the average waiting time in each queue with an additional customer based on the average number of customers in each queue from the previous loop.

2. Calculate the average throughput for the system by applying Little's result to the entire network.

3. Calculate the average number of customers in each queue by applying Little's result to the average throughput and the average waiting time of the queue from steps 1 and 2.

We can put these steps into an algorithm where w_m is the average waiting time in queue m, V_m is the visit ratio of queue m, λ is the throughput of the system (measured from the same queue as the visit ratios), and $l_m(n)$ is the average number of customers in queue m when the total number of customers is n.

Repeat steps 1, 2, and 3 for $n = 1, 2, \ldots, N$.

1. For $m = 1, 2, \ldots, M$

$$w_m = \begin{cases} 0 & \text{for IS} \\ \mu_m^{-1} l_m(n-1) & \text{for FCFS, PS, LCFS-PR} \end{cases}$$

2. $\lambda = \dfrac{n}{\displaystyle\sum_{m=1}^{m} (w_m + u_m^{-1})V_m}$

3. For $m = 1, 2, \ldots, M$

$$l_m(n) = V_m \lambda w_m$$

So we now have a simple algorithm to compute the average queue length l_m, the average waiting time w_m, and the system throughput λ from the visit ratios V_m and the average service times μ_m. We can compute the average throughput for each queue, λ_m, directly from the system throughput and the visit ratios, $\lambda_m = \lambda V_m$.

We can improve the performance of the code for this algorithm by noting a few things about the operations. First, we see that the algorithm constantly adds the service time to the waiting time for each queue in the throughput calculation and must use the visit ratios times the average waiting times in several locations.

So, in the following code, we have premultiplied the visit ratios and the average service times to get a single factor, the weighted service time FAC[M]. In addition, we have changed the variable for the average number of customers in the queue, LEN[M], to contain the average number of customers plus one and the variable for the average waiting time, W[M], to contain the weighted-average waiting time plus the weighted-average service time.

```
PROGRAM MVA(INPUT,OUTPUT);

(* THIS PROGRAM IMPLEMENTS THE SIMPLEST VERSION OF *)
(* THE MEAN VALUE ANALYSIS ALGORITHM               *)
```

```
CONST MAXQ = 10;
      FCFS = 1;
      LCFS = 2;
      PS   = 3;
      IS   = 4;

VAR M,N,POPULATION,NUMQ      :INTEGER;
    VISIT,FAC,LEN,SERTIM,W   :ARRAY[1..MAXQ] OF REAL;
    THRU                     :REAL;
    QTYPE                    :ARRAY[1..MAXQ] OF INTEGER;

BEGIN;       (* MVA ALGORITHM *)

WRITELN(' ENTER THE NO OF QUEUES AND THE POPULATION');
READLN( NUMQ, POPULATION );

IF NUMQ > MAXQ
 THEN BEGIN;
    WRITELN('TO MANY QUEUES');
    END
 ELSE BEGIN;

    (* INITIALIZE VARIABLES *)

    WRITELN('ENTER THE VISIT RATIO, SER TIME, & TYPE');
    FOR M:=1 TO NUMQ DO
        BEGIN;
        READLN( VISIT[M], SERTIM[M], QTYPE[M] );
        FAC[M] := VISIT[M] * SERTIM[M];
        LEN[M] := 1
        END;

    (* LOOP ON INCREASING POPULATION OF CUST. *)

    FOR N:=1 TO POPULATION DO
        BEGIN;
        THRU := 0.0; (* CLEAR ACCUM FOR SUM *)

        (* LOOP ON EACH QUEUE FOR A POPULATION *)

        FOR M:=1 TO NUMQ DO
            BEGIN;
            IF ( QTYPE[M] <> IS )  (* INF SERVER *)
               THEN W[M] := FAC[M] * LEN[M]
               ELSE W[M] := FAC[M];
            THRU := THRU  + W[M] (* RUNNING SUM *)
            END; (* QUEUE LOOP *)
```

```
      THRU := N / THRU;

      (* UPDATE QUEUE LENGTHS FOR NEXT LOOP *)

      FOR M:=1 TO NUMQ DO
         LEN[M]:= 1.0 + THRU * W[M];

      END;  (* POPULATION LOOP *)

   (* OUTPUT RESULTS *)

   WRITELN(' QUEUE  LENGTH  WAIT   THRUPUT');

   (* PRINT ONE LINE FOR EACH QUEUE AND      *)
   (* CONVERT VALUES TO REMOVE SPECIAL FACTORS *)

   FOR M:=1 TO NUMQ DO
      BEGIN;
      WRITE(M:4,(LEN[M]-1):9:2);
      WRITE(((W[M]-FAC[M])/VISIT[M]):7:3);
      WRITELN((THRU*VISIT[M]):9:2);
      END;

   END;

END.
```

Example 7.9: As an example, let us solve the same model as that used in the previous example, using the mean value algorithm instead. First, we solve for the visit ratios, which are obvious in this case.

$$V_1 = 1 \qquad V_2 = 0.7 \qquad V_3 = 0.2$$

Second, we compute the factors for each queue using the visit ratios and the average service times.

$$F_1 = 28 \qquad F_2 = 28 \qquad F_3 = 56$$

Now, we begin the algorithm for $n = 1$.

$$W_1 = 28 \qquad W_2 = 28 \qquad W_3 = 56$$

$$\text{Thru} = \frac{1}{28 + 28 + 56} = \frac{1}{112}$$

$$L_1 = \frac{140}{112} \qquad L_2 = \frac{140}{112} \qquad L_3 = \frac{168}{112}$$

Execution continues for $n = 2$ in the next iteration of the loop.

$$W_1 = 35 \qquad W_2 = 35 \qquad W_3 = 84$$

$$\text{Thru} = \frac{2}{35 + 35 + 84} = \frac{1}{77}$$

$$L_1 = \frac{112}{77} \qquad L_2 = \frac{112}{77} \qquad L_3 = \frac{161}{77}$$

And the final step for this example, $n = 3$.

$$W_1 = \frac{448}{11} \qquad W_2 = \frac{448}{11} \qquad W_3 = \frac{1288}{11}$$

$$\text{Thru} = \frac{33}{448 + 448 + 1288} = \frac{11}{728} = 0.0151$$

$$L_1 = \frac{1176}{728} \qquad L_2 = \frac{1176}{728} \qquad L_3 = \frac{2016}{728}$$

So we can now compute the unweighted average values for the waiting time, number in the queues, and throughput for each queue.

$$w_1 = \frac{140}{11} \qquad w_2 = \frac{200}{11} \qquad w_3 = \frac{3360}{11}$$

$$l_1 = \frac{448}{728} \qquad l_2 = \frac{448}{728} \qquad l_3 = \frac{1288}{728}$$

$$\lambda_1 = \frac{11}{728} \qquad \lambda_2 = \frac{11}{1040} \qquad \lambda_3 = \frac{11}{3640}$$

We can compare the results to the convolution solution to see that, indeed, the results are the same.

$$\rho_1 = 28\lambda_1 = 28\frac{11}{728} = \frac{11}{26}$$

$$= u_1 \frac{G(2)}{G(3)} = \frac{11}{26}$$

Exercise

7.7 What is the average waiting time in queue 2 for $N = 4$ in Example 7.9?

7.7.3 Multiple Server Solution Techniques

So far, we have not mentioned how to handle the case of a FCFS queue with multiple servers, or the more general load-dependent server behavior. A server is load-dependent if the rate of service varies with the number of customers in the queue. So a multiple server or infinite server is a type of load-dependent queue.

Although the computations become more complex, the fact that a server is load-dependent does not preclude the solution from having a product form as long as the dependence is only in terms of the parameter of the distribution. We are not allowing the case of dependence between success service times or more general distributions.

In the case of load dependence, the service rate will vary with the number of customers in the queue. We will define the service rate as a function of the number of customers in the queue $\mu_i(n)$. When the dependence is due to multiple servers, that function is straightforward.

$$\mu_i(n) = \begin{cases} n\mu & n < s_i \\ s_i\mu & n \geq s_i \end{cases}$$

We can now consider how each of the two solution techniques will change when we include load-dependent service rates.

Convolution with Load-Dependent Servers

Recall that for multiple servers, an extra factor was needed in the normalization constant. To get the factor $\beta_i(n_i)$ into the normalization constant, we need to multiply previous values. This product will require that the recurrence relationship now include all the previous values for smaller populations, not just the last one.

To begin, let us define a function that includes the products of the different load-dependent service rates. This will simplify our notation.

$$A_i(n) = \prod_{j=1}^{n} \frac{\mu_i(j)}{\mu_i(1)} \tag{7.23}$$

Note that $A_i(n)$ reduces to $\beta_i(n)$ for the special case of multiple servers.

Since the service rate is load-dependent, we cannot just multiply the previous value by the relative utilization. We must multiply all of the previous values by the appropriate value of $A_i(n)$, which depends on the number of customers circulating in the network. Therefore, the recurrence relation must include all of the previous values for fewer customers. The following equation is proper recurrence relationship for the partial sum of the normalization constant in the case of load dependent servers.

$$g(n, m) = \sum_{k=0}^{n} \frac{(u_m)^k}{A_m(k)} g(n - k, m - 1) \tag{7.24}$$

The initial conditions for the recurrence relationship can be determined by noting that with no customers in the network, we still have only one state.

$$g(0,m) = 1$$

The other condition is determined by noting that when there is only one queue in the network, the normalization constant can be computed easily from the definition.

$$g(n,1) = \frac{(u_1)^n}{A_1(n)}$$

The calculation of the performance measures from the normalization constants is the same as before for the load-independent queues. However, the calculations are not as simple for the load-dependent queues.

Since the service rate for the load-dependent queue will change with the number of customers in the queue, we cannot simply multiply the relative utilization times the ratio of the normalization constants. The calculation for the utilization of a load-dependent queue is 1 minus the ratio of the normalization constant for the system without that queue and the normalization constant for the system with the queue.

Since the computation requires the normalization constant for the network without the load-dependent queue, it is still easily computed if the Mth queue is the load dependent one.

$$\rho_M = 1 - \frac{g(N, M - 1)}{g(N, M)} \tag{7.25}$$

Example 7.10: As an example, consider the simple two queue, cyclic queuing network shown in Figure 7.12, where one queue is load-dependent. The first queue is a simple $M/M/1$ queue with a single service rate of 40 customers per second. The service rate for the second queue, in customers per second, is given below.

$$\mu_2(1) = 40$$

$$\mu_2(2) = \frac{160}{3}$$

$$\mu_2(3) = 60$$

$$\mu_2(4) = 64$$

$$\mu_2(5) = \frac{200}{3}$$

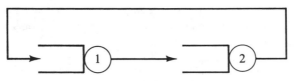

FIGURE 7.12 A Simple Two-Queue Network

First we compute the product factor, $A_2(n)$.

$$A_2(1) = 1$$

$$A_2(2) = 1 \cdot \frac{1}{40} \cdot \frac{160}{3} = \frac{4}{3}$$

$$A_2(3) = \frac{4}{3} \cdot \frac{60}{40} = 2$$

$$A_2(4) = 2 \cdot \frac{64}{40} = \frac{16}{5}$$

$$A_2(5) = \frac{16}{5} \cdot \frac{200}{120} = \frac{16}{3}$$

We must now solve for the relative utilizations [using the value of $\mu_m(1)$ for all load-dependent queues]. For this example the relative utilizations are simply $u_1 = 1$ and $u_2 = 1$.

	u_1	u_2
0	1	1
1	1	2
2	1	11/4
3	1	13/4
4	1	57/16
5	1	15/4

Table 7.3

So the utilization of queue 1 (the load-independent queue) is simply $57/60 = 0.95$. The utilization of queue 2 (the load-dependent queue) is $1 - 1 \cdot 4/15 = 0.7333$.

Exercise

7.8 What is the utilization of queue 1 and queue 2 in Example 7.10 if the population was only $N = 4$?

Mean Value Analysis with Load Dependent Servers

Since mean value analysis is simply another mechanism to compute per-formance measures for product form queuing networks, it is also extendable for the case of load-dependent servers. (Note that the infinite server queue was a special case of load-dependent service.)

The extension requires the additional calculation of the probability density function of the number of customers in the queue. This is needed to determine if the arriving customer queues in the case of multiple servers. This extension will change the computation for the weighted-average waiting time. The general form of the mean value theorem gives the average waiting time as seen by an arriving customer in terms of the average queue length as seen by an outside observer with one less customer in the network.

$$ w_m = \frac{l_m(n-1)}{\mu_m(1)} + \sum_{i=1}^{N} i \left(\frac{\mu_m(1)}{\mu_m(i)} - 1 \right) P[n_m = i - 1 | n - 1] \quad (7.26) $$

Therefore, to include load-dependent queues in the MVA algorithm will require a computation of the marginal probability density function for each load-dependent queue. This complicates the algorithm but is not a severe problem, since the MVA algorithm obtains the exact results for the current population at the end of each loop.

One can think of mean value analysis as interchanging the order of the loops from convolution. Recall that we iterated on population for each queue in the convolution algorithm, but here we loop on all queues for each addition to the population. So we note that at the end of an iteration, we have the complete information for the network with that population. Therefore, we can compute the probability density function for the network of queues with that population in terms of the probability density function for the smaller populations. Using the marginal distribution of the joint probability density function, we get the value $P[n_m = i \mid n]$ for the next iteration.

$$ P[n_m = i | n] = \frac{\mu_m(1)}{\mu_m(i)} \lambda(n) P[n_m = i - 1 | n - 1] \quad (7.27) $$

Given this more general formulation, we can extend the MVA code to include multiple server queues other than the simple infinite server case. The following Pascal code implements the algorithm for multiple servers. Note that the code is not optimized for either space (it reserves an entire array for the marginal probabilities) or speed; some subscript computations could be improved.

```pascal
PROGRAM LDMVA(INPUT,OUTPUT);

CONST MAXQ = 10;    (* ONLY TOY PROBLEMS *)
      MAXPOP = 20; (* ARE ALLOWED HERE  *)
      FCFS = 1;
      LCFS = 2;     (* USE TYPE CODES TO *)
      PS   = 3;     (* SIMPLIFY INPUT    *)
      IS   = 4;

VAR I,M,N,NUMQ      :INTEGER;
    POPULATION      :INTEGER;
    VISIT,FAC,LEN   :ARRAY[1..MAXQ] OF REAL;
    SERTIM,W        :ARRAY[1..MAXQ] OF REAL;
    THRU            :REAL;
    NSER,QTYPE      :ARRAY[..MAXQ] OF INTEGER;
    P               :ARRAY[0..MAXPOP,1..MAXQ] OF REAL;

BEGIN;
WRITELN(' ENTER THE NO OF QUEUES AND THE POPULATION');
READLN( NUMQ, POPULATION );

IF (NUMQ > MAXQ) OR (POPULATION > MAXPOP)
 THEN BEGIN;
    WRITELN('TO MANY QUEUES OR CUSTOMERS');
    END
 ELSE BEGIN;

  WRITELN(' ENTER VISIT RATIO, SER TIME & NO., & TYPE');
  FOR M:=1 TO NUMQ DO    (* GET VALUES FOR EACH QUEUE *)
      BEGIN;

      WRITELN(' FOR QUEUE ',M:3);
      READLN( VISIT[M], SERTIM[M], NSER[M], QTYPE[M] );

      FAC[M] := VISIT[M] * SERTIM[M];  (* INITIALIZE *)
      LEN[M] := 1;                      (* VALUES     *)
      P[0,M] := 1.0;
      FOR N := 1 TO POPULATION DO P[N,M] := 0.0;
      END;

  FOR N:=1 TO POPULATION DO     (* LOOP FOR ALL CUST. *)
      BEGIN;
      THRU := 0.0;
      FOR M:=1 TO NUMQ DO

      (* FIRST WE CALCULATE WAITING TIME FROM     *)
      (* PREVIOUS VALUES OF POPULATION.           *)
```

```
    IF ( NSER[M] = 1 ) THEN
      BEGIN;                 (* FOR LOAD INDEP. Q  *)
      IF ( QTYPE[M] <> IS )
        THEN W[M] := FAC[M] * LEN[M]
        ELSE W[M] := FAC[M];
      THRU := THRU + W[M]
      END

    ELSE
      BEGIN;                  (* FOR MULTISERVER Q  *)
        W[M] := 0.0;
        FOR I := 0 TO NSER[M]-2 DO
          W[M] := W[M] + P[I,M] * (NSER[M]-I-1);
        W[M] := FAC[M] * (W [M] + LEN[M])/NSER[M];
      THRU := THRU + W[M]
      END;

(* NOW WE CALCULATE THE THROUGHPUT FOR THE    *)
(* SYSTEM USING LITTLES RESULT                *)

THRU := N / THRU;

(* NOW WE UPDATE THE QUEUE LENGTHS AND MARGINAL*)
(* DENSITIES FOR EACH QUEUE BY APPLYING LITTLES*)
(* RESULT TO THE NEW WAITING TIMES AND THRUPUTS*)

FOR M:=1 TO NUMQ DO
  BEGIN;
    LEN[M]:= 1.0  +  THRU * W[M];

    FOR I := NSER[M]-1 DOWNTO 1 DO
      P[I,M] := THRU * FAC[M] * P[I-1,M] / I;
    P[0,M] := 0.0;
    FOR I := 1 TO NSER[M]-1 DO
      P[0,M] := P[0,M] + P[I,M]*(NSER[M]-I);
    P[0,M] := 1.0 - (THRU*FAC[M]+P[0,M])/NSER[M];
  END;

  END;  (* POPULATION LOOP *)

WRITELN(' QUEUE  LENGTH  WAIT  THRUPUT');

FOR M:-1 TO NUMQ DO (* PRINT OUT VALUES FOR EACH Q*)
  BEGIN;
  WRITE(M:5,(LEN[M]-1):9:2);
```

```
    WRITE(((W[M]-FAC[M])/VISIT[M]):7:3);
    WRITELN((THRU*VISIT[M]):9:2);
    END;

  END;  (* NONERROR CONDITION *)

END.  (* LDMVA *)
```

7.8 Networks with Multiple Routing Chains

We have seen how product form networks are powerful for modeling systems. So far, we have restricted our view to product form networks with customers of a single class or type. However, the product form solution holds for some networks of queues where multiple classes of customers are allowed. It is even possible to deal with multiple classes of customers and load-dependent queues. However, to keep the notation simple we will not discuss that combination in this book. (The interested reader can merge the two techniques or refer to the bibliography for more advanced textbooks.)

In a network of queues with different classes of customers, both the service rate and the routing may be class dependent. This will allow us to construct models of systems where the load on the system is characterized by a heterogeneous mixture of tasks. In a model of a time-sharing system, we might have a class of customers for interactive jobs which behave differently from the class of customers for batch jobs.

Basically, in a system with multiple classes, everything we have considered so far is replicated for each class. Each queue will have a mean service rate (or time) associated with each class. Each queue will have a potentially different set of probabilities of proceeding to any other queue for each class. The population (i.e., number of customers circulating in the system) is now a vector $\mathbf{N} \triangleq (N_1, \ldots, N_K)$ where an element N_k is the number of customers of class k circulating in the network. Since we need to consider a population with one less customer, we will use the notation $\mathbf{e}_k$ to denote the vector of all zeros except in the kth element, where there is a 1. Therefore, for some intermediate population vector $\mathbf{n}$, the population vector with one less class k customer is $\mathbf{n} - \mathbf{e}_k$.

7.8.1 Routing Chains

Recall how we described the movement of customers through the network with the routing chain $[p_{ij}]$. In a multiple-class system, the selection of which queue is next can be based on the customer's class. So we now will have multiple routing chains $1 \leq k \leq K$ within the network.* Now the description of how customers move within the network becomes a three-dimensional table $[p_{ijk}]$ for the probability of a customer of class k going from queue i to queue j.

To solve for the relative utilizations or the visit ratios, we solve each of the chains separately. So we will have a set of relative utilizations, $u_{m,k}$, for each queue for each class. Similarly, we would have a set of visit ratios, $V_{m,k}$, for each queue for each class.

7.8.2 The M $\Rightarrow$ M Property

This distinction between customers complicates the state description of the system as well. Now the state of a queue must distinguish the number of customers of each class which are currently queued. In the case of LCFS and FCFS, the actual order of the customers must be distinguished, since the customers may now differ in their service. Consider the state descriptions of each of the following types of queues.

FCFS. State $\overset{\Delta}{=} (c_0, c_1, \ldots, c_n)$

LCFS. State $\overset{\Delta}{=} (c_0, c_1, \ldots, c_n)$

Processor Sharing (PS). State $\overset{\Delta}{=} (n_1, n_2, \ldots, n_K)$

Infinite Server (IS). State $\overset{\Delta}{=} (n_1, n_2, \ldots, n_K)$

In the case of LCFS and FCFS, the state is a precise representation of the queue, where c_i is the class of the ith customer in the queue. In the case of processor sharing and infinite servers, there is no real queue, so the state is simple the number of customers of each class.

The balance requirement for the M $\Rightarrow$ M property is now much more complex. To determine if a queue with multiple classes of customers will satisfy the M $\Rightarrow$ M property, it is necessary to consider precisely how a departure can occur to result in state S_i which would balance the potential arrival in state S_j. Given a state S_i, denote as S_i^{+k}, any state where a class k customer may depart and result in the state S_i. The state S_i^{+k} is a very special state. A class k customer must be able to depart for the state S_i^{+k} and if that departure did occur, the resulting state would be precisely the state S_i. There may be many such states. Denote the set of such states as Z^{+k}. Now the balance requirement for the

---

* In this book, we will not discuss cases where customers are allowed to change classes. In general, it is possible to have customers changing class as they move from one queue to another. This implies that any chain may actually have more than one class associated with it.

$M \Rightarrow M$ property will sum of all such states to balance the arrival rate. That balance must again hold for all possible states, S_i.

$$\forall S_i, \ 1 \le k \le K \quad \sum_{S_i^{+k} \in Z_i^{+k}} \frac{P[S_i^{+k}]R(S_i^{+k} \to S_i)}{P[S_i]} = \lambda_k \qquad (7.28)$$

Example 7.11: Consider the case of the processor sharing queue.

$$S_i = (n_1, n_2, \ldots, n_k, \ldots, n_K)$$

The only state where a class k customer could depart and result in the state S_i is as follows:

$$S_i^{+k} = (n_1, n_2, \ldots, n_k + 1, \ldots, n_K)$$

The rate at which the departure could occur is given by the ratio of the number of class k customers times the rate of service for class k customers divided by the total number of customers sharing the server $n + 1$, where $n \triangleq \Sigma n_k$.

$$R(S_i^{+k} \to S_i) = \frac{n_k + 1}{n + 1} \mu_k$$

So, as before, we assume that the $M \Rightarrow M$ property holds and derive a possible steady-state solution.

$$\frac{P[n_1, n_2, \ldots, n_k + 1, \ldots, n_K] \dfrac{n_k + 1}{n + 1} \mu_k}{P[n_1, n_2, \ldots, n_k, \ldots, n_k]} = \lambda_k$$

Since this must hold for all classes k and for all states, we can back substitute to get the possible steady-state solution.

$$P[n_1, n_2, \ldots, n_K] = Cn! \prod_{k=1}^{K} \frac{\left(\dfrac{\lambda_k}{\mu_k}\right)^{n_k}}{n_k!}$$

To check to see if this really is the steady-state solution, we must check this solution in the state balance equation for the processor sharing queue.

$$P[n_1, n_2, \ldots, n_K] \sum_{k=1}^{K} \lambda_k + P[n_1, n_2, \ldots, n_K] \sum_{k=1}^{K} \frac{n_k}{n} \mu_k$$

$$= \sum_{k=1}^{K} P[n_1, n_2, \ldots, n_k + 1, \ldots, n_K] \frac{n_k + 1}{n + 1} \mu_k$$

$$+ \sum_{k=1}^{K} P[n_1, n_2, \ldots, n_k - 1, \ldots, n_K] \lambda_k$$

Substituting our possible solution into the state balance equation, we obtain the following expression.

$$
Cn! \prod_{k=1}^{K} \frac{\left(\dfrac{\lambda_k}{\mu_k}\right)^{n_k}}{n_k!} \sum_{k=1}^{K} \lambda_k + Cn! \prod_{k=1}^{K} \frac{\left(\dfrac{\lambda_k}{\mu_k}\right)^{n_k}}{n_k!} \sum_{k=1}^{K} \frac{n_k}{n} \mu_k = \sum_{k=1}^{K} C(n+1)! \cdot
$$

$$
\frac{n_k+1}{n+1} \mu_k \frac{\lambda_k/\mu_k}{n_k+1} \prod_{k=1}^{K} \frac{\left(\dfrac{\lambda_k}{\mu_k}\right)^{n_k}}{n_k!} + \sum_{k=1}^{K} C(n-1)! \lambda_k \frac{n_k\mu_k}{\lambda_k} \prod_{k=1}^{K} \frac{\left(\dfrac{\lambda_k}{\mu_k}\right)^{n_k}}{n_k!}
$$

Using the distribution law to interchange some of the summations and products, this expression can then be reduced.

$$
Cn! \sum_{k=1}^{K} \lambda_k \prod_{k=1}^{K} \frac{\left(\dfrac{\lambda_k}{\mu_k}\right)^{n_k}}{n_k!} + Cn! \sum_{k=1}^{K} \frac{n_k\mu_k}{n} \prod_{k=1}^{K} \frac{\left(\dfrac{\lambda_k}{\mu_k}\right)^{n_k}}{n_k!}
$$

$$
= \sum_{k=1}^{K} C(n+1)! \frac{\lambda_k}{n+1} \prod_{k=1}^{K} \frac{\left(\dfrac{\lambda_k}{\mu_k}\right)^{n_k}}{n_k!} + \sum_{k=1}^{K} C(n-1)! n_k\mu_k \prod_{k=1}^{K} \frac{\left(\dfrac{\lambda_k}{\mu_k}\right)^{n_k}}{n_k!}
$$

This can be reduced still further, finally resulting in an obvious equality, which proves that the processor sharing queue does satisfy the M $\Rightarrow$ M property.

$$
Cn! \sum_{k=1}^{K} \lambda_k \prod_{k=1}^{K} \frac{\left(\dfrac{\lambda_k}{\mu_k}\right)^{n_k}}{n_k!} + Cn! \sum_{k=1}^{K} \frac{n_k\mu_k}{n} \prod_{k=1}^{K} \frac{\left(\dfrac{\lambda_k}{\mu_k}\right)^{n_k}}{n_k!}
$$

$$
= Cn! \sum_{k=1}^{K} \lambda_k \prod_{k=1}^{K} \frac{\left(\dfrac{\lambda_k}{\mu_k}\right)^{n_k}}{n_k!} + Cn! \sum_{k=1}^{K} \frac{n_k\mu_k}{n} \prod_{k=1}^{K} \frac{\left(\dfrac{\lambda_k}{\mu_k}\right)^{n_k}}{n_k!}
$$

In the case of FCFS, only the single class queue has the M $\Rightarrow$ M property. In other words, the FCFS queue will only have the product form solution when used in a network of queues with multiple classes if each class has an exponentially distributed service time with precisely the same parameter. Basically, even if there are multiple classes, the FCFS queue does not distinguish between them.

7.8.3 Convolution

When more than one class of customers are considered, the recurrence relationship used to calculate the normalization constant is slightly more complex.

Basically, the computation now takes place in a multidimensional (M by N_1 by $N_2 \cdots$ by N_K) table.

$$G(m,\mathbf{n}) = G(m - 1, \mathbf{n}) + \sum_{k=1}^{K} u_{m,k} G(m, \mathbf{n} - \mathbf{e}_k) \qquad (7.29)$$

For ease of notation, we have defined all normalization constants for negative population vectors as zero. The relative utilizations, $u_{m,k}$, are obtained in the same fashion as before.

$$\sum_{i=1}^{M} u_{i,k}\mu_{i,k}p_{i,j,k} = u_{j,k}\mu_{j,k} \qquad (7.30)$$

Example 7.12: Let us return to the simple model shown in Figure 7.11 of the multitasking computer used in Examples 7.8 and 7.9 but with two classes of customers. Since queue 2 and queue 3 represented the disks with a FCFS queuing discipline, the multiclass network must have the same exponentially distributed service times for both classes. In the case of queue 1, the processor sharing discipline has the flexibility to allow different average service times for each class, but our model will not have any distinction between classes for service time. However, the multiclass model will have two different routing chains for each class, one representing CPU intensive tasks and the other representing I/O intensive tasks.

$$p_{1,1,1} = 0.1 \quad p_{1,2,1} = 0.3 \quad p_{1,3,1} = 0.6 \quad p_{2,1,1} = 1.0 \quad p_{3,1,1} = 1.0$$
$$p_{1,1,2} = 0.4 \quad p_{1,2,2} = 0.4 \quad p_{1,3,2} = 0.2 \quad p_{2,1,2} = 1.0 \quad p_{3,1,2} = 1.0$$

Solving for the relative utilizations for each class, we obtain the starting values for the tables.

$$\begin{array}{ccc} u_{1,1} = 1.0 & u_{2,1} = 0.42857 & u_{3,1} = 6.0 \\ u_{1,2} = 1.0 & u_{2,2} = 0.57143 & u_{3,2} = 2.0 \end{array}$$

We can now start filling in the multidimensional table. To keep the example small and easy to show on a page, we will assume that there are two customers of each class circulating in the network. Since $G(m,\mathbf{n})$ is really $G(m,(n_1, n_2))$, we will write down each $N_1 \times N_2$ matrix as the algorithm fills the table. Observe how the algorithm runs through combinations of population vectors to fill the table.

$G(1,\mathbf{n})$		0	n_2 1	2
	0	1.0	$u_{1,2}$	$u_{1,2}^2$
n_1	1	$u_{1,1}$	$2u_{1,1}u_{1,2}$	$3u_{1,1}u_{1,2}^2$
	2	$u_{1,1}^2$	$3u_{1,1}^2u_{1,2}$	$6u_{1,1}^2u_{1,2}^2$

Table 7.4

Substituting the values for the relative utilizations, we obtain the following table for the first queue.

$G(1,\mathbf{n})$		0	n_2 1	2
	0	1.0	1.0	1.0
n_1	1	1.0	2.0	3.0
	2	1.0	3.0	6.0

Table 7.5

Using that table and the relative utilizations we compute the table for the next queue.

$G(2,\mathbf{n})$		0	n_2 1	2
	0	1.0	1.57143	1.898
n_1	1	1.42857	3.4898	5.8076
	2	1.61224	5.4169	11.5843

Table 7.6

Finally, the exact normalization constants for all possible combinations of the population vector are obtained.

$G(3,\mathbf{n})$		0	n_2 1	2
	0	1.0	3.57143	9.041
n_1	1	7.42857	39.77552	139.60464
	2	46.1837	336.43742	1522.08698

Table 7.7

Given the normalization constants, we can proceed to compute the performance measures.

$$\rho_{1,1} = u_{1,1} \frac{G(M, \mathbf{N} - \mathbf{e}_1)}{G(M, \mathbf{N})} = 0.091719$$

$$\rho_{1,2} = u_{1,2} \frac{G(M, \mathbf{N} - \mathbf{e}_2)}{G(M, \mathbf{N})} = 0.221037$$

$$\rho_{2,1} = u_{2,1} \frac{G(M, \mathbf{N} - \mathbf{e}_1)}{G(M, \mathbf{N})} = 0.039308$$

$$\rho_{2,2} = u_{2,2} \frac{G(M, \mathbf{N} - \mathbf{e}_2)}{G(M, \mathbf{N})} = 0.126307$$

$$\rho_{3,1} = u_{3,1} \frac{G(M, \mathbf{N} - \mathbf{e}_1)}{G(M, \mathbf{N})} = 0.550314$$

$$\rho_{3,2} = u_{3,2} \frac{G(M, \mathbf{N} - \mathbf{e}_2)}{G(M, \mathbf{N})} = 0.442074$$

$$\lambda_{1,1} = \rho_{1,1}\mu_{1,1} = 0.003276$$

$$\lambda_{1,2} = \rho_{1,2}\mu_{1,2} = 0.007894$$

$$\lambda_{2,1} = \rho_{2,1}\mu_{2,1} = 0.0009827$$

$$\lambda_{2,2} = \rho_{2,2}\mu_{2,2} = 0.0031577$$

$$\lambda_{3,1} = \rho_{3,1}\mu_{3,1} = 0.0019654$$

$$\lambda_{3,2} = \rho_{3,2}\mu_{3,2} = 0.0015788$$

Similarly to the single-class algorithm, where only one column was actually used, this algorithm does not have to store all the values. The algorithm can be executed with only one $N_1 \times N_2 \times \cdots \times N_K$ matrix by starting at the element $0, 0, \ldots, 0$ and zigzagging through the matrix.

7.8.4 Mean Value Analysis

Mean value analysis can also be extended for multiple classes of customers, subject to the same restriction that the network of queues must be product form (i.e., all queues must satisfy the $M \Rightarrow M$ property).

The extension is straightforward. In the single-class algorithm, the main loop incremented the number of customers. In the multiclass algorithm, there are many customers of different classes, so there is a loop for each class. In addition, since the recurrence step was based on the mean value theorem, the multiclass algorithm must compute the mean wait for a class k customer based on the average number of customers in the queue obtained for a population with one less class k customer. That means that the average queue length must be computed for different population combinations. Finally, all the service rates, throughputs, and visit ratios are now class dependent. So the storage requirements go up significantly.

The following algorithm is the multiclass version of mean value analysis. Note the additional subscripts to denote class dependencies and the fact that the population is now a vector rather than a scalar value.

Repeat steps 1, 2, and 3 for all combinations of customer population vectors.

1. For $k = 1, 2, \ldots, K$ and $m = 1, 2, \ldots, M$

$$w_{m,k} = \begin{cases} 0 & \text{for IS} \\ \mu_{m,k}^{-1} l_m(\mathbf{n} - \mathbf{e}_k) & \text{for FCFS, PS, LCFS-PR} \end{cases}$$

2. For $k = 1, 2, \ldots, K$

$$\lambda_k = \frac{n}{\displaystyle\sum_{m=1}^{M} (w_{m,k} + \mu_{m,k}^{-1}) V_{m,k}}$$

3. For $m = 1, 2, \ldots, M$

$$l_m(\mathbf{n}) = \sum_{k=1}^{K} V_{m,k} \lambda_k w_{m,k}$$

Note that the multiclass MVA algorithm iterates on all combinations of population for each class. That is an exceptionally large amount of computation. In addition, the algorithm must use the values of the average number in each queue from various different combinations of populations, not just one. So the average number of customers in each queue for those combinations of populations must be retained for later use. Although the code below retains all previous values, that is not actually necessary. It is only necessary to retain all combinations that have the same total number of customers as the current population being computed, minus one.

Another minor point is about the limits of iteration on the loops. The loops for population must all start at zero even though the first pass is a no-op. This is the only way to guarantee that the value of zero for each class will be used with the other combinations. (It it is easier to include 0, 0, . . . , 0 so that 1, 0, . . . , 0 and 0, 1, . . . , 0 are not special cases.) This also requires special checks in the code for negative values and to define the throughput for a class with zero customers as zero.

The following Pascal code is given to illustrate the implementation of the algorithm. It is not a clever implementation and uses many brute-force constructs, but it also exposes the details of the algorithm more clearly. The maximum number of classes are fixed at 3 and the number of customers in each class is set at 5. (Note that increasing MAXCL also requires adding loops.) This is simply to keep the array for the average number of customers in queue for all population combinations a manageable size. A production implementation would not follow this structure at all, but would use dynamic allocation techniques instead.

```
PROGRAM MCMVA(INPUT,OUTPUT);

CONST
        MAXCL = 3;
        MAXQ = 10;
        MAXN = 5;
        FCFS = 1;
        LCFS = 2;
        PS   = 3;
        IS   = 4;
VAR M,K         :INTEGER;
    N1,N2,N3    :INTEGER;
    NUMCL,NUMQ:INTEGER;
    TEMP        :REAL;
    N           :ARRAY[0..MAXCL] OF INTEGER;
    VISIT,FAC   :ARRAY[1..MAXQ,1..MAXCL] OF REAL;
    SERTIM,W    :ARRAY[1..MAXQ,1..MAXCL] OF REAL;
    THRU        :ARRAY[1..MAXCL] OF REAL;
    QTYPE       :ARRAY[1..MAXQ] OF INTEGER;
    POP         :ARRAY[1..MAXCL] OF INTEGER;
    LEN         :ARRAY[1..MAXQ,0..MAXN,0..MAXN,0..MAXN]
                                          OF REAL;
BEGIN;  (* MCMVA *)

WRITELN('ENTER THE # OF QUEUES AND THE # OF CLASSES');
READLN( NUMQ, NUMCL );

  FOR M:=1 TO NUMQ DO (* INIT Q SPECIFIC STUFF *)
   BEGIN;
   WRITELN(' ENTER THE TYPE OF QUEUE ',M:3);
   READLN( QTYPE[M] );
   LEN[M,0,0,0]:=1.0
   END;

  FOR K:=1 TO NUMCL DO (* INIT CLASS SPECIFIC *)
   BEGIN;
   WRITELN(' ENTER THE # OF CUSTOMERS OF CLASS',K:3);
   READLN( POP[K] );
```

```
    WRITELN(' ENTER THE VISIT RATIO & SER TIME');
    FOR M:=1 TO NUMQ DO
        BEGIN;
        WRITELN(' FOR QUEUE NUMBER ',M:5 );
        READLN( VISIT[M,K], SERTIM[M,K] );
        FAC[M,K] := VISIT[M,K] * SERTIM[M,K];
        END;
    END;

(* NOW WE ITERATE FOR ALL POSSIBLE COMBINATIONS *)
(* OF CUST WITH ONE LOOP FOR EACH POSSIBLE CLASS*)
(* I.E. MAXCL=3                                 *)

FOR N3:=0 TO POP[3] DO
 FOR N2:=0 TO POP[2] DO
  FOR N1:=0 TO POP[1] DO
    BEGIN;

  N[1] := N1;
  N[2] := N2;  (* GET AROUND PASCAL LIMITATION *)
  N[3] := N3;

FOR K:=1 TO NUMCL DO                 (* CLASS LOOP *)
 BEGIN;
 THRU[K] := 0.0;
 N[K] :=N[K] - 1;    (* ONE LESS CUST OF CLASS *)

  IF N[K] ≥ 0 THEN     (* CHECK FOR NEG FIRST    *)
    FOR M:=1 TO NUMQ DO
     BEGIN;
     IF ( QTYPE[M] <> IS )
       THEN W[M,K] := FAC[M,K]*LEN[M,N[1],N[2],N[3]]
       ELSE W[M,K] := FAC[M,K];

     THRU[K] :=THRU[K]  +  W[M,K]
     END;

  N[K] := N[K] + 1;    (* RETURN TO PROPER POP. *)

  IF ( N[K] = 0 )      (* SINCE ZERO IS ALLOWED *)
       THEN THRU[K] := 0.0 (* DEFINE THRU AS 0  *)
       ELSE THRU[K] :=N[K] / THRU[K];

 END;     (* CLASS LOOP K *)
```

```
(* NOW APPLY LITTLES RESULT TO EACH CLASS IN    *)
(* EACH QUEUE                                    *)

FOR M := 1 TO NUMQ DO
  BEGIN;
  TEMP := 0.0;
  FOR K := 1 TO NUMCL DO
     TEMP := TEMP + THRU[K] * W[M,K];
  LEN[M,N[1],N[2],N[3]] := TEMP + 1.0
  END; (* QUEUE LOOP M *)

END;  (* POPULATION LOOPS *)

WRITELN(' QUEUE LENGTH      WAIT        THRUPUT');

(* OUTPUT RESULTS *)

FOR M:=1 TO NUMQ DO
  BEGIN;
  WRITELN(M:4,(LEN[M,POP[1],POP[2],POP[3]]-1):9:3);
  FOR K:=1 TO NUMCL DO
  BEGIN;
  WRITE('      CLASS ', K:3);
  WRITE(((W[M,K]-FAC[M,K])/VISIT[M,K]):10:4);
  WRITELN((THRU[K]*VISIT[M,K]):10:4)
  END; (* CLASS LOOP K *)
  END;  (* QUEUE LOOP M *)
END.  (* MCMVA *)
```

Example 7.13: Consider the same model we used in Example 7.12 to illustrate the multiclass convolution algorithm. Initially, we need to compute the visit ratios. For this simple problem, we can read off the visit ratios directly from the model.

$$V_{1,1} = 1.0 \qquad V_{2,1} = 0.3 \qquad V_{3,1} = 0.6$$
$$V_{1,2} = 1.0 \qquad V_{2,2} = 0.4 \qquad V_{3,2} = 0.2$$

The service disciplines for the disk queues are FCFS, so the service distributions must be exponentially distributed with the same parameter. The values used in Example 7.12 are repeated here.

$$\mu_{1,1}^{-1} = 28 \text{ ms} \qquad \mu_{2,1}^{-1} = 40 \text{ ms} \qquad \mu_{3,1}^{-1} = 280 \text{ ms}$$

Using the service times and visit ratios above, we can compute the weighted service time factors used in the algorithm.

$$FAC_{1,1} = 28 \qquad FAC_{2,1} = 12 \qquad FAC_{3,1} = 168$$
$$FAC_{1,2} = 28 \qquad FAC_{2,2} = 16 \qquad FAC_{3,2} = 56$$

Beginning the algorithm, we initialize the average number of customers in each queue for the population vector of $n = (0,0)$. The first pass through the algorithm for that population vector is a no-op, so the next pass through the algorithm is for one customer of class 1.

$n = (1,0)$

$$w_{1,1} = 28 \qquad w_{2,1} = 12 \qquad w_{3,1} = 168$$
$$w_{1,2} = 0 \qquad w_{2,2} = 0 \qquad w_{3,2} = 0$$

$$\lambda_1 = \frac{1}{28 + 12 + 168} = 0.0048077$$

$$\lambda_2 = 0$$

$$\text{len}_1(1,0) = 1.134615 \qquad \text{len}_2(1,0) = 1.0577 \qquad \text{len}_3(1,0) = 1.8077$$

The next step in the algorithm increments the number of customers of this class.

$n = (2,0)$

$$w_{1,1} = 31.7692 \qquad w_{2,1} = 12.6923 \qquad w_{3,1} = 303.6923$$
$$w_{1,2} = 0 \qquad w_{2,2} = 0 \qquad w_{3,2} = 0$$

$$\lambda_1 = \frac{2}{31.7692 + 12.6923 + 303.6923} = 0.00574$$

$$\lambda_2 = 0$$

$$\text{len}_1(2,0) = 1.134615 \qquad \text{len}_2(2,0) = 1.0577 \qquad \text{len}_3(2,0) = 1.8077$$

The inside loop is now at its limit, so the outside loop increments.

$n = (0,1)$

$$w_{1,1} = 0 \qquad w_{2,1} = 0 \qquad w_{3,1} = 0$$
$$w_{1,2} = 28 \qquad w_{2,2} = 16 \qquad w_{3,2} = 56$$

$$\lambda_1 = 0$$

$$\lambda_2 = \frac{1}{28 + 16 + 56} = 0.01$$

$$\text{len}_1(0,1) = 1.28 \qquad \text{len}_2(0,1) = 1.16 \qquad \text{len}_3(0,1) = 1.56$$

Finally, we reach an interesting point. Note that the computation for the waiting times for class 1 customers relies on the average values computed in the step for $\mathbf{n} = (0,1)$ while the computation for the waiting times for the class 2 customers relies on the average values computed in the step for $\mathbf{n} = (1,0)$. Both of the new waiting times are used to calculate the average number of customers in the queue for $\mathbf{n} = (1,1)$. So the values of $(0,1)$ and $(1,0)$ (which have a total of one customer circulating) are used to compute the values for $(1,1)$.

$\mathbf{n} = (1,1)$

$$w_{1,1} = 35.84 \qquad w_{2,1} = 13.92 \qquad w_{3,1} = 262.08$$
$$w_{1,2} = 31.7692 \qquad w_{2,2} = 16.9231 \qquad w_{3,2} = 101.2308$$
$$\lambda_1 = 0.003207$$
$$\lambda_2 = 0.00667$$
$$\text{len}_1(1,1) = 1.327 \qquad \text{len}_2(1,1) = 1.158 \qquad \text{len}_3(1,1) = 2.516$$

This would then continue with values for $(2,1)$ computed from values obtained in the steps $(1,1)$ and $(2,0)$.

The multiclass MVA algorithm has complexity equal to the product of the number of customers in each class, the number of queues, and the number of classes. So even though multiclass queuing networks provide a significant increase in the number of systems that can be modeled, the complexity makes models with a large number of classes expensive, if not impossible, to solve.

There are other extensions to reduce the complexity of the computations if small errors, or a loss of some performance measures is acceptable. There are also approximation techniques that are intended to deal with non-product-form queuing networks. These other topics are beyond the scope of this book, and the interested reader is referred to other, more advanced textbooks on these topics.

7.9 Problems

7.1 Given the following open queuing network, solve for the throughputs for each queue.

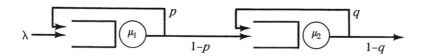

7.2 Given the following closed queueing network, solve for the visit ratios for each queue.

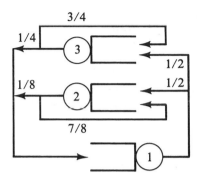

7.3 Given the following closed queueing network, solve for the relative utilization for each queue.

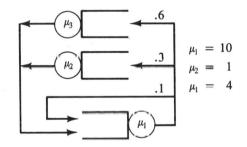

$\mu_1 = 10$
$\mu_2 = 1$
$\mu_1 = 4$

7.4 Derive the actual distribution for the interarrival times to a single queue with feedback (such as the one shown in Figure 7.4) by using Jackson's theorem, which gives the probability density function for the number in the queue (even with the feedback). *(Hint:* Start with the transform of the interarrival density conditioned on the state of the queue, and uncondition with Jackson's result.)

7.5 Show that a single-class queue, where arrivals follow a FCFS discipline on arrival with probably p or a LCFS-PR discipline on arrival with probably $1 - p$, also has the M $\Rightarrow$ M property.

7.6 For the following open queuing network, find:

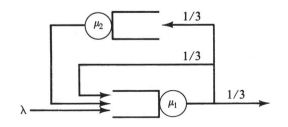

     a. The throughputs for each queue.
     b. The average number of customers waiting or in service in each queue.
     c. The total system delay for a customer.

7.7 For the following open queuing network, find:
     a. The throughputs for each queue.
     b. The average number of customers waiting or in service in each queue.
     c. The total system delay for a customer.

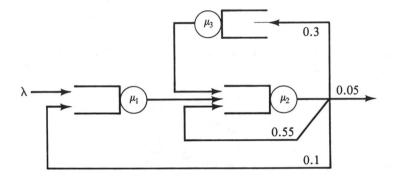

7.8 Write the code to calculate the normalization constants using the convolution algorithm for the load-independent case.

7.9 Given the following closed queuing network model with $\mu_1 = 36$, $\mu_2 = 3$, and $\mu_3 = 4$, compute the requested performance measures.
     a. The relative utilizations of each queue.
     b. The normalization constant for four customers in the network.
     c. The actual utilizations of each queue.
     d. The average number of customers in each queue (waiting or in service).
     e. The actual throughput for each queue.
     f. The average delay for each queue.

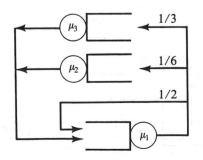

7.10 Given the following closed queuing network model with $\mu_1 = 24$, $\mu_2 = 8$, and $\mu_3 = 16$, compute the requested performance measures.
   a. The relative utilizations of each queue.
   b. The normalization constant for four customers in the network.
   c. The actual utilizations of each queue.
   d. The average number of customers in each queue (waiting or in service).
   e. The actual throughput for each queue.
   f. The average delay for each queue.

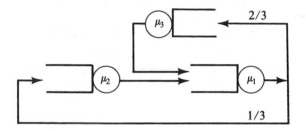

7.11 Show that the recurrence relationship for the load-dependent convolution algorithm [Eq 7.24] reduces to the same recurrence relationship as the non load-dependent case [Eq 7.19] when $A_i(n) = 1$.

7.12 Rewrite the code for the multi-server MVA algorithm given in Section 7.7.3 to avoid wasting so much space and time. *(Hint:* Break the code into two phases of load-independent and load dependent queues.)

7.13 Using the same network of queues as described in Problem 7.9 but where queue 1 is replaced by a multiple server queue with two servers, each with a rate $\mu_1 = 36$, solve for the following performance parameters.
   a. The relative utilizations of each queue.
   b. The normalization constant for four customers in the network.
   c. The actual utilizations of each queue.
   d. The average number of customers in each queue (waiting or in service).
   e. The actual throughput for each queue.
   f. The average delay for each queue.

7.14 Show that the multiclass LCFS preemptive-resume queue satisfies the $M \Rightarrow M$ property.

7.15 Show that the multiclass infinite server queue satisfies the $M \Rightarrow M$ property.

7.16 Consider a network of M queues which is a sequence of queues, the output of one being the input to the next. If the service time for each queue is deterministic and equal to D, what is the delay for a customer traversing all of the queues?

7.17 Write a simulation program for an open queuing network made up of two queues in tandem (see the accompanying figure). Assume that arrivals are from a Poisson source with parameter $\lambda = 8$. The service time of the first queue is exponentially distributed with parameter $\mu_1 = 10$. Include a special restriction where the service time of a customer in the second queue is precisely the same time that customer spent in service in the first queue, not a new value. Compare the values for the average number of customers in each queue and the average delay for a customer with the values obtained analytically by assuming that the network is a simple Jacksonian network where the service time of the second queue is independently sampled from the same distribution as the first queue.

Case 8 Studies

8.1 Introduction

This chapter is a collection of modeling problems which are solved using the techniques developed in this textbook. They are not ordered in the same fashion as the topics in the previous chapters, but in the order of increasing complexity. Each of the models developed here is an analytic model (i.e. abstract mathematical model) but a simulation is often used to validate the simplifying assumptions. The basic models presented here have appeared elsewhere in the literature as models of various systems. Some have even become the *classic* (or standard) models for such systems.

One of the most difficult problems in modeling is to first understand the process well enough to construct a model of the more important aspects of the process. It is very difficult to convey the dynamics of this creative part of modeling in such a static environment as a textbook. Therefore, each case study begins with a description of the problem, the assumptions made, and some justification for the assumptions (experimental if possible). This is not a solution to the problem of conveying the more creative aspects of modeling, but is the best that can be accomplished here in this text.

8.2 The Basic Approach to a Case

In practice, a performance analyst will begin by talking with the design engineers to get a fundamental understanding of how the system functions. Do not assume that any one engineer or manager really understands how the system works. In fact, for the performance expert to be really effective, she or he must begin by being a great systems engineer.

To have a fundamental understanding of the system, all of the possible interactions and some idea of the potential frequency of those interactions must be understood. Clearly, not all possible interactions can be anticipated or denoted, so the abstraction of the model begins at this stage. Hopefully, things that are left out are insignificant to the particular behavior the performance analyst is trying to determine. (You will be surprised how many things are really insignificant in their effect on the average performance of a system and how some seemingly simple things have a significant effect.)

Next, once the performance analyst has a good idea of the process, the particular type of modeling technique must be selected. The tradeoffs between analytical modeling and simulating come into play at this point. If a simulation is used, the system can be modeled more precisely (although not completely since the simulation must run in some reasonable time). Simulations tend to be easily accepted by clients, since they are systems people themselves. However, changes to the system are harder to reflect in the simulation, so the client will need to become an expert to adequately support the simulation. (As an alternative the client could keep the performance analyst on retainer, a useful point to remember.) That is one of the most important reasons for using standard simulation languages which let the user build a simulation in much the same way as we have constructed analytical models. These special purpose languages provide a high level interface for the user to define queues, passive resources (like memory requirements) and synchronization points. Ontheotherhand, if an analytical model is used, many different design alternatives can be quickly compared with a wide variety of parameter values. So, if an analytical model is possible (and they often are not) then it is usually the preferred option.

The next major step to actually construct the model. This entails formulating a mathematical problem, using one of the basic models described in this book, or designing the simulation program.

The last step in modeling the system is to determine the input or load specification for the model. This is often not given the appropriate attention necessary for a complete study. This means that all of the parameters for the components and their interactions must be specified. This can be a major problem if the design is not complete. Even if the design is complete, a new design can create a new environment where the actual load placed on the system is simply not quantifiable. (Consider the newer distributed systems where a large number of powerful workstations, print servers, file servers, and communication servers interact. Clearly, parameters from time-sharing systems are not directly applicable.)

The most appropriate parameters to use are obtained from experimental measures on the system being modeled. However, we immediately see that we have a chicken and egg problem with such a source of information. If you can measure it, why model it? If you can't get the correct parameters, then the model will not give the correct predictions. However, all is not lost, since some parameters can be measured correctly from other systems and still other parameters can be inferred from previous experience and knowledge of the system under study.

Eventually, the measures are obtained from the model evaluation and the analyst must summarize, interpret, and present the results. Presentation is a very important part of performance modeling. The best model or study in the world is worthless unless the results can be presented in a form which is understandable and useful to the client. Here is one common point of friction. Since the performance analyst works with all of this sophisticated mathematics and/or software, the client often expects exact answers. We have often presented exact answers in our sample problems, but that is really misleading. The idea of getting 0.135 seconds for the anticipated response time for some system does not mean that a particular run will result in 0.135 seconds of response time. Recall the section on confidence intervals in Chapter 4. An experiment will usually result in an outcome different from the expected value. In fact, since the input parameters are often an approximation there is even more of a chance for deviation from the predicted performance.

The results of a performance study should be presented to locate particularly heavily used components or subsections, to compare two different design approaches, and to uncover poorly understood designs and design assumptions. Under these conditions, a 10% to 20% error may be perfectly acceptable (especially if the various designs differ in performance by an order of magnitude).

The first case study has been selected to illustrate just that point. The model is trivial and the computations are simple applications of formulas from Chapter 6. However, it clearly illustrates the usefulness of performance modeling to support management decisions.

8.3 A Simple Capacity Planning Problem

In the April 1980 issue of IEEE *Computer* magazine dedicated to analytical modeling, this application was used by Arnold O. Allen to motivate analytical modeling. In this situation, a manager has been presented with a situation where he must decide whether or not to buy another expensive piece of equipment, as suggested by his designers, and where to put it, if he does purchase it.

8.3.1 The Problem

Consider a situation where a manager supervises a VLSI design group at some small corporation. The designers in this group must take a logic diagram and design CMOS and NMOS cells to implement the design. Much of the preliminary work and device simulation is done at simple terminals attached to a larger mainframe. There are enough such terminals for every designer to have one dedicated to his use. However, at present, there is only one high resolution graphics workstation which can be used to interactively design the cell layouts.

The designers have complained that they must often wait an hour or so just to get on the machine, even though they only use it for about a half hour. They want the company to buy another graphics workstation at a cost of 50,000 dollars. There is enough money in the budget, but if spent unwisely, it could not be spent on something else.

The problem for the manager is to decide whether another graphics workstation is really needed, and whether or not to place it at the same spot as the current one or locate it elsewhere.

8.3.2 The Model

There is no need to construct a complicated model to make a go/no-go type of decision. The model must simply distinguish between the alternatives. In this case, the simplest model is the M/M/1 queue for the designers waiting to use the workstation. Using this model includes a lot of assumptions about the actual process that may or may not be true, but it cannot be very far off.

To set up the model, we must determine the load parameters on the queue. For that, some simple observations are needed so the manager asks the systems administrator to give him the login logs and some summary information. The summary is given in table 8.1.

Number of users	10 per day
Available hours	8 per day
Average login	30 minutes

Table 8.1

More detailed information could be obtained from the log reports, but the manager wants to make a quick decision. (In addition, adding more information to an imperfect model doesn't justify the added effort.)

8.3.3 The Analysis

Putting some of the information together, we note that the system is used by 10 designers per day for an average time of 30 minutes, so the average busy time is about 5 hours per day. The system is not completely utilized. However, that utilization of 5/8 in the M/M/1 model indicates an average number of designers in queue of $5/3 - 5/8 = 25/24$, More importantly to the designers, the average waiting time is $4/3 - \frac{1}{2} = 5/6$ hours, or 50 minutes. It appears that the designers do have a valid complaint.

However, even though the average wait is long, it may be the case that only a few designers wait for a very long time while most designers wait for only a short time. To check that, the manager can use the $M/M/1$ model to compute the amount of time that 90% of the designers have to wait.

$$P[w \le t] = W(t) = 1 - \rho e^{-\mu(1-\rho)t}$$
$$0.90 = 1 - \rho e^{-\mu(1-\rho)t}$$
$$e^{-\mu(1-\rho)t} = \frac{1}{10\rho}$$
$$t = \frac{1/\mu}{1-\rho} \ln 10\rho$$
$$= \frac{30}{3/8} \ln(50/8) = 146.6 \tag{8.1}$$

So, given the measured values and the validity of the $M/M/1$ assumption, we determine that 90% of the designers would wait less than 147 minutes. Even if there is a 20% error, that is still too long to make the designers wait, so the decision to purchase the workstation has been supported.

It now remains to see if such a purchase of a single workstation will really improve the situation. Adding the second workstation changes the situation from a $M/M/1$ model to a $M/M/2$ model if we install the new workstation at the site of the current workstation. Since the same designers come to the stations just as often * and the session duration stays the same, the new system utilization becomes half of the previous value of 5/8, or 5/16. Using that value we can substitute for ρ in the following formula for the $M/M/2$ model (see Problem 6.2).

$$P_0 = P[\text{idle}] = \frac{1-\rho}{1+\rho+2\rho^2} = 0.456 \tag{8.2}$$

$$P[\text{queue}] = 1 - P_0 - P_1 = \frac{2\rho^2}{1+\rho+2\rho^2} = 0.1295$$

$$N = E[k] = 2\rho + \frac{2\rho^3}{(1-\rho)^2} P_0 = 0.684$$

$$W = N/\lambda - 0.5 = 0.684/1.25 - 0.5 = 0.0472 \tag{8.3}$$

From these calculations, we note that both systems are idle almost half the time (compared with about one third for the single system), but the probability of walking up and having to wait is only around 0.12. We can also see that the

---

* This is an approximation, since waiting less will mean that they would do more useful work and would return to the workstation more often.

average waiting time has dropped from 50 minutes to closer to 3 minutes. This should please the designers.

Therefore, installing the additional workstation should improve the situation for the designers. But the new workstation does not have to be placed beside the current one. What would we expect to see for waiting times if we separated the systems?

To model this option we assume that we can place the workstation at some site where the designers will split equally so that 5 designers per day visit each site. Secondly, we assume that the sites are separated by enough distance that when a designer sees one workstation busy, he or she will not proceed to the other site, but simply wait. (Hopefully, the wait will be short enough to keep designers from trying to move back and forth.) In this case we have two $M/M/1$ queues with half of the arrival rates.

$$\rho = 0.625/2 = 0.3125$$
$$W = \frac{0.5}{1 - 0.3125} - 0.5 = 0.227$$

So, the average waiting time for the designers when the workstations are separated is about 14 minutes. That is significantly larger than the 3 minutes for the same site case, so the manager would probably put the two workstations together unless there were other issues, such as travel time or politics, which were not included in this model.

8.3.4 Commentary

Of course, not all facets of a decision are quantitative. The manager may include many other issues in the final decision. Political, budgetary, psychological, and sociological issues often dominate the quantitative evaluation.

One question that may have already occurred to the reader is; "Why buy anything at all if it was under-utilized in the first place?" Many system managers do look at the problem from the standpoint of optimizing utilization. If one required the designers to sign up for time slots, and give up the workstation at the end of their slot whether or not they were finished, there would be no waiting for the system. (We would, in effect, change the situation from Poisson arrivals to deterministic arrivals and deterministic service, the $D/D/1$ queue.) However, that approach ignores the impact that such a scheme may have on the designers' productivity. So, there is no easy answer to the real problem of capacity planning.

Another point that may affect the actual decision is simple politics. If the designers are physically separated because of a space allocation problem, placing the additional workstation at the remote site, although less efficient, could be considered as a signal to the other designers of their importance. The loss of efficiency could easily be made up in an increase in productivity due to improved morale.

The kind of analysis illustrated in this case study is often called decision support, since it is really intended to provide quantitative support of a particular decision, not to actually determine the answer. The real purpose of modeling is to support decisions and evaluations, but not to automate them. The models are tools for the analyst to make some quantitative comparisons. The models never provide complete and precise information about the future.

8.4 A Time Sharing System

When computers first became available, they were used in a batch environment which simply queued jobs for execution, one after another. This strategy maximized the utility of the expensive computer system, but required users to wait for a significant time (turnaround) before the results of a run could be examined. Therefore, the actual time from program design to program release was usually very long. This was the motivation for a new operating system design which processed jobs on a round robin basis, spending a small amount of time on each program, allowing more than one program to be in progress at a time.

Once more than one program could be in the system at any one time, people started attaching terminals to the computer and allowing users to initiate their own programs. This allowed more than one user to be "sharing" the computer at one time. Each user was getting a share of the computer's processing time.

8.4.1 The Problem

The problem with this design is the degradation of service seen by all users when the load gets too high. So, it is necessary to configure a system carefully and to limit the number of simultaneous users to the maximum that the system can handle while maintaining a reasonable average response time.

The basic components of the time sharing system are the users at their terminals, the CPU, and the disk drives with their associated controllers (or channels). There are other components in a real time-sharing system, such as printers and plotters, but they are used infrequently enough and are usually simply output devices controlled by spooling programs. Since the spooling of a file is really disk I/O and the user does not notice that actual delay in printing the job (except for the small amount of speed decrease due the background process) we will not include those devices and their effect in this problem.

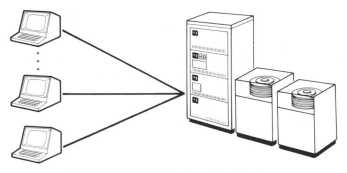

FIGURE 8.1 A Time Sharing System

In the newer time-sharing systems, all processes run with virtual memory support. Therefore, the actual amount of physical memory does not limit the number of processes explicitly, but only decreases the performance of the system. We will assume that there is enough swap space reserved in the configuration of the system to allow all of the processes initiated by users to actually run.

To handle the requirements of the swapping for the virtual memory systems, we will dedicate one special disk for that purpose. (This may be a disk with data as well as swap space, but we will consider the swap use of the disk as dominant.) One of the objectives of this study is to determine the maximum number of users that should be allowed on the system at one time to guarantee some minimal level of service (i.e. some average response time under maximum load).

Normal processing will require disk access for executable processes, input data, and output data (possible spooling). Other, less expensive, disks are selected for this purpose. Determining the proper speed and number of such disks is another objective of the study.

8.4.2 The Model

At any given time, the time-sharing system has a fixed number of users executing a particular load. Therefore, even though the number of users may change over time, we will assume that the system will reach a steady state during the period that a fixed number of users are on the system. That implies that we have a closed system to model where the number of customers (user initiated processes) is fixed. (This, of course, ignores the fact that in a modern time-sharing system a user may initiate any number of independent processes.)

So, for this problem we will select a closed network of queues as the model for the time-sharing system. The users at their terminals will sit for some period of time (think time) while they read the output of a process on the screen before they initiate a new process. This means that no user will wait for another user before deciding what to type, so a multi-server model with the number of servers equal to the number of users would be an appropriate selection. However, if we assume that only one process at a time is initiated by a user, then we can use an infinite server model for the users at their terminals, and the number of customers circulating in the network of queues represents the actual number of users.

The CPU is processing each of the tasks in its queue on a round robin basis, but that cannot be modeled exactly. However, if a process references an address which is not loaded, then a page fault will occur, requiring the operating system to read the information off of the paging area on the disk. This is slow enough for the operating system to suspend the current process and start the next one on the ready queue. Similarly, if a process requests some disk I/O directly, those devices are slow enough in comparison that the process is suspended until the I/O action completes. So, in fact, the amount of time a process is given is not always used. In this model, the amount of time given a process is exponentially distributed and the ready queue is treated as a FCFS queue. If the process does not cause a page fault, request I/O, or complete execution, then the process returns to the end of the queue for more processing.

The disks are modeled as FCFS queues, which requires the assumption of an exponentially distributed service time. This, in fact, is not correct. Actual measurements of disk response times in time-sharing systems indicate that there is less variance in disk access time than the exponential model would indicate.

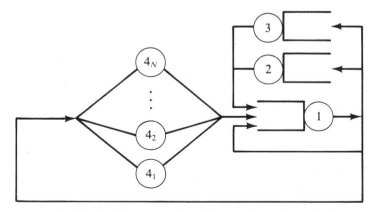

FIGURE 8.2 A Queuing Network Model of a Time Sharing System

8.4.3 The Analysis

The first step in analyzing the system is to obtain some parameters for the components in the model. For this study, we will be using the values associated with a VAX® 11/750 computer manufactured by Digital Equipment Corporation. We are assuming that the operating system is the Ultrix® operating system (a UNIX® equivalent from DEC.) The computer has two disk drives, a RA80 fixed winchester disk and a RL02 removable cartridge disk.

	RA80	RL02
Capacity	121 MB	10.4 MB
Avg. Seek	25 ms	55 ms
Avg. Latency	8.33 ms	12.5 ms
Avg. Access	33.33 ms	77.5 ms

Table 8.2

The execution of the processes in a time-sharing operating system is controlled by the scheduler. Many of the parameters are "tunable" by the system administrator, so they do not have a fixed value. We will assume that the amount of time (quantum) that the scheduler will give a process is 50 milliseconds. However, processes will usually execute for some fraction of that time since they will be suspended for I/O, while some processes will cycle in the ready queue for some time before completing or requesting I/O. In this model we are using an exponentially distributed service time with a mean value of 50 ms. Couple that with a probability of 0.1 of returning directly to the ready queue, and we have an average CPU burst time of about $50/0.9 = 55.6$ ms. Note that a large number of processes will complete execution or request I/O before the average processing time is up since the exponential distribution is "bursty."

Since the majority of commands executed by the users are very short commands, the probability that a process will complete its required execution when it leaves the CPU queue is high. Therefore, the probability that a process will leave the CPU queue and return to the infinite server queue (representing the users) is equal to 0.4 in this model. The service time in the infinite server queue is the average time a user spends thinking before entering another command. In an interactive environment, users will respond in about 5 seconds. This is characteristic of editors and simple system commands.

In the absence of any information about the disk access pattern we will assume that the disks are relatively full and that the probability that a disk is

VAX and Ultrix are registered trademarks of Digital Equipment Corporation. UNIX is a registered trademark of AT&T.

accessed is proportional to its size. So the RA80 is accessed 92% of the time when a disk access is made, while the RL02 is accessed only 8% of the time. Given the probability that a process accesses a disk is 0.5, the probability of accessing the RA80 is 0.46 and the probability of accessing the RL02 is 0.04.

The system configuration document indicates that the base VAX 11/750 system can handle about 32 users. If we use these parameters for the workload and the population size of 32, we can run the mean value analysis code from Chapter 7 to obtain the values shown in Table 8.3.

QUEUE	LENGTH	WAIT	THRUPUT
1	2.27	0.104	14.70
2	0.29	0.009	6.76
3	0.05	0.004	0.59
4	29.39	0.000	5.88

Table 8.3

Note that the throughput for the CPU queue is 14.70 processes per second. We can obtain the average CPU utilization from the relationship $\rho = \lambda \bar{x}$ for single server queues which indicates that the CPU is utilized 73% of the time for this workload. We can also obtain the average response time using Little's result applied to the queues 1, 2, and 3 as a whole, $(32 - 29.39)/5.88 = 0.444$ seconds. This would indicate that 32 users is a reasonable limit for this machine.

It is important to remember that the system can handle 32 users whose workload fits this pattern. This pattern is characteristic of highly interactive, light load users. (Almost all processes would complete in less than one half of a second.) If the users were programmers who do a large number of compiles, the probability that a process would complete after leaving the CPU queue would be an order of magnitude lower (say 0.05.) Therefore, the probability of the process returning to the CPU queue would be higher (say 0.2) and the probability of accessing the RA80 and RL02 would change to 0.69 and 0.06 respectively. Assuming this more characteristic workload for programmers, we obtain a very different table of results.

QUEUE	LENGTH	WAIT	THRUPUT
1	2.85	0.111	17.70
2	0.64	0.019	12.22
3	0.09	0.006	1.06
4	4.43	0.000	0.89

Table 8.4

We note from the results given in Table 8.4 that the CPU is utilized 89% of the time when only 8 programmers are running on the same computer. Similarly, the response time has increased to $(8 - 4.43)/0.89 = 4.01$ seconds. So, the number of users for this system could be 32 if the users are light, interactive users but must be limited to less than 8 (more like 4) if the users are more intensive users like programmers.

8.5 A Multiprocessor

There are many different designs for a multiprocessor. There may be one or more memory units, one or more communication paths, and one or more instruction streams. The one common point is that there is more than one processing element.

1. For simplicity, the system may have many different processors with private memory on one or more common buses.
2. To allow more concurrency in accessing data, the system may have an interconnection network between a collection of memory modules and the processing elements. The interconnection network can be complete (a crossbar) or incomplete (a Banyan network, Omega network, or a simple bus).

Each of these approaches emphasizes a different side of the cost/flexibility tradeoff. The bus approach is cheaper and easier to design, but the bus itself becomes the system bottleneck. The interconnection network allows more flexibility and moderate cost. The crossbar network allows complete connectivity at a very high cost.

The whole purpose of the multiprocessor is to overcome the limitation of the processing power of a single processor. If several processors can cooperate to accomplish a task, then they can either solve larger problems or solve standard problems faster. However, it is not at all clear where that cost/performance tradeoff point actually is located. In fact, at the time of the writing of this book, there is still a very active research effort pursuing the answer to this question. (Note that even though we are attempting to model one of these designs, we do not really understand how the system will be used and therefore, how it will be loaded. As we learn more, the model may be adapted to include the more appropriate load requirements.)

8.5.1 The Problem

One particular multiprocessor was designed and built in the mid-1970s. The system was developed at Carnegie-Mellon University and was called the CM.mmp. The design was made up of 16 processors connected to 16 memory modules through a crossbar interconnection. This allowed any processor to access any memory module, unless it was currently in use. (A crossbar is the kind of interconnection originally used in telephone systems. You could call anyone you wanted, but you might get a busy signal.) The processors had no local memory, so each read and write had to go across the crossbar to some memory module.

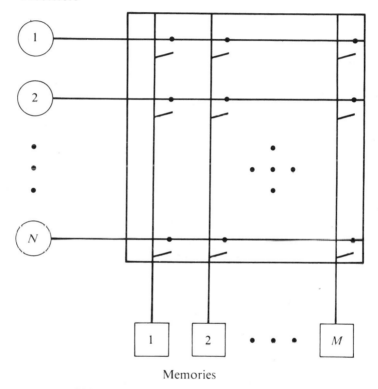

FIGURE 8.3 The CM.mmp Multiprocessor

So, during the operation of the system, each processor may be executing an instruction, decoding an instruction, reading an instruction from memory, or reading/writing data from/to memory. If, during the memory access, one of the other processors is currently accessing that memory, the processor will have to wait for the current access to complete. Clearly, we could operate the system as 16 independent processors, since if each processor accessed a different memory module, then there would be no blocking. However, in that case since the processors could not communicate, they could not cooperate to solve some task which was larger.

The problem with such a design is the difficulty in predicting how often the processors are going to get that busy signal, and wait without accomplishing anything useful. In a 1973 study at CMU, Dileep Bhandarkar suggested and analyzed several models of this architecture. One of the models was a discrete time Markov chain model which we will describe here.

8.5.2 The Model

We begin by modeling the time as a discrete quantity. Each Δt time step in the model represents the entire time to compute an address, access memory, and execute an instruction. This means that each step of the model represents several machine cycles. In the real system, this time will vary for different instructions, but we will ignore that variation in our model. (Bhandarkar also developed more complex models.)

We now define the state of the system as a vector **n** whose elements, n_i, are the number of processors currently accessing or waiting to access the ith memory module. By defining the state of the system in this way, we have assumed that the processors behave in a similar way and are not distinguishable. We have also assumed that a processor which is waiting for access to a memory module currently being accessed by another processor must wait for a full step. In the real system, because execution and memory reads may overlap, the blocking is not so complete. This makes our model a conservative one, which is often useful in the design phase where many unknown quantities still exist.

The set of states and the state transitions (omitting self loops) for a system with 3 processors and 3 memory modules is shown in Figure 8.4. Note that states like (3,0,0) only have one processor actively accessing memory. Therefore, only one processor is capable of completing execution and making another memory access. So, from a state (3,0,0) only the states (2,1,0), (2,0,1), or (3,0,0) are possible on the next step.

The probabilities assigned to each transition depend on the probability, p_m, that a processor will access a particular memory module m. If we assume that the processors access memory identically and independently then we can construct the one-step transition probability matrix.

The entries are formed by recognizing the fact that a state like (1,1,1) will have three processors ready at the end of the time step, while a state like (3,0,0) can have only one ready processor. We have assumed that processors select the next memory module independently and at random, so the transition probability is the product of the probabilities that a particular memory is selected by each of the ready processors. In some cases, there are several ways for the ready processors to select the 3 memory modules, so we multiply the probability by that number. As an example, in the case of a transition from the state (1,1,1) back to itself, there are three processors selecting memory modules such that each has its own module. That can occur in 3! different ways.

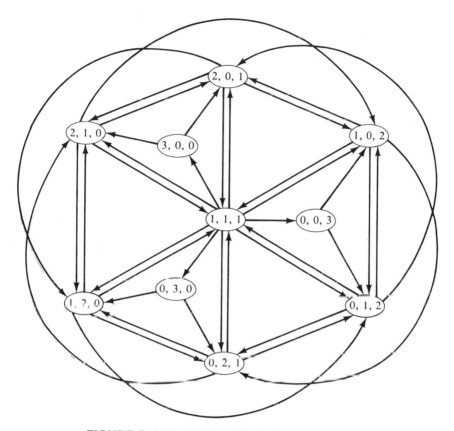

FIGURE 8.4 The Markov Chain for the CM.mmp

8.5.3 The Analysis

Note that for the simple case of 3 processors and 3 memory modules this Markov model has 10 states. In general, for a system with N processors and M memory modules, counting the number of possible states is the same as counting the number of ways of putting N identical objects into M different bins.

$$\text{Number of states} = \binom{N + M - 1}{M - 1} \tag{8.4}$$

So, for the target system of 16 processors and 16 memory modules, the number of possible states in this simple model is 300540195, which is far too large to be tractable. Therefore, some simplification is necessary if we wish to model a system larger than 8 processors and 8 memory modules.

If we consider the case where all processors access memory modules uniformly (i.e. $p_i = 1/M$), then we can reduce the state space by only considering

	(1,1,1)	(3,0,0)	(0,3,0)	(0,0,3)	(2,1,0)	(2,0,1)	(1,0,2)	(0,1,2)	(0,2,1)	(1,2,0)
(1,1,1)	$6p_1p_2p_3$	p_1^3	p_2^3	p_3^3	$3p_1^2p_2$	$3p_1^2p_3$	$3p_1p_3^2$	$3p_2p_3^2$	$3p_2^2p_3$	$3p_1p_2^2$
(3,0,0)	0	p_1	0	0	p_2	p_3	0	0	0	0
(0,3,0)	0	0	p_2	0	0	0	0	p_2	p_3	p_1
(0,0,3)	0	0	0	p_3	0	0	p_1	p_2	0	0
(2,1,0)	$2p_2p_3$	p_1^2	0	0	$2p_3p_2$	$2p_1p_3$	p_3^2	0	0	p_2^2
(2,0,1)	$2p_2p_3$	p_1^2	0	0	$2p_1p_2$	$2p_1p_3$	p_3^2	0	0	p_2^2
(1,0,2)	$2p_1p_2$	0	0	p_3^2	0	p_1^2	$2p_1p_3$	$2p_2p_3$	p_2^2	0
(0,1,2)	$2p_1p_2$	0	0	p_3^2	0	p_1^2	$2p_1p_3$	$2p_2p_3$	p_2^2	0
(0,2,1)	$2p_1p_3$	0	p_2^2	0	p_1^2	0	0	p_3^2	$2p_2p_3$	$2p_1p_2$
(1,2,0)	$2p_1p_3$	0	p_2^2	0	p_1^2	0	0	p_3^2	$2p_2p_3$	$2p_1p_2$

Table 8.5

the pattern of processor access and not the specific modules. For example, the state (2,0,1) has the same pattern as (2,1,0) since there is one queued processor and two active processors in both cases. In any particular pattern, the performance measure of the number of waiting processors is the same. In each of the states (3,0,0), (0,3,0), and (0,0,3) there are exactly two processors waiting for access. So, for states with the same pattern, the performance measure of interest is the same. We will simplify our model by considering a reduced state space where states like (3,0,0), (0,3,0), and (0,0,3) are considered as a single state, (2), for the number of blocked processors.

This technique of state reduction is called *merging* or *state aggregation*. The idea is to merge states into sets of states S_m which are replaced by a single state in the merged Markov chain. The states of a discrete time Markov chain can be merged into sets of states S_m, S_n, if the probabilities satisfy the following property.

$$\sum_{j \in S_n} p_{ij} = \sum_{j \in S_n} p_{kj} \; \forall \; i,k \in S_m \tag{8.5}$$

So, for our case, the state (1,1,1) is grouped by itself in a state denoted as 0, while the states (2,1,0), (2,0,1), (1,0,2), (0,1,2), (0,2,1), and (1,2,0) are grouped together in a state denoted as 1, and the states (3,0,0), (0,3,0), and (0,0,3) are grouped together in a state denoted as 2.

	0	1	2
0	2/9	2/3	1/9
1	2/9	2/3	1/9
2	0	1/3	2/3

Table 8.6

This can be visualized in the state transition diagram shown in Figure 8.4 as a folding of the diagram along its the radius. In the case of 16 processors and 16 memory modules, the total number of merged states is only 231, far more manageable than the original number 300540195.

The reduced state Markov chain can be solved to find the steady state probabilities.

$$\pi_0 = \frac{1}{6} \quad \pi_1 = \frac{7}{12} \quad \pi_2 = \frac{1}{4} \tag{8.6}$$

The average number of waiting processors can then be computed directly from the steady state probabilities.

$$E[k] = 1 \cdot \frac{7}{12} + 2 \cdot \frac{1}{4} = \frac{13}{12} = 1.0833 \tag{8.7}$$

So, this implies that this architecture, assuming the uniform access pattern and independence between the processors, can only achieve a two-fold speedup using three processors and three memory modules. Bhandarkar found that the ratio of active processors to available processors was roughly 0.6 for this simple model, indicating a linear speedup with the number of processors.

The main point of any study is the applicability of the results. Only a limited experimental evaluation was possible in the study since the machine had not been completed. Experiments were run with 1, 2, and 3 processors accessing a single memory module. The analytical models matched the measurements to within 10% for the few measurements that were made in 1973.

8.6 A Packet Switching Network

Time sharing systems, since they allowed many people to be attached at one time, could permit users at remote sites to share the computer, if there was some way to physically connect the terminals at the remote site to the host computer. This was normally accomplished with a system of modulator/demodulators (*modems* for short) which converted the characters used by terminals and computers to analog signals which could be transmitted over telephone lines. However, such methods had problems with errors and the expense of having to use a dedicated circuit for the transmission. (The use of dialup lines means that the circuit is only dedicated during the call, but even if there are no characters being transmitted, it is not usable by anyone else during the call.) These problems, while tolerable for humans connected to computers which were relatively close, were not tolerable for computers connected to other computers which were some distance away.

In the early 1960's, a different kind of network, a packet switching network, was suggested for connecting computer systems. In the packet switching network, information to be transmitted is broken up into small pieces called packets which can use redundancy to detect errors and additional information to label the packet with a particular source and destination. Since the packets are identified with labels, many packets from different sources and to different destinations could share the same physical connection. All that was required (this is definitely an oversimplification) was for the receiver to sort the packets based upon the source and destination information. If a packet had a destination other than the sorting site, the Interface Message Processor (IMP) would forward the packet. The human analogy is the postal system where lots of different people communicate using the same transmission medium (postal trucks, boats, and airplanes) by labeling their information.

If the IMPs are connected by point to point connections in an arbitrary manner, a direct connection may not be exist for some source destination pairs. In that case, the processors in the network would receive, store, and sometimes forward a message, this type of network is called a *store and forward network*. If the unit being stored and forwarded is a packet, it is packet-switching network. If the unit being stored and forwarded is an entire message, it is a message-switching network. An important property of store and forward networks is the fact that packets or messages will traverse many different communication links in the process of being sent from a source to a destination. The particular series of communications links traversed by a packet or message is called the *transmission path*.

8.6.1 The Problem

The circuit switching idea means that the either a physical circuit must always be available (wasting resources when it is not in use), or the circuit must be set up (incurring some delay) when the computer needs to send a message. Since the circuit is dedicated, once it is set up, the source and destination are known and no overhead on the transmission is required and no additional delay at any intermediate points is incurred.

The packet switching idea trades off the additional overhead and the fact that the entire packet must be received before it can be forwarded against the increased efficiency of many packets being sent over the same physical medium. In addition, if a message is very long and is broken up into many packets, the first packet can be forwarded while the next packet is being received. One way of viewing this is to consider the circuit switching environment as many slower servers (a source destination pair may be connected by many different circuits) where queues are not allowed, while the packet switching environment is one faster server where queues are used.

8.6.2 The Model

The development of packet switching networks required a model to allow engineers to compare different designs. Several queuing models of telephone networks (circuit switching) had been in use for some time, but the packeting switching network was different enough that it required a different model. Based upon the work of Jackson, Kleinrock developed a queuing network model of a packet switching network which could be used to design such networks. The model is based upon the fact that each packet is transmitted separately (a customer) and at each intermediate node in the path of a packet from its source and destination, it must be requeued for transmission on the next link.

The model uses a queue to represent each direction of each transmission link (full duplex) in the network. The service at a queue is the actual transmission of the packet and is proportional to the length of the packet. So the movement

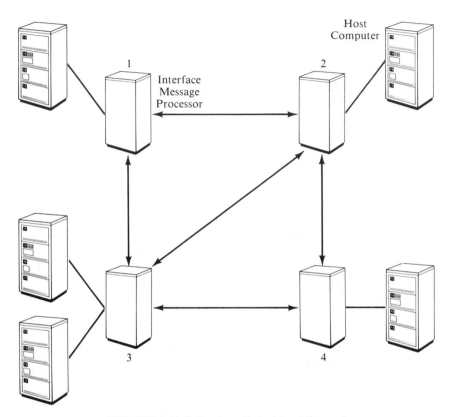

FIGURE 8.5 A Packet Switching Network

of a packet from its source to its destination amounts to having the packet queued for transmission at the source, received by the node at the end of the link when service is complete, requeued for transmission if the node is not the destination, and so on until it is finally received at its destination.

In this model we have some external workload that is offered to network. We denote this workload, γ_{jk}, in packets per second indexed by their source, j, and destination, k. The sum of the workloads for all source destination pair is simply denoted by γ.

$$\gamma \triangleq \sum_{j=1}^{N}\sum_{k=1}^{N} \gamma_{jk} \qquad (8.8)$$

Since a packet may be stored and then forwarded, the actual load on any of the individual links in the network may be higher than the load offered to the network. We will define the load on a link, i, in the network as λ_i and the sum of the offered loads to the links as λ.

$$\lambda \triangleq \sum_{i=1}^{L} \lambda_i \tag{8.9}$$

Clearly, this load will depend on the actual path taken by packets through the network. Therefore, we will assume that a routing algorithm is given such that the loads on the individual links, λ_i, can be determined from the offered load, γ_{jk}, to the network. In our example shown in Figure 8.6, if packets arrive to the network such that $\gamma_{1,4} = 2$ packets per second, then one routing algorithm may require the packets to traverse the intermediate site, 2. This would result in the loads on the links from both 1 to 2 and from 2 to 4 to be increased by 2 packets per second.

For any particular routing assignment, we can characterize the average number of links that a packet will traverse from these workload parameters. Since

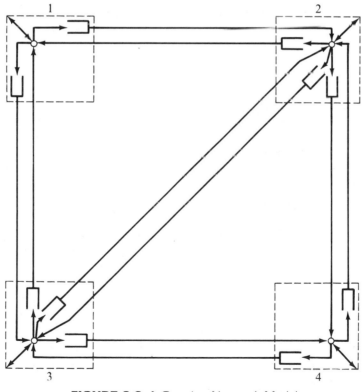

FIGURE 8.6 A Queuing Network Model

the values of loads on the links increase by γ_{jk} for each link, i, that the packets must traverse on their path from site j to site k, the average length for all paths is given by the simple formula given in equation 8.10.

$$E[\text{number of links in a path}] = \frac{\lambda}{\gamma} \qquad (8.10)$$

8.6.3 The Analysis

The objective of this analysis is to obtain an analytical model for the average delay, T, seen by a packet when it traverses the network. This will require some significant assumptions, which we will attempt to justify in this section.

We begin the analysis with our most powerful tool for general systems. We know from Little's result that the average number of packets in the network is simply γT. We can also apply Little's result to each of the queues in the network, so the average number of packets in each queue is $\lambda_i T_i$ where T_i is the yet-to-be-determined queuing delay on each link. Since the sum of the averages is the average of the sum, we have the first part of the model.

$$T = \frac{1}{\gamma} \sum_{i=1}^{L} \lambda_i T_i \qquad (8.11)$$

To analyze the delay incurred by packets as they traverse the network we need to solve for the queuing delays, T_i, at each link in the network. We assume that the communication links have the capacity to transmit C_i bits per second and that packets have a geometrically distributed length with a mean of $1/\mu$ bits, so the time to transmit a packet can be modeled as an exponentially distributed random variable with a rate μC_i.

At this point, we may be tempted to simply assume that this is an open network of FCFS queues and apply Jackson's theorem. Unfortunately, this system violates the important requirement that each queue must have an independent service distribution, not just an exponential one.

Since the length of a packet is the same at each transmission link, the arrival process to each queue is correlated to the service process. This means that this model is not a product form queuing network and accurately computing the value of T_i would be very difficult.

However, even though the arrival process from some other link and the corresponding service times are correlated, the arrival process to the outgoing link is a merged process from many other links and the offered load. Here we note that the merging of the arrivals and splitting of the arrivals according to the routing algorithm reduces the dependence between the service time and the interarrival time of packets to each link. The real question for this model is whether or not, for the number of incoming and outgoing links in our model, assuming an independent service time is a good approximation.

Kleinrock simulated many combinations of incoming and outgoing links and found that single incoming and single outgoing combination was the only poor approximation case. To justify this for yourself you may want to rerun these different cases.

We have now assumed that the system can be approximated by an open network of queues model under the reasonable assumption that the network does not have a linear topology. Using Jackson's theorem, we can now describe the delay in each queue for each link as an independent M/M/1 queue.

$$T_i = \frac{\dfrac{1}{\mu C_i}}{1 - \dfrac{\lambda_i}{\mu C_i}}$$

$$= \frac{1}{\mu C_i - \lambda_i} \tag{8.12}$$

Putting the two results together, we have an analytical model for the average delay of packets sent through a packet switching network. The model is given in terms of the communication link speeds, C_i, the average message length, $1/\mu$, the total offered load to the network, γ, and the routing dependent loads on the individual links, λ_i.

$$T = \frac{1}{\gamma} \sum_{i=1}^{L} \frac{\lambda_i}{\mu C_i - \lambda_i} \tag{8.13}$$

8.7 A Terminal Access Controller Model

The previous model is useful for analyzing packet switching networks. However, not all components in a network support large block transfers to properly use packet switching. Access to a network must be provided for humans who use keyboards and displays (a terminal) and use characters as the basic unit of transfer. This can be accomplished by having all users on host computers which are then connected to the network. However, many times users want to use a network to access the host computer. If they already had a large computer, they wouldn't need the network so badly. So, access to the network could be provided by some more dedicated, less expensive, but limited device.

One such example is found in the X.3 standard for X.25 packet switching networks. To interface a simple asynchronous terminal to a packet switching network, it is necessary to have some device which takes the characters generated by the terminal and puts them into the packets required by the X.25 network. Similarly, packets received from the network must be converted into individual characters for the asynchronous terminal. Such a device is called a packet assembly/disassembly device (PAD).

8.7.1 The Problem

To model a PAD we must understand more about how it actually works. In one direction, a PAD collects characters from the terminals attached to it and puts them into packets. There are several variations on which characters to put in a packet and when to actually form a packet.

Different conditions can be used to trigger the formation of a packet.

1. Build a Packet whenever a fixed packet size is reached. (A size of one amounts to building a packet for every character received.)
2. Build a Packet whenever a special character (such as a carriage return) is received.
3. Build a Packet whenever the maximum packet size is reached or whenever no character has been received for some period of time (a character interarrival timeout).

When a packet is built, the packet can contain characters grouped in different ways.

1. Put all queued characters into one packet, tagging each group with the terminal number.
2. Put all characters from one terminal in one packet. Use separate packets for different terminals.

In the case of the X.25 network, the actual routing of messages through the network is done by a technique called virtual circuits. This requires a path through the network to be defined for each communication session, and each packet associated with that session will have an identifier, the virtual circuit

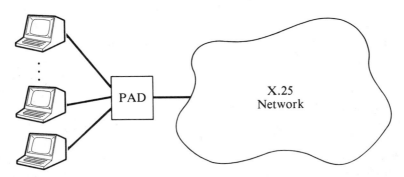

FIGURE 8.7 A Packet Assembly Device on a X.25 Network

number. Therefore, in the X.25 network, PADs must use a separate packet for each terminal.

So, the problem is to model the delays for characters being input into the PAD, assembled into packets, and then transmitted on the network. Note that since a packet must be completely received (for the error checking to be complete) before the characters in the packet can be used, all characters in the packet suffer the same delay as the packet itself. Therefore, the delay a particular character will see is the sum of the delay for waiting for the packet formation and the transmission of the entire packet.

8.7.2 The Model

To model the PAD we will use a special queuing network model. The first queue models the delay for characters waiting to be put into a packet. The second queue models the delay for the packets (containing those characters) to be transmitted into the network. The first queue is completely emptied when service is accomplished. The second queue is a more normal FCFS queue, but with the unusual arrival process from the first queue.

This problem is very complicated, since both the delay in the first queue and the arrival process to the second queue are determined by the selection of the method for triggering packet formation. We will make the same two assumptions as the previous model. Since the input to the second queue is the merging of serveral sources, we will assume that the interarrival process to the second queue is both independent and Poisson. The approximation improves with the number

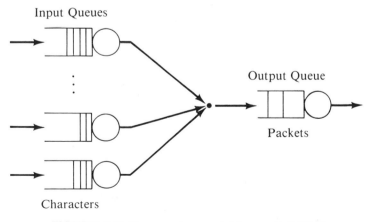

Input Queues

Output Queue

Packets

Characters

FIGURE 8.8 The queuing model for an X.3 PAD

of terminals and is validated by a simulation which models the proper interarrival process to the second queue.

1. Model 1—For the case a fixed packet size, the delay in the first queue is simply the time it takes to collect the appropriate numbers of characters. So the average delay is simply the number of characters in the packet times the average interarrival time. The arrival process to the second is then the merging of a collection of Erlang processes (one for each terminal), which we are approximating as a Poisson process. The service process is simply deterministic. So the delay in the second queue requires the solution to the $M/D/1$ queue.

2. Model 2—For the case of a special character triggering packet formation, the first queue has a delay for characters waiting for the arrival of the special character. We will assume that the probability of an arriving character being the special character is independent and random. So each of the characters in the queue must wait, on the average for the interarrival time of the special character which is the random selection from a Poisson process which is again Poisson. The interarrival process to the second queue is determined by the arrival process of the special character so in this case the arrival process really is Poisson. The service process is distributed as the number of characters between arrivals of the special character, which is geometrically distributed (so we use the continuous analog, the exponential distribution). Therefore, the delay in the second queue requires the solution to the $M/M/1$ queue.

3. Model 3—For the case of the character interarrival timeout, the delay in the first queue is the sum of random variables with truncated exponential distributions. The resulting probability density does not have a closed form and is not easily approximated by any distribution. Because of the complexity of this case, even with our simplifying assumptions, we will not try and solve this model in this book.

8.7.3 The Analysis

The analysis for the first two models is straightforward, due to our simplifying assumptions. We use the following notation in both models.

λ	Poisson input rate of characters from each terminal
C	Rate of transmission on the output channel in char/sec
M	The number of characters in a packet
K	The number of terminals
p	The probability that a character is the special character
H	The number of overhead characters needed to form a packet

Model 1

In the input queue, the first character in a M character packet must wait an average of $M - 1$ character interarrival times. Similarly, the last character does not wait at all. We can pair each of the waiting times of the first and last, the second and next to last, etc. resulting in a total waiting time of $M(M - 1)/(2\lambda)$ for all of the characters. Dividing by the the number of those characters, M, we get the average waiting time for a character in the input queue.

$$W_i = \frac{M - 1}{2\lambda} \tag{8.14}$$

The waiting time in the output queue, W_o, can be computed directly from the M/G/1 formula knowing that packets arrive at an average rate of $k\lambda/M$ and, for a deterministic service $(M + H)/C$, the second moment is simply the square of the service time.

$$W_O = \frac{K\lambda(M + H)^2/(C^2 M)}{2 - 2K\lambda(M + H)/(MC)} \tag{8.15}$$

Adding the service time for a packet and putting the delays together, we obtain an expression for the average time spent by a character from when it leaves the terminal to when it leaves the PAD.

$$T = \frac{M - 1}{2\lambda} + \frac{K\lambda(M + H)^2}{2MC^2 - 2K\lambda C(M + H)} + \frac{M + H}{C} \tag{8.16}$$

In the graph shown in Figure 8.9 we can see the general behavior of the model as a function of the input load (normalized to a percentage of the input line rate) and various packet sizes specified under the X.25 standard. Note the simulation results, denoted by dots, where the simplifying assumptions were not made. The good correspondence between the simulations and the analytical model increase our confidence in the analytical model.

The simulation results do not completely agree with the analytical results, since some of the analytical curve lies outside the 90% confidence intervals of the simulations. This is most pronounced in the region of heavy loads. The assumption of independence gives an upper bound since the dependence between the arrival process and service process in the output queue of this system tends to make it self-regulating. So the output queue acts more like a D/D/1 queue than a M/D/1 queue at the higher load values.

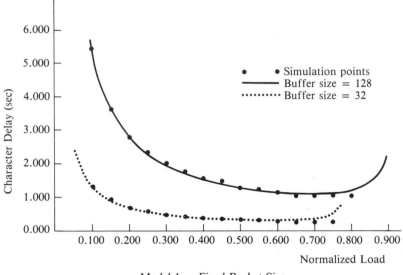

Model 1 — Fixed Packet Size

FIGURE 8.9 Character Delays using PAD Model 1

Model 1 — Buffer size 32		
Activity	Analytic	Simulation [90% Confid.]
0.1	1.2946	1.3560 ± 0.0223
0.2	0.6736	0.6990 ± 0.0171
0.3	0.4708	0.4869 ± 0.0036
0.4	0.3750	0.3783 ± 0.0055
0.5	0.3264	0.3223 ± 0.0022

Table 8.7

Model 1 — Buffer size 128		
Activity	Analytic	Simulation [90% Confid.]
0.10	5.4001	5.5188 ± 0.0962
0.30	1.9248	1.9713 ± 0.0223
0.40	1.5065	1.5631 ± 0.0465
0.50	1.2719	1.3009 ± 0.0131
0.60	1.1412	1.2349 ± 0.0883
0.70	1.0973	1.0613 ± 0.0665
0.80	1.1993	1.0179 ± 0.0743

Table 8.8

Model 2

In the second model, the number of characters in a packet is no longer a constant. The number of characters in the packet is now a geometrically distributed random variable. We have determined the total waiting time for all characters in the input queue for a fixed packet length and we know the distribution of packet length in this case, so we can remove the conditioning on the average waiting time in the input queue.

$$W_i = \frac{1}{m} \sum_{m=1}^{\infty} mW_{i|m}P[m] = \frac{1}{m} \sum_{m=1}^{\infty} m \frac{m-1}{2\lambda} P[m]$$

$$W_i = \frac{p}{2\lambda} \sum_{m=1}^{\infty} m(m-1)p(1-p)^{m-1} = \frac{1}{\lambda p} - \frac{1}{\lambda} \tag{8.17}$$

This result should not be surprising, since we noted that the arrival process of special characters was Poisson with a rate λp. So the average time between special characters is $1/(\lambda p)$. Since the Poisson process has memoryless interarrival times, the average time seen by each character is the same. The additional term appears because a character does not wait for its own interval time. (Notice, if $p=1$ then every character is a special character, and the average waiting time is zero, not $1/\lambda$.)

To model the delay in the output queue, we use the M/M/1 queue model. This is a simplification since, even though the arrival of packets is a Poisson process, the service time is not actually an independent exponential process. First, note that the service time is really a shifted geometric distribution. So, as the probability of an arriving character being the special character, p, increases, the service distribution becomes more deterministic than exponential. Second, the service time is not independent of the arrival process. The longer the message, the more time is spent collecting characters in the input queue, and the longer the interarrival time. Therefore, the assumption of service times independently sampled from an exponential distribution in the M/M/1 model is violated. However, since the longer the service time the longer the interarrival time, the system is self-regulating and the results of the M/M/1 model are an upper bound on the real system. This is evident when you look at the results from the simulations compared with the analytical model in Figure 8.10.

$$W_O = \frac{(1/p + H)/C}{1 - \lambda Kp(1/p + H)/C} = \frac{1 + Hp}{pC - \lambda Kp(1 + Hp)} \tag{8.18}$$

In this model the assumption of independence is even less valid since the service time of packets in the output queue really is a random variable. We have assumed that the output queue acts like an M/M/1 queue which has more variance, and a higher delay, than the M/D/1 queue we used in Model 1. So,

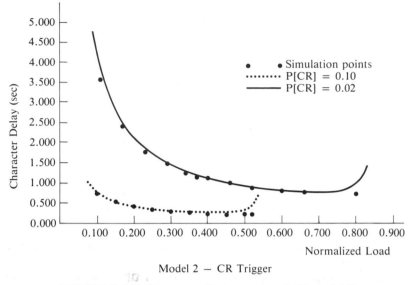

Model 2 − CR Trigger

FIGURE 8.10 Character Delays using PAD model 2

we note that the simulation values start to vary from the analytical model at lower loads than in model 1 and are well out of the 90% confidence interval for loads close to saturation.

Model 2 − P[CR] = 0.1		
Activity	Analytic	Simulation [90% Confid.]
0.10	0.7729	0.7841 ± 0.0300
0.25	0.3341	0.3387 ± 0.0108
0.40	0.2545	0.2321 ± 0.0030
0.50	0.3375	0.2109 ± 0.0021

Table 8.9

Model 2 − P[CR] = 0.02		
Activity	Analytic	Simulation [90% Confid.]
0.1	4.1517	4.0918 ± 0.1476
0.3	1.4538	1.5040 ± 0.1572
0.4	1.1336	1.1693 ± 0.0443
0.5	0.9605	0.9418 ± 0.0666
0.6	0.8793	0.8730 ± 0.0512
0.7	0.9047	0.7552 ± 0.0405

Table 8.10

Simulation Program

This simulation program was used to generate the simulation points shown in Figures 8.9 and 8.10 and the confidence intervals described in Tables 8.7, 8.8, 8.9, and 8.10. The same program is used for both models, since setting the probability of a special character equal to zero is equivalent to simulating the situation for model 1.

The real purpose of the simulation is the validation of the independence assumption. Since the simulation also assumes that characters arrive as a Poisson process, it cannot be used to determine how appropriate that assumption was in the model. In reality, character interarrivals in a real system vary from the Poisson assumption. In fact, the character arrival process is very stylistic and seems more dependent on the individual than on the activity in which the individual is engaged.

```
PROGRAM MODEL2(INPUT,OUTPUT);
(* IN THIS MODEL, A PACKET WILL BE CONSTRUCTED WHEN   *)
(*   <1> THE BUFFER OF INPUT QUEUE OVERFLOWS; OR       *)
(*   <2> A SPECIAL CHARACTER (USUALLY , A CARRIAGE     *)
(*       RETURN) COMES TO THE INPUT QUEUE.             *)

CONST
    INFINITY = 1.0E|39;
    MAXQNO = 10;
    MAXEVENTNO = 10000;
    TRANSIENT = 1000;
    NUMBATCH = 3;
    MAXBATCH = 10;
    BITSINCHAR = 10; (* BITS IN EACH CHARACTER *)

TYPE
    PTR = ^OUTQTYPE;
    OUTQTYPE = RECORD
    (* OUTPUT QUEUE MARKS DOWN THE ARRIVAL TIME AND  *)
    (*      THE NUMBER OF CHARACTERS OF EACH PACKET   *)
                INTIME : REAL;
                SIZE : INTEGER;
                INQDELAY : REAL;
                NEXT : PTR
              END;

VAR
    TERMNO : INTEGER;      (* NO. OF TERMINALS IN SYSTEM *)
    BUFFER : INTEGER;      (* SIZE OF THE BUFFER [CHAR]  *)
    OVERHEAD : INTEGER;    (* NO. OF OVERHEAD CHARACTERS *)
    LAMBDA : INTEGER;      (* TERM. BAUD RATE [BITS/SEC] *)
```

```
    C : INTEGER;            (* TRUNK BAUD RATE [BITS/SEC] *)
    A : REAL;               (* ACTIVITY OF THE TERMINAL   *)
    P : REAL;               (* PROB A CHAR IS A SPEC CHAR *)
    OUTQHEAD : PTR;         (* PTR TO HEAD OF OUTPUT QUEUE*)
    OUTQTRAIL : PTR;        (* OUTPUT QUEUE TAIL POINTER  *)
    TOTALDELAY : REAL;      (* DELAY SEEN BY ALL CHAR     *)
    TOTALNOCHAR : INTEGER;(* TOTAL NO. OF CHAR PROCESSED*)
    DELAY : REAL;           (* AVERAGE CHARACTER DELAY    *)
    VARDELAY : REAL;        (* UNBIASED VAR. OF CHAR DELAY*)
    ERROR : REAL;           (* 90% CONFIDENCE INTERVAL    *)
    SAMPLE : INTEGER;       (* THE BATCH COUNTER          *)
    BATCHDELAY : REAL;      (* SUM OF DELAY FOR A BATCH   *)
    BATCHDELAYSQ : REAL;  (* SUM OF SQUARES FOR BATCH   *)
    CLOCK : REAL;
    PACKETNO : INTEGER;     (* # OF PACKETS OUT OF SYSTEM *)
    EVENTNO : INTEGER;
    NEXTEVENT : INTEGER;
    LAST : INTEGER;
    TRANSRATE : REAL;       (* ACTUAL PAD OUTPUT RATE     *)
    ARRIVERATE : REAL;      (* ACTUAL TERMINAL INPUT RATE *)

  (* # OF CHAR IN QUEUE   *)
  CHARINQ : ARRAY[1..MAXQNO] OF INTEGER;
  (* STUDENT T VALUES     *)
  STUDENT : ARRAY[1..MAXBATCH] OF REAL;
  (* SUM OF ARR TIME IN QUEUE *)
  SUMARRIVAL : ARRAY[1..MAXQNO] OF REAL;
  (* NEXT EVENT FOR QUEUES*)
  TNE : ARRAY[1..MAXQNO] OF REAL;
(* ********************************************** *)
FUNCTION EXPON(RATE : REAL) : REAL;

VAR RN : REAL;
    X : REAL;

BEGIN
    RN := RANDOM(X);
    EXPON := -(1 / RATE) * LN(RN)
END;
(* ********************************************** *)
PROCEDURE READIN;

BEGIN
    READLN(TERMNO,BUFFER,OVERHEAD,LAMBDA,C,A,P);
    ARRIVERATE := (LAMBDA * A) / BITSINCHAR;
    TRANSRATE := C /BITSINCHAR;
```

```
        LAST := TERMNO + 1;
END;
(* **************************************************** *)
PROCEDURE INITIALIZE;

VAR I : INTEGER;

BEGIN
    FOR I := 1 TO TERMNO DO
    BEGIN
        CHARINQ[I] := 0;
        SUMARRIVAL[I] := 0;
        TNE[I]:= EXPON(ARRIVERATE); (* FIRST ARRIVAL *)
    END;
    (* SET OUTPUT PACKET DEPARTURE TIME TO INFINITY *)
    TNE[LAST]:= 10*INFINITY;
    OUTQHEAD := NIL;
    OUTQTRAIL := NIL;
    TOTALDELAY := 0;
    TOTALNOCHAR := 0;
    PACKETNO := 0;
    EVENTNO := 0;
    CLOCK := 0;
END;
(* **************************************************** *)
PROCEDURE DECIDEEVENT(VAR NEXT : INTEGER);

VAR
    CRITERIA : REAL;
    EVENT : INTEGER;

BEGIN
    CRITERIA := INFINITY;
    FOR EVENT := 1 TO LAST DO
        IF TNE[EVENT] < CRITERIA THEN
        BEGIN
            NEXT := EVENT;
            CRITERIA := TNE[NEXT]
        END;
    EVENTNO := EVENTNO + 1;
    CLOCK := TNE[NEXT]
END;
(* **************************************************** *)
PROCEDURE PACKETARRIVE(DELAY : REAL; CHARNO : INTEGER);

(* WHEN THE BUFFER OF INPUT QUEUE OVERFLOWS, OR A SPEC*)
```

```
(* CHARACTER COMES A PACKET IS THEN CONSTRUCTED.    *)
(* HERE, DELAY IS THE AVERAGE WAITING TIME OF A     *)
(* CHARACTER IN THE INPUT QUEUE, AND CHARNO IS THE  *)
(*  PACKET SIZE. *)

VAR
    P : PTR;

BEGIN
    NEW(P);
    P^.INTIME := CLOCK; (* SAVE PKT CONSTRUCTION TIME *)
    P^.SIZE := CHARNO;
    P^.INQDELAY := DELAY;
    P^.NEXT := NIL;
    IF OUTQHEAD = NIL THEN
    BEGIN (* THE OUTPUT QUEUE IS EMPTY NOW *)
        OUTQHEAD := P;
        TNE[LAST] := CLOCK +
                (OUTQHEAD .SIZE + OVERHEAD) / TRANSRATE;
    END
    ELSE OUTQTRAIL^.NEXT := P;
    OUTQTRAIL := P;
END;
(* ************************************************** *)
PROCEDURE CHARARRIVE(Q : INTEGER);

(* WHEN THE SCHEDULED ARRIVAL TIME OF A CHARACTER    *)
(* OCCURS THIS CHARACTER COMES TO THE INPUT QUEUE    *)

VAR
    RAN : REAL;
    X : REAL;
    INQDELAY : REAL;

BEGIN
    CHARINQ[Q] := CHARINQ[Q] + 1;
    SUMARRIVAL[Q] := SUMARRIVAL[Q] + CLOCK;
    RAN := RANDOM(X);
    IF (RAN ≤ P) OR (CHARINQ[Q] = BUFFER) THEN
    BEGIN
        (* INPUT QUEUE OVERFLOWS OR A SPECIAL CHAR   *)
        (* COMES SO A PACKET IS THEN CONSTRUCTED     *)
        INQDELAY := CLOCK * CHARINQ[Q] - SUMARRIVAL[Q];
        PACKETARRIVE(INQDELAY,CHARINQ[Q]);
        CHARINQ[Q] := 0;
        SUMARRIVAL[Q] := 0;
    END;
```

```
      TNE[Q] := CLOCK + EXPON(ARRIVERATE)
END;
(* ***************************************************** *)
PROCEDURE PACKETDEPART;

(* WHEN A PACKET HAS BEEN FINISHED TRANSMISSION       *)

VAR
    P : PTR;
    OUTQDELAY : REAL;

BEGIN
    P := OUTQHEAD;
    OUTQDELAY := CLOCK - OUTQHEAD^.INTIME;
        (* CALCULATE THE WAITING TIME OF THIS PACKET  *)
        (* IN THE OUTPUT QUEUE                         *)
    TOTALDELAY := TOTALDELAY + P^.INQDELAY
                                    + OUTQDELAY * P^.SIZE;
    TOTALNOCHAR := TOTALNOCHAR + P^.SIZE;
    PACKETNO := PACKETNO + 1;
    OUTQHEAD := OUTQHEAD^.NEXT;
    IF OUTQHEAD <> NIL
    THEN TNE[LAST] := CLOCK
                + (OUTQHEAD^.SIZE + OVERHEAD) / TRANSRATE
            (* THE OUTPUT QUEUE IS STILL NOT EMPTY SO  *)
            (* SCHEDULE THE NEXT DEPARTURE TIME        *)
    ELSE
        BEGIN
            OUTQTRAIL := NIL;
            TNE[LAST] := 10*INFINITY
        END;
    DISPOSE(P);
END;
(* ***************************************************** *)
PROCEDURE REPORT;

VAR MEAN : REAL;

BEGIN
    WRITE(' ' : 1, TERMNO : 2,
          ' ' : 1, BUFFER : 5,
          ' ' : 3, OVERHEAD : 2,
          ' ' : 3, LAMBDA : 5,
          ' ' : 3, C : 5,
          ' ' : 3, A : 2 : 2,
          ' ' : 3, P : 5 : 2);
    MEAN := TOTALDELAY / TOTALNOCHAR ;
```

```
    WRITELN(' ' : 2, MEAN : 5 : 5);
END;
(* ************************************************** *)
PROCEDURE CLEAROUTQ;

VAR P : PTR;

BEGIN
    WHILE OUTQHEAD <> NIL DO
        BEGIN
        P := OUTQHEAD;
        OUTQHEAD := P^.NEXT;
        DISPOSE(P)
        END
END;
(* ************************************************** *)
PROCEDURE STARTUP;

BEGIN
    STUDENT[1] := 1.0;
    STUDENT[2] := 6.314;
    STUDENT[3] := 2.920;
    STUDENT[4] := 2.353;
    STUDENT[5] := 2.132;
    STUDENT[6] := 2.015;
    STUDENT[7] := 1.943;
    STUDENT[8] := 1.895;
    STUDENT[9] := 1.860;
    STUDENT[10] := 1.833;

    WRITELN(' ' : 1, 'MODEL 2');
    WRITELN(' ' : 1, '------------------',
                     '------------------',
                     '------------------');
    WRITELN(' ' : 2, 'K', ' ' : 4, 'M', ' ' : 5,
                     'O', ' ' : 3, 'LAMBDA',
              ' ' : 4, 'C', ' ' : 6, 'A', ' ' : 5,
                     'P[CR]', ' ' : 4, 'W');
    WRITELN(' ' : 1, '------------------',
                     '------------------',
                     '------------------');
    WRITELN(' ' : 1, '------------------',
                     '------------------',
                     '------------------');
END;
(* ************************************************** *)
```

```
BEGIN (* MAIN *)
   STARTUP;
   WHILE NOT EOF DO
      BEGIN
      READIN;
      BATCHDELAY := 0.0;
      BATCHDELAYSQ := 0.0;


      FOR SAMPLE := 1 TO NUMBATCH DO
       BEGIN
         INITIALIZE;


         WHILE EVENTNO < MAXEVENTNO DO
            BEGIN
              IF TRANSIENT = EVENTNO
                  THEN BEGIN (* RESET STATS *)
                       TOTALNOCHAR := 0;
                       TOTALDELAY := 0.0;
                       END;
               DECIDEEVENT(NEXTEVENT);
               IF NEXTEVENT <= TERMNO
               THEN CHARARRIVE(NEXTEVENT)
               ELSE PACKETDEPART;
            END;


         CLEAROUTQ;
         DELAY := TOTALDELAY / TOTALNOCHAR;
         BATCHDELAY := BATCHDELAY + DELAY;
         BATCHDELAYSQ := BATCHDELAYSQ + DELAY * DELAY;
         REPORT
       END;


      DELAY := BATCHDELAY / NUMBATCH;
      IF NUMBATCH > 1 THEN
         BEGIN (* COMPUTE UNBIASED VARIANCE *)
         BATCHDELAYSQ := BATCHDELAYSQ - NUMBATCH
                                       * DELAY * DELAY;
         VARDELAY := BATCHDELAYSQ /(NUMBATCH - 1)
         END;
      ERROR :=STUDENT[NUMBATCH]*SQRT(VARDELAY/NUMBATCH);
      IF NUMBATCH > 1 THEN
         WRITELN( ' ':50, DELAY:7:4, ' +- ', ERROR:6:4);
   END
END.
```

8.8 A Token Ring

In this case study, we are looking at a local network architecture called a token ring. Since there are not many such systems installed, and of those that are, few are heavily loaded, we wish to have a model which will give us some idea about how the network will perform under increasing loads. We already know something about the other major local area network, the carrier sense, multiple access with collision detection (CSMA-CD) bus, which has a much larger installed base at the time of this writing. We have the advantage of several measurement studies of loads on a local area network (most of them are on the CSMA-CD bus architecture) so we can infer something about the actual load the network will encounter.

8.8.1 The Problem

A token ring local area network is made up a group of N stations, each attached to a loop of wire (or fiber optics), called the ring, by a ring interface unit (see Figure 8.11). The ring interface unit can forward bits that arrive on

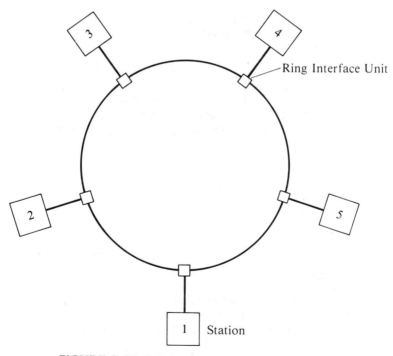

FIGURE 8.11 A Token Ring with 5 stations

the ring to the next interface, insert bits into the ring, or remove bits (i.e. not forward them) from the ring. All bits travel in a single direction around the ring.

Each station will have some messages to send to other stations on the ring. Messages, if they are very long, are broken up into pieces which are individually sent on the network, called packets, which will be reassembled at the receiving station. Since we are concerned with the lower level of the system, the token ring itself, we will consider the load to be made of packets, not messages.

Since the ring is a single communication medium, access to the ring must be controlled or else everyone may send packets on top of each other, destroying all of the packets. This is normally referred to as the *multi-access* problem. To solve the multi-access problem some protocol must be followed by each station to guarantee proper behavior of the network as a whole. There are several approaches to the problem; CSMA-CD is one and token passing (used in the token ring and token bus) is another.

Contention protocols like CSMA-CD simply allow stations to transmit at any time and regulate the behavior when something unusual happens. CSMA-CD is similar to the behavior of people at a dinner party. There is no particular time when you are to talk, you can talk any time you want, but it is impolite to talk on top of someone and if two people start at the same time they both stop and defer to each other until one of them starts without interference.

The token ring is the opposite extreme. In a token ring, precisely when a station can attempt to transmit is regulated. It is then possible to avoid all collisions at the expense of waiting for your turn. A turn is defined by the possession of a special, unique object called a token. It is similar in concept, to the baton used in the Roman Senate to distinguish the individual with the right to speak.

So, a station on the token ring cannot insert bits until a token is received along the ring. To maintain fairness, only one packet may be sent when the token is held and then the token must be passed on to the next station. Therefore, the token circulates around the ring and any station with a packet will send the packet when the token reaches the station.

Since a station will send its packet and then send the token, the next station will append its packet to the end of the first and put the token at the end of that group of packets. This will continue around the ring making the actual transmission on the ring look like a train of packets with the token as the caboose. Messages are removed (i.e. not forwarded) by the original sender of the packet. If the packet makes it all the way around the ring, it must have passed the destination station. So, there is no reason to leave it on the ring. Although packets could be removed from the ring by the destination, this complicates the algorithm and leads to other problems without improving the system throughput that much, so the current standard is to make the sending station remove its own packets.

If the network is small, the first bits of the train will return to the sending station before it has even finished sending the packet, but from the viewpoint of another station passively watching the ring, the bits going by do, indeed, resemble the train analogy. Regardless of how fast the bits get around the ring, the observing station must wait for the time it takes the train to make it around before it can get the token and transmit.

Since a token will be more than one bit long to allow for a unique pattern, a station cannot recognize the token until the last bit has been seen. However, the first bits of the token may have already been forwarded (if the internal storage in the ring interface is small) by the time the token is actually recognized. So, the common practice is to change the last bit of the token and use that new pattern as a *connector* between packets. Then the packet is inserted in the ring followed by a new token. Under this scheme, all packets are followed by a fixed length field of bits which is either a connector (and another packet will follow that) or the token (at the end of the train). So even though a token does actually take time to send, our model will include that time in every packet as either the connector or the actual token.

8.8.2 The Model

As a model of the token ring, consider each station as a queue with Poisson arrivals from the outside world. Then service at each queue depends upon the amount of time for the end of the "packet train," denoted by the token, to reach the station. Since collisions cannot take place, we consider service complete when the packet is inserted into the ring.

To simplify the problem we want to consider only one of the queues (stations). If we assume that all arrivals to the stations have the same arrival process, we can use a symmetry argument to consider only one queue and infer that all others behave the same on the average. So, we have a single queue with Poisson arrivals and a single, general type of server (i.e. the ring).

Therefore, this model, originally proposed by Adarshpal Sethi and Runcay Saydam in 1984, will use the $M/G/1$ model. Since service requires the station to wait for a token, the service time is a function of the token rotation time, T. The amount of time it takes the token (or the packet train) to circulate around the ring is increased or decreased by stations inserting packets into the train. Since every station will eventually receive the token within one token rotation time (a very nice property of token rings) then the station will insert a single packet if it has any to send. We could calculate the distribution of token rotation time, if we knew how many stations would have a packet ready and the size of the packet. Given the distribution of token rotation, we can compute the average time and the variance which can then be substituted into the $M/G/1$ equations for the average waiting time.

If we knew the average token rotation time, $E[T]$, then we could calculate the average utilization of the queue as $\rho = \lambda E[T]$. Conversely, if we knew the average number of non-empty queues on the ring, we could compute the average length of a packet train and therefore the average token rotation time.

To get an expression for the average number of non-empty queues (i.e. busy stations) we will make a simplifying assumption. We will assume that the probability that a random observer (and therefore a Poisson arrival) will find each of the queues empty is an independent random variable. Since the probability of a single server queue being busy is ρ, the probability that precisely n of them are busy is binominally distributed.

$$P[n \text{ queues are busy}] = \binom{N}{n} \rho^n (1 - \rho)^{N-n} \quad 0 \le n \le N \quad (8.19)$$

This assumption is, in fact, not true since the service of each queue depends on the status of the other queues. (However, as we have seen in the previous case studies, there is a trade-off between the accuracy of the assumptions and the tractability of the computations. Assumptions that do not introduce large errors are acceptable if they significantly reduce the computational complexity.) To validate the assumption, we would compare the results of an experimental distribution obtained from a simulation which does not assume independence and the distribution derived under the independence assumption.

We have also assumed that the system is ergodic and therefore has some steady state behavior. This may not, in fact, be the case. It is quite possible that such a system may not be ergodic, but be periodic and still function perfectly well. The only way to understand this more completely is to create a more detailed model, such as a Markov chain with a complete state space, which could then be studied for periodicity and independence.

8.8.3 The Analysis

Using the fact that the number of busy stations is binomially distributed, we can write down (see problem 3.5) the mean and variance for the number of busy stations (and, therefore, the number of packets in the train).

$$\bar{n} = N\rho \quad (8.20)$$
$$\sigma_n^2 = N\rho(1 - \rho) \quad (8.21)$$

Since the token rotation time is the time it takes a station to observe the passing of a fixed length packet times the number of such packets, the random variable T for the token rotation time can be defined in terms of the random variable n for the number of packets. In addition, since it takes some time for a single bit to move around the ring (due to actual propagation delays and the delays built into the ring interface units) the token rotation time is increased by a constant amount of delay d at each station. Therefore, we can immediately write down an expression for the the average token rotation time in terms of the average number of active stations $\bar{n}$, the time to transmit a fixed length packet τ, and the fixed delay d for each of the N stations on the ring.

$$E[T] = \bar{n}\tau + Nd = N\rho\tau + Nd \qquad (8.22)$$

Since the value of the forwarding delay (internal delay in the ring interface and propagation delay) is not a random value (i.e. it is a scalar) the variance is simply the variance of the number of stations times the scalar value of the time it takes to send a message, τ, squared.

$$\sigma_T^2 = \sigma_n^2\tau^2 = N\rho(1 - \rho)\tau^2 \qquad (8.23)$$

We now have some expressions for the average token rotation time in terms of the utilizations of the queues. However, the utilization, ρ, of each queue is, by definition, $\lambda E[T]$. So, substituting this into our equation for $E[T]$, we can derive an expression for the utilization of a station.

$$\frac{\rho}{\lambda} = N\rho\tau + Nd$$

$$\rho = \frac{N\lambda d}{1 - N\lambda\tau} \qquad (8.24)$$

Substituting this back into the expressions for the average and variance of the token rotation time we get the following equations.

$$E[T] = \frac{\rho}{\lambda} = \frac{Nd}{1 - N\lambda\tau} \qquad (8.25)$$

$$\sigma_T^2 = \frac{\lambda N^2 d\tau^2}{(1 - \lambda N\tau)^2}[1 - \lambda N(\tau + d)] \qquad (8.26)$$

Recalling that the second moment $E[T^2]$ is the variance σ_T^2 plus the square of the average $(E[T])^2$ we immediately obtain an expression for the second moment.

$$E[T^2] = \frac{\lambda N^2 d\tau^2}{(1 - \lambda N\tau)^2}[1 - \lambda N(\tau + d)] + \frac{N^2 d^2}{(1 - N\lambda\tau)^2}$$

Recall how the M/D/1 queue was different from a queue with a fixed cycle of service, since an arrival to an empty queue in the M/D/1 model began the deterministic amount of service immediately while a customer arriving to the cyclic queue had to wait for the residual lifetime of the cycle (i.e. latency). In this case we have a similar situation, except the service is not deterministic. So, in this case, if the latency is high because of a large number of packets, the probability that an arriving packet will see an empty queue is low. Conversely, if the probability of an arriving packet finding the queue empty is high, then the value of the latency is low.

To check our assumption that the latency effect was negligible, we can compute the latency weighted by the probability that an arriving customer will see an empty system.

$$\text{Error} - (1 \quad \rho) \frac{E[T]}{2} = \frac{Nd[1 - \lambda N(\tau + d)]}{2(1 - \lambda N\tau)^2} \tag{8.27}$$

So, if the ring is not busy (i.e. $\lambda \cong 0$), then the error is simply $Nd/2$, half of the time it takes to rotate the token. If the ring is busy (i.e. $\rho \cong 1$), then the error is zero. As long as $\tau >> d$ the error will be small. If, for a particular set of values, we find that the value of the latency error is low, we can ignore the latency effect and use the average waiting time and number in the queue equations we derived for the M/G/1 queue.

$$W = \frac{\lambda^2 N^2 \tau^2 d}{2(1 - \lambda N\tau)} + \frac{\lambda N^2 d^2}{2(1 - \lambda N\tau)[1 - \lambda N(\tau + d)]} \tag{8.28}$$

$$N_q = \frac{\lambda N^2 \tau^2 d}{2(1 - \lambda N\tau)} + \frac{N^2 d^2}{2(1 - \lambda N\tau)[1 - \lambda N(\tau + d)]} \tag{8.29}$$

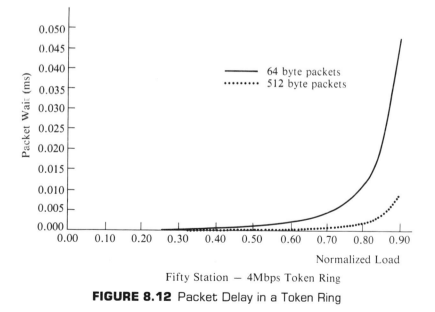

Fifty Station — 4Mbps Token Ring

FIGURE 8.12 Packet Delay in a Token Ring

APPENDIX

Useful Formulas*

A1.1 Sums

A1.1.1 Arithmetic Series

$$\sum_{k=0}^{n} k = 0 + 1 + 2 + \cdots + (n-1) + n = \frac{n(n+1)}{2} \quad (A1.1)$$

A1.1.2 Geometric Series

$$\sum_{k=0}^{n} a^k = 1 + a + a^2 + \cdots + a^{n-1} + a^n = \frac{1 - a^{n+1}}{1 - a} \quad (A1.2)$$

$$\sum_{k=0}^{\infty} a^k = 1 + a + a^2 + a^3 + \cdots = \frac{1}{1 - a} \quad (A1.3)$$

A1.1.3 Exponential Expansion

$$\sum_{k=0}^{\infty} \frac{a^k}{k!} = 1 + a + \frac{a^2}{2} + \frac{a^3}{6} + \cdots = e^a \quad (A1.4)$$

*The formulas in this section are reprinted with permission from *Standard Mathematical Tables, 24th Edition* © 1976 by CRC Press, Boca Raton, FL.

A1.2 Partial Fractions

$$\frac{f(x)}{\Psi(x)} \text{ where } \Psi(x) = \prod_{k=1}^{K} (x - a_k)^{n_k}$$

$$\frac{f(x)}{\Psi(x)} = \sum_{k=1}^{K} \sum_{j=1}^{n_k} \frac{A_{j,k}}{(x - a_k)^{n_k - j + 1}}$$

$$A_{j,k} = \frac{1}{(j - 1)!} \left(\frac{d^{j-1}}{dx^{j-1}} \frac{f(x)(x - a_k)^{n_k}}{\Psi(x)} \right)_{x = a_k} \quad \text{for } 1 \le j \le n_k \quad (A1.5)$$

A1.3 Quadratic and Cubic Equations

$$Ax^2 + Bx + C = (x - a_1)(x - a_2)$$

$$a_1 = \frac{-B + (B^2 - 4AC)^{1/2}}{2A}$$

$$a_2 = \frac{-B - (B^2 - 4AC)^{1/2}}{2A} \quad (A1.6)$$

$$x^3 + Ax^2 + Bx + C = (x - a_1)(x - a_2)(x - a_3)$$

$$a_1 = P + Q - \frac{A}{3}$$

$$a_2 = -\frac{P + Q}{2} + \frac{P - Q}{2}(-3)^{1/2} - \frac{A}{3}$$

$$a_3 = -\frac{P + Q}{2} - \frac{P - Q}{2}(-3)^{1/2} - \frac{A}{3} \quad (A1.7)$$

where

$$P = \left[-\frac{R}{2} + \left(\frac{R^2}{4} + \frac{S^3}{27} \right)^{1/2} \right]^{1/3}$$

$$Q = \left[-\frac{R}{2} - \left(\frac{R^2}{4} + \frac{S^3}{27} \right)^{1/2} \right]^{1/3} \quad (A1.8)$$

where

$$R = \frac{3B - A^2}{3}$$

$$S = \frac{2A^3 - 9AB + 27C}{27} \quad (A1.9)$$

A1.4 Linear Algebra

A1.4.1 A Matrix

$$\mathbf{A} = [a_{i,j}] = \begin{bmatrix} a_{1,1} & a_{1,2} & a_{1,3} & \cdots & a_{1,m} \\ a_{2,1} & a_{2,2} & a_{2,3} & \cdots & a_{2,m} \\ a_{3,1} & a_{3,2} & a_{3,3} & \cdots & a_{3,m} \\ \vdots & \vdots & \vdots & \vdots & \vdots \\ a_{n,1} & a_{n,2} & a_{n,3} & \cdots & a_{n,m} \end{bmatrix} \tag{A1.10}$$

A1.4.2 Transpose of a Matrix

$$\mathbf{A}^T = [a_{j,i}] = \begin{bmatrix} a_{1,1} & a_{2,1} & a_{3,1} & \cdots & a_{m,1} \\ a_{1,2} & a_{2,2} & a_{3,2} & \cdots & a_{m,2} \\ a_{1,3} & a_{2,3} & a_{3,3} & \cdots & a_{m,3} \\ \vdots & \vdots & \vdots & \vdots & \vdots \\ a_{1,n} & a_{2,n} & a_{3,n} & \cdots & a_{m,n} \end{bmatrix} \tag{A1.11}$$

A1.4.3 Determinant of a n by n Matrix

$$|\mathbf{A}| = |a_{i,j}| = \sum_{perm} (-1)^{|perm|} a_{1,perm(1)} \cdot a_{2,perm(2)} \cdots a_{n,perm(n)} \tag{A1.12}$$

Where *perm* is a function that produces all permutations of the sequence $1, 2, \ldots, n$.

$$|\mathbf{A}| = \begin{vmatrix} a_{1,1} & a_{1,2} \\ a_{2,1} & a_{2,2} \end{vmatrix} = a_{1,1}a_{2,2} - a_{1,2}a_{2,1} \tag{A1.13}$$

A1.4.4 Cofactors of a Matrix

$$\mathbf{A}^c = [a_{i,j}^c] \text{ where } a_{i,j}^c = (-1)^{i+j} |\hat{\mathbf{A}}_{i,j}| \tag{A1.14}$$

Where $\hat{\mathbf{A}}_{i,j}$ is the matrix $\mathbf{A}$ with the ith column and jth row removed.

Note that cofactors can be used to compute the determinant.

$$|\mathbf{A}| = \sum_{i=1}^{n} a_{ij}a_{ij}^c = \sum_{j=1}^{n} a_{ij}a_{ij}^c$$

A1.4.5 Inverse of a Matrix

$$\mathbf{A}^{-1} = \frac{\mathbf{A}^+}{|\mathbf{A}|} \tag{A1.15}$$

$$\mathbf{A}^+ = [\mathbf{A}^c]^T \tag{A1.16}$$

A1.5 Integrals

For the following functions u and v of the variable x, integer n and the scalar constants α and C the following hold.

$$\int (u + v)\, dx = \int u\, dx + \int v\, dx \tag{A1.17}$$

$$\int \alpha u\, dx = \alpha \int u\, dx \tag{A1.18}$$

$$\int u\, dv = uv - \int v\, du \tag{A1.19}$$

$$\int x^n\, dx = \frac{x^{n+1}}{n+1} + C \tag{A1.20}$$

$$\int e^{\alpha x}\, dx = \frac{e^{\alpha x}}{\alpha} + C \tag{A1.21}$$

$$\int \frac{dx}{x} = \ln(x) + C \tag{A1.22}$$

$$\int_0^\infty e^{-x} = 1 \tag{A1.23}$$

APPENDIX

Z-Transforms

Function	$\Leftrightarrow$	Transform
δ_n	$\Leftrightarrow$	1
u_n	$\Leftrightarrow$	$\dfrac{1}{1 - z}$
$A\alpha^n$	$\Leftrightarrow$	$\dfrac{A}{1 - \alpha z}$
n	$\Leftrightarrow$	$\dfrac{z}{(1 - z)^2}$
$\dbinom{n + m - 1}{m - 1}\alpha^n$	$\Leftrightarrow$	$\dfrac{1}{(1 - \alpha z)^m}$
$\dfrac{1}{n!}$	$\Leftrightarrow$	e^z
$f_{n+k} \quad k > 0$	$\Leftrightarrow$	$\dfrac{F(z)}{z^k} - \displaystyle\sum_{n=1}^{k} z^{n-k-1} f_{n-1}$
$f_{n-k} \quad k > 0$	$\Leftrightarrow$	$z^k F(z)$
$f_{n/k} \quad n = 0, k, 2k, \cdots$	$\Leftrightarrow$	$F(z^k)$
$n f_n$	$\Leftrightarrow$	$z \dfrac{d}{dz} F(z)$
$\dfrac{n!}{(n - m)!} f_n$	$\Leftrightarrow$	$z^m \dfrac{d^m}{dz^m} F(z)$

Note: δ_n is the unit function which is 1 for $n = 0$ and 0 for $n \neq 0$ and u_0 is the unit step function which is 1 for $n \geq 0$ and 0 for $n < 0$.

This table is reprinted with permission from *Standard Mathematical Tables* © 1976 CRC Press, Boca Raton, FL.

APPENDIX

Laplace Transforms

Function	⇔	Transform
$\delta(t)$	⇔	1
$u(t)$	⇔	$\dfrac{1}{s}$
$\dfrac{t^{n-1}}{(n-1)!}$	⇔	$\dfrac{1}{s^n}$
$Ae^{-\alpha t}u(t)$	⇔	$\dfrac{A}{s+\alpha}$
$\dfrac{t^n}{n!}e^{-\alpha t}u(t)$	⇔	$\dfrac{1}{(s+\alpha)^{n+1}}$
$t^n f(t)$	⇔	$(-1)^n\dfrac{d^n}{ds^n}F^*(s)$
$f(t-a)\quad a\geq 0$	⇔	$e^{-as}F^*(s)$
$e^{-\alpha t}f(t)$	⇔	$F^*(s+\alpha)$
$\dfrac{d}{dt}f(t)$	⇔	$sF^*(s)-f(0^-)$
$\displaystyle\int_{-\infty}^{t}f(t)\,dt$	⇔	$\dfrac{F^*(s)}{s}+\dfrac{1}{s}\dfrac{d}{dt}f(t)\Big|_{t\to 0^-}$

Note: $\delta(t)$ is the unit impulse function centered at 0 and $u(t)$ is the unit step function at 0.

This table is reprinted with permission from *Standard Mathematical Tables* © 1976 CRC Press, Boca Raton, FL.

APPENDIX

Chi-Squared Distribution

nF	.010	.050	.100	.250	.500	.750	.900	.950	.990
3	.115	.352	.584	1.21	2.37	4.11	6.25	7.81	11.3
4	.297	.711	1.06	1.92	3.36	5.39	7.78	9.49	13.3
5	.554	1.15	1.61	2.67	4.35	6.63	9.24	11.1	15.1
6	.872	1.64	2.20	3.45	5.35	7.84	10.6	12.6	16.8
7	1.24	2.17	2.83	4.25	6.35	9.04	12.0	14.1	18.5
8	1.65	2.73	3.49	5.07	7.34	10.2	13.4	15.5	20.1
9	2.09	3.33	4.17	5.90	8.34	11.4	14.7	16.9	21.7
10	2.56	3.94	4.87	6.74	9.34	12.5	16.0	18.3	23.2
11	3.05	4.57	5.58	7.58	10.3	13.7	17.3	19.7	24.7
12	3.57	5.23	6.30	8.44	11.3	14.8	18.5	21.0	26.2
13	4.11	5.89	7.04	9.30	12.3	16.0	19.8	22.4	27.7
14	4.66	6.57	7.79	10.2	13.3	17.1	21.1	23.7	29.1
15	5.23	7.26	8.55	11.0	14.3	18.2	22.3	25.0	30.6
16	5.81	7.96	9.31	11.9	15.3	19.4	23.5	26.3	32.0
17	6.41	8.67	10.1	12.8	16.3	20.5	24.8	27.6	33.4
18	7.01	9.39	10.9	13.7	17.3	21.6	26.0	28.9	34.8
19	7.63	10.1	11.7	14.6	18.3	22.7	27.2	30.1	36.2
20	8.26	10.9	12.4	15.5	19.3	23.8	28.4	31.4	37.6
21	8.90	11.6	13.2	16.3	20.3	24.9	29.6	32.7	38.9
22	9.54	12.3	14.0	17.2	21.3	26.0	30.8	33.9	40.3
23	10.2	13.1	14.8	18.1	22.3	27.1	32.0	35.2	41.6
24	10.9	13.8	15.7	19.0	23.3	28.2	33.2	36.4	43.0
25	11.5	14.6	16.5	19.9	24.3	29.3	34.4	37.7	44.3
26	12.2	15.4	17.3	20.8	25.3	30.4	35.6	38.9	45.6
27	12.9	16.2	18.1	21.7	26.3	31.5	36.7	40.1	47.0
28	13.6	16.9	18.9	22.7	27.3	32.6	37.9	41.3	48.3
29	14.3	17.7	19.8	23.6	28.3	33.7	39.1	42.6	49.6
30	15.0	18.5	20.6	24.5	29.3	34.8	40.3	43.8	50.9

APPENDIX

Student-t Distribution

	Confidence Probability			
ν	.80	.90	.96	.98
1	3.078	6.314	15.895	31.821
2	1.886	2.920	4.849	6.965
3	1.638	2.353	3.482	4.541
4	1.533	2.132	2.999	3.747
5	1.476	2.015	2.757	3.365
6	1.440	1.943	2.612	3.143
7	1.415	1.895	2.517	2.998
8	1.397	1.860	2.449	2.896
9	1.383	1.833	2.398	2.821
10	1.372	1.812	2.359	2.764
11	1.363	1.796	2.328	2.718
12	1.356	1.782	2.303	2.681
13	1.350	1.771	2.282	2.650
14	1.345	1.761	2.264	2.624
15	1.341	1.753	2.249	2.602
16	1.337	1.746	2.235	2.583
17	1.333	1.740	2.224	2.567
18	1.330	1.734	2.214	2.552
19	1.328	1.729	2.205	2.539
20	1.325	1.725	2.197	2.528
25	1.316	1.708	2.167	2.485
30	1.310	1.697	2.147	2.457
40	1.303	1.684	2.123	2.423
50	1.299	1.676	2.109	2.403
75	1.293	1.665	2.090	2.377
100	1.290	1.660	2.081	2.364
∞	1.282	1.645	2.054	2.326

This table is reprinted with permission from *Standard Mathematical Tables* © 1976 CRC Press, Boca Raton, FL.

APPENDIX

Bibliography

A6.1 Books on Probability and Statistics

Hoel, Paul G.; Port, Sidney C.; Stone, Charles J. *Introduction to Probability Theory* Houghton Mifflin, Boston, MA, 1971

Feller, William *An Introduction to Probability Theory and Its Application* Vol. I and II John Wiley & Sons, New York, NY, 1958

Karlin, Samuel; Taylor, Howard M. *A First Course in Stochastic Processes, 2nd Ed.* Academic Press, New York, NY, 1975

Drake, Alvin *Fundamentals of Applied Probability Theory* McGraw-Hill, New York, NY, 1967

Miller, Irwin; Freund, John E. *Probability and Statistics for Engineers* Prentice-Hall, Englewood Cliffs, NJ, 1977

Hogg, Robert V.; Craig, Allen T. *Introduction to Mathematical Statistics* Macmillan, New York, NY, 1970

Walpole, Ronald E. *Introduction to Statistics* Macmillan, New York, NY, 1982

A6.2 Books on Simulation

Law, Averill M.; Kelton, W. David *Simulation Modeling and Analysis* McGraw-Hill, New York, NY, 1982

Payne, James A. *Introduction to Simulation* McGraw-Hill, New York, NY, 1982

Solomon, Susan L. *Simulation of Waiting-Line Systems* Prentice-Hall, Englewood Cliffs, NJ, 1983

Iglehart, Donald L.; Shedler, Gerald S. *Regenerative Simulation of Response Times in Networks of Queues* Lecture Notes in Control and Information Sciences, No. 26 Springer-Verlag, New York, NY, 1980

Fishman, George S. *Concepts and Methods in Discrete Event Digital Simulation* John Wiley and Sons, New York, 1973

Bratley, Paul; Fox, Bennett L.; Schrage, Linus E. *A Guide to Simulation* Springer-Verlag New York, NY, 1983

A6.3 Books on Markov Theory

Kemeny, John G.; Snell, J. Laurie *Finite Markow Chains* D. Van Nostrand Co., Princeton, NJ, 1960

Kemeny, John G.; Snell, J. Laurie; Knapp, Anthony W. *Denumerable Markov Chains* Springer-Verlag, New York, NY, 1976

Howard, Ronald A. *Dynamic Probabilistic Systems* John Wiley and Sons, New York, NY, 1971

Ross, Sheldon M. *Applied Probability Models with Optimization Applications* Holden-Day, San Francisco, CA, 1970

A6.4 Books on Queuing Theory

Cohen, J. W. *The Single Server Queue* North-Holland, London, 1969

Cooper, Robert B. *Introduction to Queueing Theory* North-Holland, New York, 1981

Saaty, Thomas L. *Elements of Queueing Theory* McGraw-Hall, New York, NY, 1961

Kleinrock, Leonard *Queuing Systems, Volume I: Theory* John Wiley and Sons, New York, NY, 1975

Kleinrock, Leonard *Queuing Systems, Volume II: Computer Applications* John Wiley and Sons, New York, NY 1976

Allen, Arnold O. *Probability, Statistics, and Queuing Theory with Computer Science Applications* Academic Press, New York, NY, 1978

Neuts, Marcel F. *Matrix-Geometric Solutions in Stochastic Models* John Hopkins University Press, Baltimore, MD, 1981

Borovkov, A. A. *Stochastic Processes in Queueing Theory* Springer-Verlag, New York, NY, 1976

A6.5 Books on Performance Modeling

Trivedi, Kishor S. *Probability and Statistics with Reliability, Queuing, and Computer Science Applications* Prentice Hall, Englewood Cliffs, NJ, 1982

Lazowska, Edward D.; Zahorjan, John; Graham, G. Scott; Sevcik, Kenneth C. *Quantitative System Performance* Prentice-Hall, Englewood Cliffs, NJ, 1984

Lavenberg, Stephen S. (editor) *Computer Performance Modeling Handbook* Academic Press, New York, NY, 1983

Sauer, Charles H.; Chandy, K. Mani *Computer Systems Performance Modeling* Prentice-Hall, Englewood Cliffs, NJ, 1981

Kobayashi, Hisashi *Modeling and Analysis* Addison Wesley, Reading, MA, 1981

Courtois, P. J. *Decomposability* Academic Press, New York, NY, 1977

Bruell, Steve; Balbo, Gianfranco *Computational Algorithms for Closed Queueing Networks* North-Holland, New York, NY, 1980

Agrawal, Subhash C. *Metamodeling* MIT Press, Cambridge, MA, 1985

Coffman, Edward; Denning, Peter *Operating Systems Theory* Prentice-Hall, Englewood Cliffs, NJ, 1973

Spirn, Jeffrey R. *Program Behavior: Models and Measurements* North Holland, New York, NY, 1977

Ferrari, Domenico *Computer Systems Performance Evaluation* Prentice-Hall, Englewood Cliffs, NJ, 1978

A6.6 Selected Journal Papers

Allen, Arnold O. "Queueing Models of Computer Systems" *Computer* IEEE Press, Vol 13, No. 4 (April 1980): 13–24

Baskett, F., et al. "Open, Closed and Mixed Networks of Queues with Different Classes of Customers." *Journal of the ACM* April 1975.

Buzen, J. "Computational Algorithms for Closed Queueing Networks with Exponential Servers." *Communications of ACM* September 1973.

Reiser, M., and Lavenberg, S. S. "Mean Value Analysis of Closed Multichain Queuing Networks." *Journal of the ACM* Vol 27, No. 2 (April 1980): 313–322.

Towsley, Don. "Queuing Network Models with State-Dependent Routing." *Journal of the ACM* Vol. 27, No. 2 (April 1980): 323–337.

Lam, Simon S. "Dynamic Scaling and Growth Behaviour of Queuing Network Normalization Constants." *Journal of the ACM* Vol 29, No. 2 (April 1982): 492–513.

Jackson, J. R. "Jobshop-like Queuing Systems." *Management Science* Vol 10, No. 1 (October 1963): 131–142.

Gordon, W. J., and G. F. Newell. "Closed Queueing Networks with Exponential Servers." *Operations Research* Vol. 15, No. 2 (April 1967): 244–265.

Muntz, R. "Analytic Modeling of Interactive Systems." *Proceedings of IEEE* Vol. 63, No. 6 (June 1975): 946–953.

Sethi, Adarshpal S.; Saydam, Tuncay "Performance Analysis of Token Ring Local Area Networks" *Ninth Conference on Local Computer Networks* (October 1984): 26–31.

APPENDIX

Answers to Exercises

2.1

    a. {1,2,3,4,5,6}
    b. {3,4}

2.2 $A \cap B'$

2.3   {1,2,3,4,5,6} where each number is the count of dots showing on the top face of the die.

2.4   The real numbers between 0 and 4.

2.5

    a. Invalid. $P[b] > 1$
    b. Invalid. $P[c] < 0$
    c. Possibly valid.
    d. Invalid. $P[\{a,b\}] \neq P[\{a\}] + P[\{b\}]$

2.6

    a. Invalid. $P[0 \leq x < 1] = -1$
    b. Invalid. $P[0 \leq x < 1] = 2 > 1$
    c. Valid.
    d. Invalid. $P[0 \leq x < 1] \neq 1$

2.7 $\dfrac{1}{9}$

2.8   0.5

2.9   .3

2.10   .44

2.11 $\dfrac{8}{104} = \dfrac{1}{13}$

2.12 $52 \times 52 = 2704$

2.13 $52 \times 51 \times 50 \times 49 \times 48 = 311{,}875{,}200$

2.14 $\dfrac{311{,}875{,}200}{5!} = 2{,}598{,}960$

2.15 2, 3, 4, 5, 6, 7, 8, 9, 10, 11, 12

2.16 $f(x) = \begin{cases} 0 & x < 0 \\ x & 0 \le x \le 1 \\ 1 & x > 1 \end{cases}$

2.17 $P[1/3 < X \le 2/3] = \dfrac{1}{3}$

2.18 $P[X = 1/2] = 0$

2.19 $(1 - p)[p^4 + p^5 + p^6]$

2.20 $\lambda\tau$

2.22 $5/12$

3.1 $e^{\lambda(z-1)}$

3.2 $f_k = k^2 \quad k \ge 0$

3.3 $f_k = \dfrac{2}{3}\left(\dfrac{1}{3}\right)^k$

3.4 $f_k = k^2$

3.5 $\mu e^{-\mu t} + 2\mu e^{-2\mu t} \quad t \ge 0$

3.6 $\lambda\tau$

3.7 $F(t) = \dfrac{r\mu(r\mu t)^{r-1}e^{-r\mu t}}{(r-1)!}$

4.1 (1,7,6,9,0,11,10, . . .)

4.2 (7,15,7,15,7,15,7,15, . . .)

4.3 (1,7,6,9,10,1,7,0,10,11,2,2, . . .)

4.4 $\chi^2 = 2.2$ with 9 degrees of freedom. So we can reject at 1% confidence, so we can not accept at 99%. We can not reject at 2.5% confidence so we accept with confidence 97.5%. We can easily accept with confidence 90%.

5.1 The system is reducible. States 1 and 2 are transient. States 3, 4, 5, 6, and 7 are recurrent nonnull. States 3, 4, and 5 are periodic, while states 6 and 7 are aperiodic.

5.2

$$p(1) = [0.00, 0.55, 0.40, 0.05, 0.00]$$
$$p(2) = [0.165, 0.385, 0.325, 0.100, 0.025]$$

5.3

$$\pi = \left[\frac{4}{17}, \frac{6}{17}, \frac{3}{17}, \frac{4}{17}\right]$$

5.4

$$\mathbf{P}^n = \begin{bmatrix} \frac{1}{3} & \frac{2}{3} \\ \frac{1}{3} & \frac{2}{3} \end{bmatrix} + \left(-\frac{1}{2}\right)^n \begin{bmatrix} \frac{2}{2} & -\frac{2}{3} \\ -\frac{1}{3} & \frac{1}{3} \end{bmatrix}$$

6.1 $\mu = \dfrac{\lambda}{\mu}$

6.2 $\rho - \dfrac{\lambda}{2\mu}$

6.3 No. $12.356 \neq 25.6*7.34$

6.4 $N = 1$ and $\rho = 1/2$

6.5 $\rho = 2(2^{1/2} - 1)$

6.6 $p_k = \dfrac{\left(\dfrac{\lambda}{\mu}\right)^k \dfrac{1}{k!}}{\displaystyle\sum_{k=0}^{m} \left(\dfrac{\lambda}{\mu}\right)^k \dfrac{1}{k!}}$

6.7 $p_k = \dfrac{1 - \lambda/\mu}{1 - (\lambda/\mu)^{L+1}} \left(\dfrac{\lambda}{\mu}\right)^k$

7.1 $\begin{bmatrix} 0.1 & 0.7 & 0.2 \\ 1.0 & 0.0 & 0.0 \\ 1.0 & 0.0 & 0.0 \end{bmatrix}$

7.2 $\lambda_1 = 1.0 \quad \lambda_2 = 0.7 \quad \lambda_3 = 0.2$

7.3 $\dfrac{26}{57} = 0.456$

7.4 $2\dfrac{26}{57} = 0.912$

7.5 $2* 502 + 9 = 1013$

7.6 $\dfrac{502}{1013} = 0.496$

7.7 24.615 *msec*

7.8 $\rho_1 = 1 \cdot \dfrac{13}{4}\dfrac{16}{57} = 0.912$

$\rho_2 = 1 - \dfrac{16}{57} = 0.719$

Index